MW00640074

DANGEROUS FICTIONS

DANGEROUS FICTIONS

The Fear of Fantasy and the Invention of Reality

KEEP AWAY FROM CHILDREN

Lyta Gold

Soft Skull
New York

DANGEROUS FICTIONS

First Soft Skull edition: 2024

Library of Congress Cataloging-in-Publication Data
Names: Gold, Lyta, author.
Title: Dangerous fictions : the fear of fantasy and the invention of reality / Lyta Gold.
Description: First Soft Skull edition. | New York : Soft Skull, 2024. | Includes bibliographical references.
Identifiers: LCCN 2024025624 | ISBN 9781593767709 (hardcover) | ISBN 9781593767716 (ebook)
Subjects: LCSH: Fiction—Moral and ethical aspects. | Fiction—Political aspects. | Books and reading—United States. | Moral panics—United States. | Censorship—United States. | Literature and morals—United States. | Literature and society—United States.
Classification: LCC PN3347 .G65 2024 | DDC 174/.980883—dc23/eng/20240612
LC record available at https://lccn.loc.gov/2024025624

Jacket design and illustration by Farjana Yasmin
Book design by Laura Berry
Matchbook © Adobe Stock / BillionPhotos.com; matches © Adobe Stock / chones

Soft Skull Press
New York, NY
www.softskull.com

Printed in the United States of America

10 9 8 7 6 5 4 3 2 1

To Adrian Rennix, the most dangerous reader I know

CONTENTS

INTRODUCTION

Moral Panics Old and New

In 2015, a young man came home from a movie to find a pan of brownies that had been made, in part, from dog shit. His mother hadn't approved of the movie he'd chosen to see, and in an act of retaliation she'd baked him two pans of brownies: one that was normal and one where the batter had been blended with, according to her note, "a small amount of dog poop." This dog-shit dessert, her note continued, was intended as a symbol of the corrosive influence of the wicked Hollywood film that the young man had chosen to watch against his mother's will, taking sin into his body along with the sugar. Poop brownies are a common image in certain evangelical circles, illustrating a belief that consuming fictional stories can be as dangerous as eating literal shit. The young man's mother was proud of her dog-shit brownies, the baked-in literalness of her metaphor; she'd already posted pictures with the caption "Poo, anyone?" on her Facebook page.[1]

This event really happened in real life, but still, let's imagine it as though it happened in a novel. We could tell the story from the son's point of view, but I think the mother makes a more interesting choice. Limited but distant third person: Her movements brisk and cheery, described in simple language and without strong narrative judgment. The woman leaves her house. She finds a piece of dog shit in the yard, out there in the dark. Bringing it inside, she leaves the dog shit lying on her countertop in a plastic bag while she beats the eggs and measures the flour. And when all the ingredients have been mixed and the batter is ready, she opens the plastic bag, and—

It's nauseating to imagine, which is exactly how you know it's the right narrative choice. This is what fiction does best: provides access to the forbidden and the dark and the strange, the impossible inner life of a woman who would bake dog-shit brownies in her own oven, using her own pans and bowls and utensils. A woman who's convinced that her child is the one in danger; her child is the one whose behavior needs to be curtailed, before he's seduced by a fictional story into doing something disgusting and terrible.

The woman's name is Monica Brown, and in 2022 Mike Hixenbaugh of *ProPublica* wrote about her dog-shit brownies because Monica's son Weston—the one who had watched the forbidden movie some years before, and was later disowned when he came out as gay—recognized her as a loud public figure in the sudden rise of book bans across the United States.[2] The book-banning efforts have largely targeted works by LGBTQ+ and Black authors in schools and public libraries, usually on the grounds that the books are pornographic or upsetting or both. As is typical with this type of censorship, most of the challenged books are novels: fictional stories, more so than nonfictional narratives about real people, have long been believed to have an uncanny power over hearts and minds, especially those of young people.[3] Monica Brown claimed on a right-wing radio show in 2022 that the books at her local middle school library contained material that was "negative, dark—things nightmares are made of."[4] These books weren't just

frightening: they were dangerous, transforming previously innocent psychic space into an evil shadow realm.

Throughout recorded history, particularly in the cultures that
make up what we call the "west," fiction has often been labeled
as negative, dark, immoral, frightening, poisonous, diseased,
plague-ridden, and a form of evil sorcery. The current wave of book
bans may be the worst since the 1980s, but we've seen this sort of
thing before, and we'll see it again.[5] The fear of fiction waxes and
wanes, spiking every couple of decades like some kind of hysterical cicada. The book bans of the early 1980s, which were driven
by religious conservatives, dovetailed with the "Satanic Panic" over
books and games involving magic, like Dungeons and Dragons.[6]
Before that, in the 1950s, the anxiety was centered on trashy paperback novels and comic books, which were said to cause "moral
damage" and bring about a "loss of ideals" in young people that
would invariably lead to a life of crime.[7] In the late 1920s and 1930s,
the fictional culprits were sexy Hollywood movies and modernist
novels such as *Ulysses*, which—lest people engage in too much sex
and modernism—resulted in the Hays Code and more book bans.
Earlier still, at the turn of the twentieth century, America's problems
were blamed on dirty books and illustrations that could be ordered
through the mail.[8] In the centuries before that, there were successive
waves of concern over penny dreadfuls, women's novels, all kinds of
novels, chivalric romances, any romances, comedic plays, all kinds
of plays, back and back through the ages to the fourth century BCE,
where Plato declared in the *Republic* that all stories and artistic imi-
tations of any kind—including poetry, music, and painting—were
unacceptable in an ideal society unless they could be proved to im-
part rational, healthy, wholesome values.

While the specific context changes and evolves, the fear of fiction seems to always boil down to the fear of one's current society
and the people who live in it. Other people's minds are frightening

because they are inaccessible to us; in fact, we can only know them fully and objectively through fictional representation, which is to say, not at all. And fictional representation is very powerful— art being generally more compelling than reality—which means it's always possible that art could seduce our fellow citizens into wicked beliefs. Moral panics over fiction are common in democracies, because the inner lives and motives of others matter a great deal in a democracy: more so than in other types of government, where people have less direct control over their political fate. In a democracy, your fellow citizens—if united as a majority or an energetic plurality—can organize for social progress or encourage the passage of draconian laws that terrorize minorities. Fear of other people, and how they might work together to shift reality, is the reason that the contest over written language so often extends beyond the grounds of nonfiction and history (the present and past being obviously and reasonably politicized territory) into that which is definitionally *not* real. Fictional stories are imaginary things that didn't happen to people who never existed; we're all perfectly aware of that fact. But we're also aware that fiction affects us profoundly and mysteriously, to an extent that we can't tabulate or fully understand. And we know that other people are affected just as strongly and unpredictably as we are.

Fiction is, in fact, the story of other people. That, more than anything else, is what makes it dangerous.

At the same time, however, the panics over fiction are never fully *about* fiction: they're almost always deflections of some other, more formless anxiety. Anxiety about the body politic, anxiety about the next generation, anxiety about who gets to make and control art, anxiety about what kinds of people get to exist in the public imagination, and, at its deepest level, anxiety about what kinds of human activity can be categorized as valuable and therefore worthy of attention (and compensation) in the first place. The debate over "dangerous fiction" is never about such simple questions as "Is fiction good for us?" or "Is fiction bad for us?" No matter what we're saying, we're always speaking in metaphor and allusion: we're always talking about something else.

Nothing Ever Changes (Except the Internet)

This book is going to focus on "western" anxiety about the power of fiction, partly for geographic convenience and partly because these ideas have a clear and traceable lineage. The arguments about whether fictional stories are dangerous for us are essentially identical through time and on both sides of the Atlantic:[9] people in nineteenth-century France fretted over the impact *Madame Bovary* would have on fragile minds in basically the same terms that people now fret about the impact of young adult (YA) novels. This doesn't mean that conservative book banners have read *Madame Bovary* (or YA novels either—they're not big readers) or are remotely familiar with any of the historic writing on this topic. Moral panics tend to repeat themselves in basically identical language simply because they arise from the same perennial sets of concerns.

These concerns—and the concerned—have tended to be conservative, since fear of "other people" looms large in the conservative imagination, but they've never been exclusively right wing. Jonathan Gottschall, a centrist academic who studies literature and evolutionary psychology, argued in his 2021 book *The Story Paradox* that stories are like evil oxygen: an "essential poison" that is necessary for existence but also "a highly volatile compound" that "does great cumulative damage" to our fragile souls.[10] This image is somewhat classier than the dog-shit brownie, but it's really the same thing: stories are *bad* for us, and they need to be tightly regulated. This is something that many people tacitly agree with, regardless of their politics: the swarms of Goodreads reviewers condemning novels for causing "harm" concur with conservative book banners that books can be harmful—they just disagree on what that harm consists of and who should regulate it. The same ideas about the risk and power of fiction tend to pop up all along the political spectrum, reinforcing one another, while their base assumptions are rarely challenged.

Before we go any further, I want to be very clear: in this house, we will not be engaging in false equivalencies. There can be no comparison whatsoever between the organized, coordinated, and highly lucrative censorship drives of the religious right and the loose collection of internet anecdotes generally referred to as "cancel culture."[11] They aren't entirely unrelated: the right has pursued its own cancellation drives (such as Gamergate) and they have used—and possibly fueled through bot activity—cancellation activity on the left to disguise or justify their own culture battles. But when YA novelists scrap with one another on Twitter over faults of representation, when college students ask for a trigger warning on Ovid's *Metamorphoses*, when a random person on the internet expresses a stupid opinion about the message of a movie—these aren't remotely in the same league as the book bans. They aren't even using the same level of equipment: they're peewee football to the right wing's NFL (at least, I suppose, when the right isn't trying to cancel the NFL itself for excessive wokeness). The conservative book bans have barred access to huge swaths of literature in libraries and school districts across the country, and many librarians have been harassed and threatened, some to the point of quitting their jobs for their own safety. Meanwhile, in the worst version of left cancel culture, a handful of novelists have lost their book deals.[12] But although these occurrences are totally different in terms of scale, scope, effect, and imagined intent, I still think it's important to explore how they arise from the same misguided presumptions about what fictional stories do, how they can or should be regulated, and whether they can be justified, especially in a democracy.

There are a few different images and assumptions that make up this set of beliefs, and I'll attempt to tease them out briefly in the rest of this introduction before exploring their implications in later chapters of this book. But first, a quick note on scope: I am using "fiction" throughout to refer to stories that are made up, which are understood by both storyteller and audience to involve fictional people and events or imaginative retellings of real (or mythic) people and events. Distinctions between mediums—epic poems, plays, novels, comic books, movies, TV shows, video games—are relevant insofar as the birth of new mediums causes an absolute freak-out each time, but otherwise I'm choosing to treat them as independent bodies inhabited by the same spirit. Stories—even before the days of endless compulsory rehashes and remakes—have historically leapt across mediums, being adapted and reinterpreted in new and different forms. The line between storytelling and music is often blurry as well (lyrics being a form of poetry and often accused of being dangerous, especially when the genre is new, or new to the ears of a hegemonic culture or an older generation). So we'll jump around a bit through mediums and across time and cover everything I think is interesting or important, or just funny and dark and strange.

And while this book could easily have been a thousand pages or more, I've been informed by sensible people that nobody's going to read all that, so I'm necessarily leaving out some perfect examples, side channels, and internecine academic debates. It isn't just that people who live in the "west" have been nervous about the effects of fiction for centuries; they've been *writing* about this nervousness from one point of view or another, and in the meantime, other people have been writing many more fictional stories to get upset about. This conversation is so old, and so constant, that it may precede writing itself: at least in the democratic city-states of classical Greece, where it seems to begin.

The Worst Form of Government (Except for All the Others)

Most histories of dangerous fiction begin with Plato, though anxiety about the pernicious effect of stories can be found in fragments of work by earlier Greek philosophers, who criticized the epic poetry of their day for portraying the gods as murderous, adulterous assholes.[13] In the *Republic*, Plato expands upon and clarifies these early concerns: When people encounter stories about gods and heroes behaving badly, what stops them from imitating what they hear? When the poets sing about Achilles mourning Patroclus, won't the audience get the impression that it's okay to cry too much over dead loved ones, like a *woman*? When Achilles looks Agamemnon in the face and calls him a "wine-bibber, with the eyes of a dog and the heart of a deer"—I mean, what if you said that to your dad?[14] A cop? The president??? To Plato, depiction is always endorsement and a social license for bad behavior. "We must put a stop to such stories," his version of Socrates declares, "lest they produce in the youth a strong inclination to do bad things."[15]

The Greek word for imitative behavior is "mimesis," and most of the time, when we get anxious about the effects of fiction, we're worried about mimetic responses—not so much from ourselves but from other people.[16] Plato specifies that the wise among us are mostly safe from the temptations of poetry, but "children and foolish people" are in danger, because they can't tell the difference between images and reality.[17] The wise are supposedly an elite few, while children and the foolish are everywhere. This is why you have to cut the heart out of fiction: all vice, all cruelty, anything that might tempt the masses by example. But of course, vice and cruelty are the fun parts: the Greek gods and heroes do appear in myth as murderous, adulterous assholes, which is why we still enjoy ancient Greek literature over two thousand years later and remain on a first-name basis with their gods.

Plato worries about the negative effect of art on children and the foolish because he's concerned about shaping people—specifically, a social elite—into good and useful citizens. He's not a fan of democracy: it's the second-worst system he can imagine, and only tyranny holds greater horrors for him. He does allow that a person who lives in a democracy might be a happy and interesting person: "a complex man, full of all sorts of characters, fine and multicolored, just like the democratic city."[18] In other words, the democratic city itself is a lot like a good story, full of all sorts of characters: complex, multihued, lively, and interesting. But including exciting characters naturally means including wicked characters too, and as such, democracy inevitably gives way to tyranny.

To be fair to Plato, the transition from democracy to tyranny and back again happened in his lifetime, and the *Republic* is partly an attempt to imagine a society designed so perfectly that the political turmoil he witnessed could never happen again. There are many other examples of democracies, up to and including the United States, where a majority or plurality has managed to tyrannize the rest—and they have done it, in part, through storytelling. There are documented instances of stories that have done harm, where mimesis has had at least some awful effect. The continued existence—and belligerence—of far-right racist extremism in the South can be traced in part to Lost Cause novels and films such as *Gone with the Wind* and the infamous *Birth of a Nation*.[19] Medievalish epics like Sir Walter Scott's nineteenth-century fantasies have also been targeted for blame, helping to inspire a goopy romantic racism that dovetailed neatly with the Ku Klux Klan's self-conception as heroic white knights battling a dark and evil horde.[20]

More recently, the racist dystopian French novel *The Camp of the Saints* (1973) has been credited with partly inspiring a legion of anti-immigrant politicians and intellectuals, most famously Stephen Miller of the Trump administration (a matter that will be covered in more detail in chapter 3).[21]

Other novels have had more beneficial or ambiguous effects. *Uncle Tom's Cabin* is credited with rallying previously ignorant northerners to the abolitionist cause, though critics such as James Baldwin have noted that it did so on the back of racist stereotypes.[22] Upton Sinclair's *The Jungle* (1906) led to outrage and activism against industrial food production (and was harmful if you were a meat-packing baron, I guess). Nikolai Chernyshevsky's novel *What Is to Be Done?* (1863) directly influenced Lenin and his contemporaries, to the point where Lenin borrowed the title of his famous pamphlet from the novel.[23] Mimesis is a real and documented phenomenon, and yet it's often difficult to sort out how much influence it really has over world events. People are not mindless automata receiving programming instructions from fiction; much proudly political art has little measurable effect on actual political events. With any direct transformation of a particular story into real political action there's always going to be a strong element of choice, not to mention the influence of many other factors.

Still, influence is hard to prove in one direction or another: and there are all sorts of hypothesized mimesis events in western cultural history whether the works in question are fairly targeted or not. Goethe's hugely popular book *The Sorrows of Young Werther* was blamed for a rash of suicides across Europe; at least one young woman drowned herself in 1778 with a copy of *Werther* in her pocket.[24] Much more recently, a study blamed the Netflix TV show *Thirteen Reasons Why* for a spike in teen suicides, though another study disagreed with the findings.[25] The controversial novel *American Dirt* was accused of, among other things, helping to spread false and bigoted ideas about what the drug war and immigration are really like, which theoretically could have had a knock-on effect when it comes to U.S. policy.[26] The broader controversy over who gets to write about a given culture is partly about power and access, but also about the devastating effects on social policy and internal self-perception that come from flooding the public imagination with bigoted stereotypes written by outsiders. One book on its own may have little influence; a flood of stories that are all the same, and all push the same demeaning ideology, are another matter entirely.

So there may be reason for concern; reason to lock up the poets and tear down their works. But once censorship of art begins, it's hard to find an end, hard to reach a place of perfect safety, where other people—who we always imagine to be foolish, unlike ourselves—can no longer possibly develop the wrong ideas. Obviously you and I are safe from the influence of bad stories full of wrong ideas, but what about *other people*? Fear of other people and their wrong ideas has, like censorship, waxed and waned over the years; much of it has had to do with literacy and the ready availability of popular stories. By the early modern era, with the rise of the printing press and the bourgeoisie, this fear became a pressing concern. There were so many more readers: What were they reading, and what was their reading doing to them? They were vanishing into secret, silent worlds: What were these worlds, and what relation did they have to reality? Were they seeing the world not as it is and should be but as it isn't and shouldn't?

As novelist and literature professor Margaret Anne Doody writes in *The True Story of the Novel*, her magisterial history of fiction in the west: "Anything that encourages women, the young, and the poor to dream, to imagine things otherwise, may well be destructive of the civic order and of civic virtue as imagined by the dominant political theory . . . The rise of civic virtue leads to a lot of nasty talk about the 'mob.'"[27] Reading has always been a potentially liberatory practice: there were plenty of efforts in the early modern period to ensure that certain populations—slaves, in particular—were prevented from learning to read anything at all. Clarence Lusane, a Howard University professor of political science, has said that by the 1830s, it was commonly and increasingly believed that "an educated enslaved person was a dangerous person."[28] Any reading, fiction or otherwise, could theoretically help slaves imagine themselves out of their condition and into a different reality.

Fiction is then "dangerous" in all sorts of ways and in all sorts of political directions. But it's always going to be a response to the perceived threat of other people, especially when it comes to participatory societies where the opinions of *other people* make a difference. Other people can be unruly, undisciplined, and ungovernable; they can be made up of a fine and multicolored and frustrating and hateful and even vicious individuality, as in a novel, or a democracy. And that's why Plato's *Republic* doesn't offer any suggestions for democracies: it's a blueprint for educating an elite class in an ideal, authoritarian civilization, one that Plato's fellow citizens would have found bizarre and inhuman.[29] There's no version of "control the poets" that's easily compatible with a free society.

Let's Go Eat a Goddamn Snack[30]

Maybe, you may think, the poets don't have to be wholly censored in a free society; maybe we can just try to encourage the creation of good stories that are good for our well-being and discourage the creation of bad ones that cause us harm. But in the United States, it's almost impossible to separate the concept of a free society from that of a consumer society, and it's equally impossible to separate our abstract worries about fiction from more earthbound anxieties about health and wellness. In fact, the language we use to talk about fiction is nearly inseparable from the language we use to talk about food. "We consume stories gluttonously throughout our lives," warns Gottschall in *The Story Paradox,* "and we become what we eat."[31] British writer Rick Gekoski admitted in *The Guardian* that he sometimes reads what he calls "fast-food fiction"—genre fiction, like *Harry Potter* or *Fifty Shades of Grey*—which he says "provides the same kind of transient pleasures as eating fast food, and is probably equally good or bad for you."[32] We're so used to comparing fiction to food that we rarely stop to consider whether the analogy actually makes sense. There is, in fact, no hard evidence that reading a light novel is anything like eating a candy bar or that reading Dostoyevsky is anything like eating asparagus. And there's no way to collect data that could be easily separated from socioeconomic factors. But none of this has ever stopped people from pulling out their imaginary doctorates in the field of edible media studies and declaring that *some* stories are junk food, while others are "eating your vegetables."

Anyone who says that reading Dostoyevsky resembles the dull but necessary work of eating vegetables has clearly never read Dostoyevsky (or understands how to roast vegetables, for that matter). But we live in a wellness culture that places moral and social value on weight and health, and so the image of "healthy fiction" retains a powerful hold over us. Great Books, we're often told, are important for our mental development: they make us more complex, more interesting, and better critical thinkers. It's absolutely true that reading great literature and analyzing great TV shows can help you become a better *writer,* but plenty of dull and tendentious people have read classic novels and watched the best-regarded prestige dramas. Those who advocate for fine fiction like fine dining tend to consider their diet superior to that of others, even if they also enjoy some lowbrow art—and they always do, though fortunately junk genres contain zero calories for the discerning. It's always *other people* who are mere consumers, other people who are overdoing it, other people who are mindlessly stuffing their faces with the cultural slops. Those sloppy, lazy, disgusting *other people* . . .

It really is always other people.

Now, it's true that some people—sadly, way too many people— avoid things like classic novels and critically acclaimed films because they think they won't like them, because the constant comparison to healthy vegetables has made these great works of art sound limp and unpleasant. The command to "eat your vegetables" is never going to convince them, because it's a condescending phrase we reserve for children. And I don't think it's ever really said in order to convince but rather for the speaker to maintain a kind of lonely superiority, to establish his position as one of the small number of the tragically wise, living high above the mass of children and the foolish. This view of art also manages to keep the speaker in a lofty position above the great works themselves; imagine reducing *Ulysses* to a fiber supplement! Well, James Joyce, with his scatological fetish, might have approved.[33] But *Ulysses* was also famously banned for being too filthy and too sexy: the opposite, in fact, of a healthy diet.[34]

Advocating for great fiction as just another wellness diet doesn't indicate any sort of respect for it but rather instrumentalizes it into something positive and improving—that is, something that can be justified as worthy of our time. And when so much of modern life has already been boxed up and packaged into something that's good for us, that makes us better citizens and better workers, it's no wonder that so many people turn to what they themselves call "trash TV" instead. The quickest way to kill many grown-ups' interest in a work of art is to label it as healthy and useful, to turn it into another productive chore. And the quickest way to kill fiction more generally is to declare that it exists to make you a better person, to train you into shape.

The Empathy Gym, or Do You Even Lift Compassionately, Bro?

In 2021, a British judge passed an unusual sentence. When presented with the case of a young neo-Nazi who had been caught with thousands of pages of white supremacist manifestos and how-to guides for making bombs, the judge ruled that the neo-Nazi should—instead of receiving jail time—simply read the classics of British literature, such as Shakespeare, Austen, Dickens, Hardy, and Trollope. The neo-Nazi did a little bit of the reading, and then—if you can believe it—he turned around and became a Nazi again.[35] Austen and Shakespeare didn't de-Nazify him; they didn't turn him into a compassionate or anti-racist person. The only real question here is why the judge believed they might.

This judge, whether he knew it or not, was caught up in what critic Jennifer Wilson has called "the Empathy Industrial Complex," a process by which fictional stories are extolled and valued for their supposed ability to produce empathy.[36] Gottschall enthuses that stories are "an empathy generator" and function as "empathy machines," cribbing from Roger Ebert's famous description of cinema as "a machine that generates empathy."[37] The pop psychology writer Johann Hari has referred to novels as "a kind of empathy gym," as if literature is something to be suffered through in the gym of the mind, turning those pains into gains.[38] (It's never clear how much empathy-iron we should pump—how *much* should we read to produce optimal levels of empathy? Could we overdo it, and end up contorted into abject messes of compassion?)

Regardless, fiction is supposed to be useful for our moral development, and the moral development of liberal white people specifically. This is another presumption, like the food analogy, that's rarely questioned: the 2023 PEN America banned books report casually describes YA novels as a tool for teaching empathy.[39] The image has been around for a while, but Wilson describes how the empathy-industrial complex really kicked off in 2016, tied to the related industry of the sympathetic Trump voter profile.[40] Gottschall promotes the empathic value of anti-racist literature in particular, saying that reading books like *Uncle Tom's Cabin* doesn't just help white people feel kindlier toward Black people (despite or against its anti-Black stereotypes) but that "empathy is a kind of muscle, and the more exercise we give it by consuming fiction, the stronger it gets."[41]

This is, of course, another fitness metaphor, closely related to the image of great art as healthy vegetables. Fiction is something we consume to make us better, wiser, stronger: white people are supposed to devour stories about people of color "as a kind of ethical protein shake," in the sardonic words of writer Elaine Castillo. In an essay titled "Reading Teaches Us Empathy, and Other Fictions," Castillo points out how writers of color, celebrated by the larger publishing world—and often by themselves—for their empathy-generating qualities, can sometimes find themselves diminished in the process: they're expected to continually provide stories of trauma and violence "the way their ancestors once provided spices, minerals, precious stones, and unprecious bodies."[42] There's no end to this expected provision, as there's no end in any kind of wellness culture: only more and more gains, more and more empathy-muscles to show off. And much like a gym, like a factory, like imperialism, the empathy-industrial complex can never stop on its own: it will always need more and more ethnic tragedy to feed into the careless maw of whiteness. The frustrations experienced by writers of color at the hands of well-meaning but condescending white readers—Castillo herself provides several anecdotes—are good evidence that the empathy-industrial complex is ineffective, or at least is effective at building something other than empathy. It certainly provides the semblance of having done some kind of interior political work, without having to change external material conditions.

Several studies claim to show that reading increases empathy, even when controlling for external factors (such as being naturally interested in learning about the lives of other people); there are also studies that contradict the pro-empathy findings.[43] Even if the pro studies are correct, there's a clear outer limit to how far this learned empathy can go. If reading novels—or watching films, as Ebert suggests—increases empathy, then the publishing industry and Hollywood ought to be full of the kindest, most empathetic people alive, instead of being legendary hotbeds of personal cruelty, misogyny, racism, and low wages for writers.[44] And if enjoying fiction does somehow increase empathy but the work of *making* fiction is a nightmare of backstabbing and inequality, it's worth asking why the difference between consumption and creation is so stark. If art produces empathy, it clearly hasn't been enough to overcome capitalism on its own. At best, it's just a feeling, a nice vibe, one which has not resulted in much-needed change.

Empathy, however, is no mean value, and not all readers are condescending and devoid of true feeling. It may indeed be healthy—or at least not bad—for white readers or members of other dominant groups to feel morally compelled to seek out perspectives that they might otherwise not have considered trying. If nothing else, it helps marginalized writers sell books, against the still semi-prevailing wisdom in the industry that such literature isn't profitable. But encouraging wider reading, as well as the further diversification of a still majority-white publishing industry, is a different goal than the kind of moral wellness promised by the empathy-industrial complex and the expectation placed on literature to "fix" people, especially racists.

In the case of the sentencing of the neo-Nazi, Austen et al. seem to stand in for a kind of secular gospel, and the god in question is Education, in keeping with the common liberal belief that only the stupid and uneducated are evil, with evil being simply a confusion of manners (and who better to teach manners than Austen?). One does not say Nazi slogans in public; one's white supremacy is far more sublimated than that. Consuming fiction by people of color can end up being just another development of this sublimation; whether reading inculcates empathy or not, it at least creates the appearance of doing the ethical work that fiction is supposed to do, that it *must* do, to justify its existence.

This kind of moral guilt and moral work—guilt without materially addressing the reasons for the guilt, work without fixing anything—dates back to at least the sixteenth century. Doody explains this as another fallout of the printing press: as soon as novels and romances became more readily available, it started to become "*necessary* to defend the fictional; a certain guilt [became] attach[ed] to reading stories." This guilt even crossed highly charged Catholic and Protestant lines, as literature everywhere was expected to teach moral lessons and inculcate good values, providing fine exercise for the mind.[45] Nobody used gym imagery because gyms as such didn't exist yet, and they rarely argued for the good news of empathy because that wasn't a key social value of the time. But the argument in defense of fiction is more or less the same. Fiction must demonstrate that it's doing the work, that it's absolving the guilt of self-indulgence in a fun activity as well as the guilt of social sin, whatever the important sin of the day might be.

But it would go too far to argue, as the right often does, that this amounts to "virtue signaling" and that nobody cares about representation beyond a kind of social performance. There are plenty of good reasons to care about representation: the personal (whatever your identity is, you want to see yourself represented, to know that you exist); the empathetic (you care that other people see themselves represented, to know that they exist, an empathy that doesn't begin in fiction but necessarily predates it); and the artistic (you want everyone to create the art they want to create, and you want that art to be of the very highest quality and judged accordingly; that is, you care about art for its own sake).

Castillo cautions against taking a nonpolitical "arts for art's sake" approach to fiction in response to the empathy-industrial complex, on the grounds that it leads to "reading the same white Europeans forevermore," but I think the term "arts for art's sake" has often been misappropriated and misunderstood.[46] It's not always a demand to seek falsely "neutral" and "apolitical" (i.e., white and male) art; it can also be a demand to approach all art with the aesthetic seriousness it deserves. The phrase itself is associated most often with Oscar Wilde—a white European, to be sure, but also a gay man who was persecuted for his sexuality and wrote moralizing fairy tales, comedies of manners, and a novel of sublimated gay desire. In the preface to *The Picture of Dorian Gray*, Wilde wrote that "there is no such thing as a moral or an immoral book. Books are well written, or badly written. That is all."[47] Insisting on being judged *as an artist*, on your own merits, not based on whether you provide high-quality moral instruction to a dominant social group and inculcate the right social values of the day—that isn't some sort of anti-political statement but a highly political one. It tells readers to go and get their values elsewhere, to stop demanding that their fiction provide the difficult labor of soul-making, to do the work *themselves*. A book isn't a gym; it doesn't exist for you, to fix you, but for itself alone. Austen and Shakespeare can't cure a neo-Nazi, because great literature exists for its own sake, not to make us better people.

Wilde's argument is difficult and provocative—not least because he made several difficult and provocative statements about art, many of which contradict one another, contradictions he

merrily acknowledged without resolving them—but also because
the politics or nonpolitics of art may be the most dangerous terms
on which fiction is evaluated.[48] We know that propaganda has real
effects and consequences, and in times of social crisis, we often see
a call for art to be openly and obviously "political"—meaning that
it demonstrates opposition to a dominant ideology—or "apolitical," meaning that it loudly or tacitly supports status quo values
perceived to be under attack. When cultural change is either too
slow or too fast (depending on your perspective), it's easy to pick
out stories and hold them accountable for the social change they
are imagined having caused or prevented. Especially if those stories are very, very popular, and the machinery of capitalist mega-
production only makes them worse.

Art for Politics' Sake

It turns out that the movie that Weston Brown went to see, the one
that earned the ire of his mother and her dog-shit brownies, was
Marvel's *Avengers: Age of Ultron*. Now, many leftist critics would
likely describe Marvel movies much like dog shit in brownies: a
stinking pile of political and economic propaganda rolled around in
a tasty filling of likable actors.[49] (Although when it comes to the ex-
ecrable *Age of Ultron* itself, I think even the most committed Marvel
fan would agree that one's a bit dog shit.) The far right, on the other
hand, has targeted Marvel and Disney for their supposed "wokeness" and threatened Disney with boycotts, particularly on the
grounds of the studio's occasional gay representation—often limited to a single line of dialogue or a blurry lesbian kiss in the background of a shot. The right's outrage over Disney's "wokeness" is
matched only by leftist contempt for the multiconglomerate's feeble
twitches toward creating a rainbow of characters (often praised by
liberal critics) and the way that the popularity of Disney's products

has led to an arms race among the other media conglomerates, degrading the quality of all movies everywhere.

It may be my lingering Stockholm syndrome talking—some years ago, I worked for Marvel in its consumer products division—but this last charge, of degrading filmmaking, has never seemed entirely fair. Disney has certainly built a despicable template, and Marvel is well-known for its horrible treatment of visual effects (VFX) workers (which leads to dreadful CGI as well as labor abuses), but neither company invented capitalism, nor did they invent capitalism's lack of creativity, the tendency of all media conglomerates to copy-paste the last popular thing again and again until the ink wears out.[50] The corporate capture of every single piece of the entertainment sphere didn't begin or end with Disney, but Disney is, for now, the largest of these conglomerates, and many people on the left and the right have decided to hold it and its subsidiaries uniquely responsible for many of the great cultural evils of American society. Whatever the company happens to be propagandizing for today, it could be promoting something else; the issue isn't *really* that Disney is a giant evil organization (though it is), but that it hasn't been aiming its fully armed and operational battle station in the right directions.

Pop culture has always been a problem. Any work of fiction is potentially dangerous as a carrier of ugly politics that could spread among the masses (we use the term "going viral" for a reason). But a popular movie or TV show or totalizing franchise is perceived as especially contagious, particularly if it's designed to be fun, exciting, and easily comprehensible. Virality and contagion, the language of disease: here we have another common set of images that have often been used to describe the effect of fiction.[51] Like health food and empathy gyms, what's suggested by the negative image of illness has little to do with the way stories actually migrate through the world; it tells us much more about our social anxiety regarding *other people* and the diseased ideas they might carry. It's absolutely true, of course, that developing a more discerning approach to analyzing fiction and a broader knowledge of a medium's possibilities can prevent you from being sucked in by mediocre and propagandistic storytelling, but it's easy to assume that as soon as you've been successfully inoculated, you're immune, while other people remain foolishly vulnerable forever.

Pop culture discourse often falls back on the reflexive fear and contempt for *other people*: it's only *other people* who fall for propaganda and illusion; only other people are subject to the viral effects of mimesis. And because other people can and will be infected by propaganda and illusion, it's important to isolate them from any potentially viral particles. A mass audience lacks the intelligence to parse out capitalist messaging or will simply explode in a burst of gayness if they see two ladies kiss. The Marxist sociologist Stuart Hall wrote in his famous essay on pop culture that when you imagine working people as a mindless herd of "cultural dopes" (and oneself as obviously "right, decent and self-satisfied" in comparison), you've surrendered some of the basic tenets of socialism.[52] This doesn't mean that pop culture is automatically noble or artistically interesting or anything like that—it just means the presumption that other people who enjoy popular culture are permanently stupid, with lowbrow tastes and no discernment, remains difficult to square with the belief that working people deserve a greater share of political power. It also implies a presumption of being yourself at least middlebrow, if not highbrow: positioned somewhere above the stupid masses. This may be perfectly fine for the right, but it's deadly for the left—at least, the part of the left that's compatible with and interested in mass participation in politics.

This is a tetchy issue—which I will cover in greater detail in later chapters—but I want to be clear that there's no horseshoe theory in play here, just some critics on the left and right united by a casual contempt for other human beings that sometimes masquerades as care. And they've been recently joined in this by liberals as well. Whereas the dominant liberal position for the past several decades has been that art should be "apolitical" and supporting the status quo (in supposed contrast to didactic, change-oriented communist political art), the rise of Trump caused liberal writers and story makers to rethink their roles and reposition themselves as educators of the feeble-minded masses. Conservatives have often disingenuously pretended to be against political art wholesale (by which they mean any politics other than their own), but otherwise there's now a nearly perfect agreement across all political tendencies that fiction should be not only political but didactically so, and is best interpreted and valued solely for its politics (and the more obvious the messaging, the better). Other people, in this view, are almost wholly susceptible to cultural messaging, and the culture is the best or even the only battleground on which the war for or against social change can be waged (as opposed to direct action, social movements, legislation, etc.). The presumption that art should be created and interpreted as clear political allegory has increasingly become the only kind of practicable politics, and one that's rarely good for either art or politics. Pop cultural tentpoles are supposed to, somehow, make a strong political stand while simultaneously bringing in a tidy profit for the media conglomerate that created and distributed them. That seems like a nearly impossible job.

Get a Job

Every assumption about the purpose of fiction so far—opiate for the democratic masses, healthy snack, empathy dumbbells, propaganda viruses that can infect for good or evil—has rested on the same assumption: fiction must *do* something; it must demonstrate value. If it doesn't serve a clear, healthy purpose—if it doesn't educate, improve, or convince—then either it's serving evil purposes or it's a waste of time, not to mention money (money which is of course equal to time, which could be spent making money!!!). For decades, important newspapers and magazines have relentlessly debated whether colleges and universities are justified in teaching the humanities—that is, how can you be expected to pay for something if it doesn't demonstrate an immediate, obvious return on investment?[53] The usual defense of the humanities has been some combination of healthy snacks and empathy dumbbells, plus the utilitarian value of the critical thinking skills learned from great literature, presented as an unimpressive bulwark against the tide of much more obviously profitable studies such as economics, business, marketing, and communications (famously rigorous and totally not bullshit disciplines). The sciences are also offered as practical, utilitarian options, mostly based on a fantasy about the lifestyle of respected scientists and not on the reality of what being a low-level researcher is like and what it pays. We're so accustomed to the terms of this repetitive conversation about the "value" or "purpose" of literature that it's over before it begins. Obviously, reading and creating fiction is *not* justifiable in comparison to other activities, not when you've already surrendered the basic premise that everything must demonstrate immediate practical value if it wants to exist.

Does fiction have value? Should it prove itself? The way that fine art has been turned into a mere investment vehicle in the twenty-first century seems like the dead end of the idea that artistic expression ought to have a measurable value, that it only matters if it can be put to use. A painting in a billionaire's storage space doesn't really need any paint, any labor, any intention, any art or artistry at all. In the age of NFTs, it doesn't even need a physical body, and in the age of AI, it doesn't even need a human creator. All it needs is a price tag.

Everything has a price tag now, including leisure, rebranded as "self-care": something you do to fix up the machine of your body and mind for harder labor in the future. I live with two cats who engage *only* in leisure, unless you want to call it self-care. Sometimes I look at them, lazing about while a fly crawls on the wall. "Do something!" I yell. "Earn your keep!" My cats only blink, and yawn, and settle down for another nap. Westerners have a real problem when things don't earn their keep, when the existence of something has no clear return on investment. My cats refuse to catch mice or insects: they don't even pay rent. They lie about, like my piles of unread novels lie about, because I need to work. I ran across a meme online that ruined my life; it said, "Human beings are the only species that pays to live on Earth."[54] So much went wrong when it was decided that everything had to pay its way: that all things must demonstrate their value or be replaced by something that does. The discussion of fiction has thus far required a presumption of *some* sort of value. What does fiction do to us, for us? Does it pay the rent?

Stories, right now, don't pay very much at all. Writing—the incomes of a handful of wealthy novelists and film writers excepted—is an increasingly devalued art. So why bother to talk about fiction at all if its value can't be determined, if it's either so dangerous it must be controlled or so pointless that it doesn't pay the bills? We're long past the part of a nonfiction introduction where I'm supposed to explain why the problem I'm discussing is the *biggest* problem, the most important issue facing America today, the one that must be resolved before we can tackle any of the rest. Gottschall asks, breathlessly, whether the problem of fiction is "the problem of problems? What if stories are the master factor driving so much of the world's chaos, violence, and misunderstanding?"[55]

I think the problem of fiction is probably just the problem of fiction, which is perfectly important on its own. In fiction we set the parameters of reality: as with the impossible inner life of the dog-shit brownie mom, we imagine what can't be known. What we imagine—or, more specifically, what the publishing and film and TV and comic and video game development industry will fiscally allow to be perceived in the public sphere—separates what is taken to *be* reality and what must remain a dream. When we worry about mimesis, that other people will imitate what they see and read, we don't ask what's so wrong with established reality that our fellow citizens might prefer to imitate art, might make incorrect assumptions about reality based on art, and might rest their view of human history on art. And who can afford to make that art, and why, and what remains unsaid, or at least unpublished, tells us a great deal about the limits of the social imagination and ourselves. The danger of fiction isn't so much that it changes us (though it does); the danger is that it reveals—and conceals—the limitations of our reality that is only itself a fiction, which is a set of conditions we have agreed to for now and can be rewritten at any time.

Fiction, even of the most "realistic" kind, represents what never happened, what isn't, but what maybe yet could be, in a different world than this. It's always moving in opposition to reality. All art is motion, and *in* motion. A good story goes in a direction that we were unable, previously, to see.

Could this be dangerous? Sure. But life is dangerous. The opposite—death, stagnation, stasis—is very boring. If American culture seems to be stagnant right now, it's partly because at the supposed end of history, it's more profitable to pretend there's nothing more to be said and all that remains, culturally, is to jostle for different ideological positions: to look at art not just as something that invariably *has* politics but something that's supposed to *do* politics, for us, so we don't have to. The "culture war" is a convenient frame for many political tendencies: leftist intellectuals can pin their failure to communicate with working people on a supposedly lobotomizing pop culture; liberals can turn political theater into literal theater, where a meme or a gesture *totally destroys* their opponents, thereby obviating the need to ever do anything at all; and conservatives can avoid addressing the fact that the entirety of their political ideology besides the culture war basically amounts to "kill the poor."[56]

There's great danger in pretending that fiction is the only danger, that the culture war is of such singular importance it's worth crushing art into little boxes for the sake of some future victory. Fiction may be dangerous to us, but we are also dangerous to it; we can turn art into a cause when it's often more of a symptom, we can praise writers as vital to the healthy functioning of democracy and then make sure only those who are born wealthy get to participate; we can shame people for their "low" tastes and therefore guarantee they never take pleasure in—and ownership of—a rich culture that belongs to them and everyone. We can be so invested in explaining why fiction is Important to Society that we forget that it's—most importantly—*fun*, and that's why we care about it in the first place.

And we love it. We really do *love* our favorite stories with a sincere and intense affection. When someone hates a book we had a profound emotional connection with, the effect is visceral, like hearing "You shouldn't love your boyfriend, he sucks." And maybe you shouldn't love your boyfriend, and he does suck, but love is rarely a question of "should." If we didn't fall in love with fiction, we wouldn't spend so much time worrying about how it affects other people, which is to say, displacing our worry about its effect on us.

The most loudly policed group of readers has always been women and young people, women historically having been viewed in this context as psychological minors.[57] Gottschall, helpfully, claims that science *proves* women are indeed more helpless in the sexy grip of literature.[58] On the other hand, legendarily "colorful"

New York mayor Jimmy Walker said in blunt response to the moral panic over novels in the 1920s: "No woman was ever ruined by a book."[59] This fear of ruination still lingers, a hundred years later, and so that's where we'll start. The most prominent elements of the current moral panic over fiction center around the fear that delicate girls and women (and boys) won't just fall in love with what they read—but be destroyed by it.

DANGEROUS FICTIONS

CHAPTER ONE

Get a Load of These Crazy Broads

Manatee County was so afraid of books they covered them up. In early 2023, the Florida school district ordered classroom books to be hidden or removed until each one could be vetted as safe for the delicate minds of children. The books were literally papered over, and a mocking sign read: "CLOSED by Order of the Government."[1] Florida had just passed the Stop WOKE Act, a conservative bill that was designed to curb the teaching of Black history and racial injustice as well as to block student access to "pornographic" material. The act even went so far as to make it a felony in Florida for teachers to share anything pornographic or obscene with students. Porn is, famously, something you know when you see it, meaning that it's always in the eye of the censor, and censorious right-wing parents across the country have managed to find it mostly in novels about gay, trans, and Black characters who fall in love or just learn to love themselves.[2] Only certain kinds of books, in their eyes, can ruin kids' minds. Only certain kinds of characters are obscene.

There are and have always been novels in school libraries that discuss or depict sex: they usually feature straight white characters.[3] In some cases, white and heterosexual material has also been challenged by conservatives—Sarah J. Maas's romantic fantasy series *A Court of Thorns and Roses* has been banned from at least eleven schools to date.[4] A 2022 Virginia lawsuit tried to stop Barnes & Noble from selling the second *Court* volume to minors, on the grounds that it contains sex scenes and "normalizes" abuse (it actually depicts a woman *leaving* an abusive relationship, rather movingly so for a series that has been succinctly dubbed "faerie smut").[5] The other book targeted by the attempted Barnes & Noble lawsuit was *Gender Queer*, Maia Kobabe's graphic novel–memoir about growing up nonbinary.[6] *Gender Queer*, the reigning champion of challenged books from 2021 to 2023, certainly could be considered obscene if you wanted to think of it that way: it contains scenes of masturbation and adult sex.[7] Obscenity standards, however, do allow for a book to contain sexual content if it has "literary value"—literary value being, apparently, also something you know when you see it.[8]

Librarianship is always a question of curation, and when it comes to obscenity it may feel practical to split the difference: children, you could argue, shouldn't be exposed to any sort of sexual material, whether heteronormative or otherwise.[9] But even if you set aside the subjectivity of the obscenity standard, the truth is that the supposedly pornographic books on the challenge list are almost always being read by high schoolers, who are often sexually active whether their parents want them to be or not and almost certainly didn't learn about sex from a book. Most of them probably learned it from the internet, something most kids have access to at home, with parental blockers that (sorry, parents) can be easily superseded. Given the ready availability of so much pornography online—Anthony Comstock, the censor-general of the late nineteenth century who tried to remove any potentially masturbatory material from public life, would simply have *died*—it seems strange that conservative parents would go after novels in the first place. Whether we like it or not, twenty-first-century children are easily able to view sex acts on the internet that are far beyond anything their parents can imagine, let alone what they might find in a novel. But "moral entrepreneurs" like Moms for Liberty have chosen to go after books, a perennially attackable and therefore safer subject.[10] As we find with any panic over the power of fiction, novels function here as a symbol of a deeper anxiety. In this case, Moms for Liberty confesses their real concern on their own website: their true crusade is about "parental rights."[11] Parents—or so these conservative moral entrepreneurs believe—have the right to decide what educational material their child encounters in a public school, over and above the expertise of teachers and librarians; a parent also has the right to decide what medical guidelines their child should follow, over and above the rules mandated by public health departments. Many of the newly prominent censorship organizations, including Moms for Liberty, began as anti-masking advocacy groups that campaigned to send their children to school without adequate protection during the worst of the COVID-19 pandemic. This may seem like a strange reversal of the disease/virality framework that's often associated with the fear of fiction—these parents were fine with a *literal plague* but they're hysterical over *books?*—but in many ways it's perfectly consistent. The *real* plague, the one to be concerned about, is the plague of books that contain damaging ideas, and the real fear, the one to have nightmares about, is not that your children might get sick and die (in which case they would still have been your children) but that these ideas might change your children beyond recognition (in which case they wouldn't belong to you anymore).[12]

In 1876, one of the members of the New York Society for the Suppression of Vice—Anthony Comstock's censorship organization—declared that, when it came to reading or viewing obscene material, he would prefer "that my boy and girl were brought home to me corpses than that these terrible suggestions of wrong should enter their bosoms."[13] *Better dead than changed* comes up often in conservative thought; the sentiment isn't directed just at their children but at the march of history itself. Conservatism is, so often, a fear of the passage of time. The next generation is always at mortal risk of change, which is why right-wing parenting is rife with concerns about social reproduction (and especially about girl children, since uteri are the loci of the future). If strict heterosexuality isn't observed, then the familiar, orderly, expected patterns of life might fall away, replaced by something new and uncomfortable. Old values could be discarded; traditions could be trampled; girls might make mistakes; they might experience the mortification of the flesh in all senses of the term; they might have too much sex with the wrong people, and not enough with the right ones.

Much like the persistent anxiety about fiction, anxiety about the generations repeats and repeats, varying in detail but never in theme. Back in seventeenth-century France, for example, social conservatives freaked out over the idea that young bourgeois women would decide, based on their reading of popular romantic novels, that they deserved love and marriage on their own terms. Today, social conservatives worry that their children—mainly, but not exclusively, girl children—will read the wrong novels and decide that they deserve to live their entire lives on their own terms, even if that means transitioning away from their assigned gender or pursuing same-sex relationships or not having sex at all (therefore literally putting physical reproduction, i.e., future social reproduction, at risk).[14] After decades of anxiety about sexually depraved and pregnant teenage girls, the entirety of the respectable U.S. commentariat is suddenly panicked that the kids aren't fucking enough.[15] This dovetails with media nervousness about the supposedly declining birth rate—it's actually a declining *white* birth rate, though articles on the subject rarely admit this directly.[16] The sexual and reproductive anxiety of the 2020s is at root a racial anxiety, and the generational death they fear is that of white generations specifically.

Coverage of the conservative book bans has largely skipped over the fact that most (though not all) of the agitated parents are white: the white supremacist "fourteen words" are never far behind anything they're saying.[17] This is why the other major target of censorious right-wing parents has been stories featuring Black and brown characters, even if these books don't contain anything that could be construed as sexually inappropriate. Depictions of people of color could still be damaging to the conservative mind: stories that address race in terms of historical wrongs or continued oppression might, in the words of right-wing Texas state representative Matt Krause, "make students feel discomfort, guilt, anguish, or any other form of psychological distress because of their race or sex."[18] There's no amount of discomfort, guilt, or anguish that conservatives can allow their children to experience: even momentary discomfort with the reality of white supremacy would be too much. (For some well-off, advantaged people, the worst thing that can ever happen to them is that they might feel passing psychological discomfort: they will avoid it at all costs.) The Virginia mother who claimed that reading Toni Morrison's *Beloved* gave her son night terrors—a claim opportunistically featured in a 2021 gubernatorial campaign ad for Glenn Youngkin—likewise couldn't tolerate the idea that her son felt bad for a moment, and that a great work of literature had caused it.[19]

The rhetoric about harm in Krause's bill to ban books in Texas was repeated, nearly word for word, in Florida's Stop WOKE Act; the conservative book bans and much of their language originates with right-wing "consultant" Christopher Rufo, who has tried to leverage the culture war to improve Republican prospects.[20] Rufo has even done so while acknowledging that his project is itself a type of fiction: he admitted in an interview with Zach Beauchamp of *Vox* that he deliberately communicates in an "artful and kind of narrative manner," which is not meant to be taken as the literal truth, and that his recent nonfiction book (which accuses the left of brainwashing the country through media and education) may employ a "kind of literary device" to win its cultural battles.[21] Beauchamp's article is titled "Chris Rufo's Dangerous Fictions," since a total indifference to truth is really one of the most dangerous imaginable fictions.

In fact, Rufo has generally been open on social media whenever he's inventing a narrative in real time for his stated purpose, which is to gain power for the Republican Party.[22] His war on fiction, however, has had mixed political results; it's certainly stirred up a lot of anger and anxiety, but going after children's education also tends to trigger a strong counterresponse. The Moms for Liberty school board candidates saw big gains in their early years only to be absolutely trucked in more recent elections.[23] The Central Bucks School District in Pennsylvania was so delighted to have overthrown the dominance of Moms of Liberty that it threw a celebratory tailgate (this is Pennsylvania excellence), and the new Bucks County school board president was sworn in on a stack of banned books.[24] Ron DeSantis, who chained his presidential aspirations to the culture war, was dragged down by it into the abyss. The lowest moment of DeSantis's campaign may have been his show debate against California governor Gavin Newsom, in which Newsom railed against DeSantis for banning writers such as Toni Morrison, and DeSantis could only wheeze, "False narratives!" (a narrative that was itself, of course, false).[25]

But though I could go on at length about the book banners and their hilarious failures, the unfunny part is that they don't care. Even if they're beaten, they'll be back. The battle over children's reading is so important to Rufo and his ideological progeny that it doesn't matter if it's a political loser; it doesn't matter if they're only inventing their claims that reading certain books makes children feel dangerously bad, or if they have to lie and pretend that they aren't actually banning the books that have made their children feel so dangerously bad. It doesn't even matter that they often haven't read the books they find so obscene or that many high-profile members of Moms for Liberty have been caught up in sex scandals and allegations of child abuse.[26] Their hypocrisy means nothing to them: it doesn't damage their self-conception as guardians of purity. This isn't ultimately about what's true, but about the ideological fortifications these moral entrepreneurs need to fend off the passage of time. They are desperate to maintain a picture of a world with only themselves in it.

Do No Harm

Rufo's dangerous fiction is, put plainly, the pretense that children's books are pushing unacceptable Marxist ideology that harms children; the actual truth is that, if children's books have previously had a hegemonic ideology, it's usually been a conservative one. The fear of books causing political harm and psychological distress has contributed to the (much fewer and far less organized) cases of censorship on the left and liberal side of the spectrum. *Huckleberry Finn* and *To Kill a Mockingbird* have often been targeted for bans by liberal parents, on the grounds of the former's usage of racial slurs and the latter's use of the racist "white savior" motif.[27] In 2023, Roald Dahl's popular children's books were expurgated of their fatphobic and otherwise offensive material, on the grounds that these images could harm children's developing minds.[28] Many (though not all) of the infamous Twitter book "cancellations" have centered around YA and children's literature, particularly those written by marginalized people, and have argued that these stories can do measurable psychological damage to young people. In principle, book cancellations are an attempt to protect children from the white supremacy and patriarchal ideology that's already so common in literature—in practice, unfortunately, it often looks a lot more like bullying marginalized writers, especially women writers.

I'm bringing this up not to draw false structural equivalencies between the enormous problem of conservative book bans and the very tiny problem of cancellations, but because I think it's genuinely dangerous to agree with the right's basic principles about the threat of fiction and simply apply them differently according to a different set of political priorities. If there's no ideological stand against censorship as a concept, then all we have is a contest of power, and whoever wins just happens to be whoever is politically stronger at the moment. I think it's much wiser to invalidate the grounds for the right's entire argument: otherwise, they'll always have a justification for papering over fiction they find uncomfortable. PEN America agrees with me; in 2023 it issued a report about cancellations that situates the issue in its proper minor context but emphasizes that "critics who apply a rhetoric of harm in their evaluation of YA books risk playing into the hands of book banners, who also use the language of harm and describe books as 'dangerous.'"[29]

That being said, the left and liberal rhetoric of harm is still more interesting and nuanced than the right-wing variety. And if I give the left side of the scale more weight in this chapter relative to its share as a public problem, it's only because I think these arguments are more seriously intended and deserve more thoughtful treatment. The left-wing book cancelers are trying to address real and complicated concerns; the right-wing book banners simply love power and hate time.

And since the word "cancellation" tends to get slapped over a huge variety of situations, I want to be extremely clear about what I mean by a "book cancellation." A book cancellation happens when the following conditions are met: (1) a writer has published or is about to publish a book or other work of fiction; (2) another writer or reader argues on social media that the book is racist or problematic in some way; (3) other writers and readers (who have usually only encountered contextless quotes and not read the book itself) add their voices to the call that the book is offensive; (4) the writer faces some degree of harassment and questioning of their identity; (5) often there's a direct effort to cancel the book, especially if it hasn't been published yet; and (6) the book is either canceled by the publisher or writer or pulled and reissued after an edit, or the cancellation attempt is ignored and the anger dies down, usually fairly quickly. A book cancellation of this sort does not include, in my view, writers who are criticized for extracurricular bigoted statements, called out for a pattern of sexual harassment or abuse of their colleagues, or panned in the normal way by critics who read their work and disliked it.[30] I'm only interested in the specific scenario where the work *itself* is labeled dangerous or inappropriate, with the implication or demand that something must be done about it. Declaring something dangerous is always a call to action, especially when the safety of children is at stake. "Books are dangerous," novelist Daniel José Older wrote in *The Guardian* regarding his participation in the cancellation of a children's book which he and others said was racist. "That's why we love them. Stories matter, and the stakes are higher in children's literature."[31]

For different reasons, and with different political motives, a basic framework is held in common by different actors on different sides of the political spectrum: that books are inherently threatening ideological envelopes, and stories told to young people need to be policed and controlled, lest the children develop the wrong beliefs. There's just disagreement on *which* beliefs, how many resources should be devoted to the fight, and who has the right to decide which books are healthy and safe.[32] Should it be parents, teachers, librarians, writers, or readers? Who watches the watchmen: Should parents monitor teachers and librarians, or should a loosely affiliated community of writers monitor one another on social media, writers who are competing against one another to sell books in a tight market and may have unspoken material interests in play as well as legitimate differences of opinion over whether a given story can be considered harmful?

The cancellation Older was writing about was of the very literal sort, where the children's book *A Birthday Cake for George Washington* was pulled by its publisher shortly before its debut. Critics (who mostly only saw an image of the cover, the art, and the jacket copy circulating on social media) said that the book depicted "happy slaves" and gave a false impression of history. The author, Ramin Ganeshram, who has both Trinidadian and Iranian ancestry, claims that her book was misread (if people read it at all) and misunderstood, while acknowledging that she herself wasn't pleased with the soft-focus illustrations, the ending, and the cheerful jacket copy forced on her by the publisher. She was also frustrated by critics who denied her race, particularly those "who insisted a non-white creative team would never produce such a book, took away my status as a person of color and glossed over the fact that the illustrator and editor are both African American."[33]

Most of these online cancellations have involved—as this one did—marginalized writers denouncing the work of other marginalized writers, whether they've ended with a book being literally canceled, self-pulled and reissued, or heavily criticized to the point of harassment and psychological distress. In fact, there's a notable discrepancy in whom these book cancellations choose to target and whom they choose to avoid. Extremely few living cis, heterosexual white men have had a book canceled—certainly the number of op-eds by white male novelists writing about their fear of some future cancellation wildly outstrips the number of actual books that have been removed or threatened with removal.[34] Living white male writers might be mocked for their problematic writing: you may see jokes about Stephen King's tendency to write magical Black people or George R. R. Martin's use of racist stereotypes and his penchant for rape scenes, but there have been few if any serious campaigns to get their books removed or altered. The idea of going after either King or Martin is laughable: these are *very* wealthy and famous guys, and they feel untouchable. This, I think, is unconsciously understood by everyone involved: the only writers who can be accused of harm are those who are socially precarious enough to be harmed themselves—and are also most likely to listen and take the criticism seriously in the first place.

It's true that a decent number of the book cancellations have been directed at cis, heterosexual white women, and, in the context of book publishing, it's fair to ask whether cishet white women can be truly categorized as marginalized. But if they don't face discrimination, we would expect them to be subject to cancellation in the same proportion as cishet white men, at least relative to their share in various genres. Children's, young adult, and speculative fiction seem to be the genres most often subject to cancellation efforts, but literary fiction has had its own occasional bout (such as with *American Dirt*, which involved accusations of harm and calls for the book to be pulled, but no actual action by the publisher). There is, however, no cishet white male version of *American Dirt*; no cishet white male version of something like Elizabeth Gilbert's novel *Snow Forest*, a book which was indefinitely delayed after a public outcry over the fact that it was going to be set in Russia (Russia had invaded Ukraine some months previously, and readers seem to have decided that any remotely positive portrayal of Russians by a sufficiently famous woman was offensive). Gender is really the defining factor, as books by non-white and non-famous women are just as likely to be targeted for cancellation: *Everything's Fine*, the debut novel by Black writer Cecilia Rabess—which is partly about an interracial romance—was labeled anti-Black by critics who mostly hadn't read it.[35] In fact most of these books have been condemned without being read, on the grounds that they *could* have negative political consequences for unwise readers. In fact, writers these days are increasingly being held responsible for any ways their book could be read, even if unfair and sloppy, even if based on a two-sentence excerpt briefly glimpsed on Twitter. In an increasingly feminized literary profession, the writer is usually conceptualized as a woman and women are still responsible for other people's feelings, impressions, and moral hygiene.

If online cancellations are almost exclusively a matter of readers targeting writers they perceive as vulnerable, this suggests that—as always—something else is in play beyond simply criticizing bigoted books and trying to prevent the spread of bigotry among the reading public. Ganeshram expressed frustration with a publisher who betrayed her best interests and that of the book: when it came to that problematic jacket copy, she says that the publisher "ignored or refused" every one of her suggested changes. Her account of events may be self-serving, but it's true that most authors   and workers in artistic industries more generally—have little recourse when it comes to disagreements with mainstream producers, other than to seek less-lucrative indie publishers or to take on self-publishing with all its risks. Writers from especially marginalized backgrounds may reasonably feel they have less freedom than most, and a narrower path toward success.

The book cancellations, generally imagined as being perpetrated solely by a hysterical horde of angry, childlike women and/or people of color, arise from genuine frustrations at the state of the industry; they also have tended to fall hardest on those who are already most damaged by the industry. Older, in response to PEN America's condemnation of the response to *A Birthday Cake for George Washington*, asked PEN and other organizations to turn their focus toward the lack of diversity in publishing.[36] The problem he points to is genuine, though it's not clear that lack of diversity was the specific issue for the book in question or that individual social media callouts will solve what is ultimately a crisis of power and money.

These callouts might be best understood as a reflexive frustration, a last-ditch effort by marginalized writers and readers who feel shut out from any real power in the publishing world (and elsewhere), turning their energy toward an attempt to fix the social reproduction of the generations. Maybe, if children are exposed to the right literature—and only the right literature—the world of the future might be more equitably distributed; maybe through strict standards of appropriate character behavior, we can rewrite reality. It's a nice idea, though it reveals itself by its own faithlessness; surely there would be efforts to cancel problematic work by living white men (and there's plenty) first and hardest, rather than focusing on work by the marginalized, just as the conservatives do in their book bans, and using a similar rhetoric of harm. And "harm" is hardly an invention of the social media age: there's a long history of children—especially girls—being designated as uniquely vulnerable readers, and women writers (and women characters) classed as uniquely responsible for educating them. What's actually at stake in this particular history—which dates back to the seventeenth century at least—is the depiction of reality, and who gets to determine what that means.

Think of the (Rich Girl) Children

Molière's first play—*Les précieuses ridicules* (1659)—isn't often performed, which is a shame because the play and the metanarrative of its creation presages so much about our current moment. Often translated as "the ridiculous ones" or "the affected ladies," *Les précieuses* is a farce about a pair of teenage bourgeois girls who have read silly romantic novels and developed all the wrong ideas about gender and sexuality. Thanks to these dangerously bad books, they've decided that they should have a choice in the men they marry, and that their marriages should wait "until after the other adventures."[37] To a contemporary audience, this is more or less baseline feminism, but to a seventeenth-century one it was a ridiculous violation of social norms. Sure, a *story* might feature an aristocratic heroine who deserved to be loved and respected, but respectable bourgeois girls in real life were bred for marriage and reproductive labor: they weren't much better than pretty cattle. If a novel could theoretically lead them to expect otherwise, that wasn't just funny to imagine; it was a threat to social reproduction. By the end of the play, the girls are humiliated, the patriarchal order is restored, and the threat posed by silly novels is averted—for now.

The play was a huge hit, and it made Molière's career: Louis XIV himself saw it several times.[38] It clearly appealed to the well-heeled audience's anxieties about literate young women who had too high an opinion of their own intelligence and agency. It's unclear if the "précieuses" ever existed as a group or a real social threat; nobody appears to have ever used that word for themselves, and scholars are divided on whether the term refers to a genuine proto-feminist movement or a bunch of YA girls made up to get mad at, a sort of public fiction.[39] Given how sheltered bourgeois women were at the time, there were probably at least a few girls who lived their lives through books and said some silly and pretentious things, but as often happens with moral panics, a handful of real examples are blown up into a horde, a hysteria, an irrational and all-consuming enemy that must be destroyed. It's a lot like the blame placed on "YA Twitter" or "puriteens" or "tenderqueers" as the lone source of silly readers and book cancellation efforts: when adult literary and speculative fiction novelists are also scrapping on social media over problematic books, the problem probably lies elsewhere, including in the design of the platforms themselves.

New technology also lay behind the précieuse panic: by the mid-seventeenth century the printing press was well established, and more women were reading than ever before, taking part in what could legitimately be considered a popular culture. It's worth noting how deliberately limited this culture was: there's no extant Molière play about what would happen if, say, slaves in the French Atlantic possessions of the time started reading novels and developing ideas about freedom and the social order. Some anxieties, it seems, can't be turned into laughs. What was happening with the précieuses, however, was a manageable fear. Literate teenage white girls had new and unprecedented access to information and diversion that lay outside of their parents' homes, and while that was scary, there were solutions. The parental right (in this era, the father's right) to shape children's minds and behavior could be reasserted over the pernicious influence of fiction—specifically over the pernicious influence of one woman's fiction.

Molière never mentions her directly, but the enthusiastic teen girls in his play constantly reference their favorite books by Madeleine de Scudéry, who was a kind of seventeenth-century literary pop star, famous for her lengthy romantic adventure novels.[40] Every era of western history seems to have a wildly popular woman novelist who disappears from public memory, and it's possible Scudéry would have disappeared anyway, since the vast majority of novelists don't survive the churn of the centuries.[41] But in Scudéry's case there was also a deliberate attempt to bury her, a sort of conservative proto-cancellation campaign by other writers, on the grounds that her books represented characters in ways that were both wrong and dangerous.

Molière's play was the start, but the full attack came from

another writer. Nicholas Boileau—a poet, classicist, friend of Molière's, and rival of Scudéry's—claimed that her novels (and all novels of any kind) were both bad and dangerous art.[42] He said they failed to represent male heroes with *vraisemblance*, i.e., the men were unrealistic. This is a hugely important claim, based on a presumption that we tend to accept without really thinking about it: fiction is bad when it falsely represents reality, ergo fiction's job is to present people realistically. "Realistic," however, is and has always been a political category: much of the time, it's prescriptive rather than descriptive. In Boileau's case, he felt that Scudéry's men were unbelievably loving and romantic; they should be tough and manly, like the real heroes of the past so obviously were.[43] Scudéry had actually based one of her male protagonists on a friend of hers, a prince who had famously been involved in a doomed romance with a woman he couldn't marry, but this, to Boileau, was irrelevant: it was Scudéry's job as a writer, especially as a popular one, to provide tough and manly exemplars for men to imitate and women to fall in love with, for the sake of civic order and social reproduction.[44] It wasn't about what was "real" and really happening in the world at the time of the writing—realism rarely is—but what was normative: the social values that ought to be imparted to readers to shape the world of the future.

Boileau's critique went beyond mockery and personal dislike—every writer's prerogative—into a now-familiar accusation of public harm. He accused Scudéry of setting a dangerous precedent, of infecting readers with the wrong ideas. What if women decided, based on their reading of novels, that men should be kind and romantic? What if, say, a girl in the twenty-first century reads Sarah J. Maas's *A Court of Mist and Fury* and decides that it's okay to leave her abuser? Whatever the era, the fear is the same: that cis, heterosexual men will lose their power to set the terms of relationships; that cis, heterosexual men will no longer control social reproduction. The problem is only magnified when the broader matrix of gender and heterosexuality itself is called into question, threatening patriarchal control not just directly but also existentially. Scudéry's novel *Clélie* references a sort of joking board game about courtship called the Carte du Tendre (the Map of Tenderland), and in *Les précieuses ridicules*, the girls take this game literally, as if it were a factual depiction of the necessary stages of courtship.[45] What *would* happen, the play suggests, if silly girl readers started interpreting the Carte du Tendre as strict rules that must be followed? Why, if they had their way, the map of Tenderland would be unrolled over the map of France. Night would become day; women would rule men; what had begun in fiction would grow to subsume reality. Girls would run the world.[46]

It didn't matter whether this was actually happening, or was expected to happen, or whether the précieuses even existed in a force that could make anything happen in the first place: the fear that they might have, and that novels could lead them there, was enough. A good part of western fiction and criticism over the next two centuries would move toward conceiving of novels as moral objects, in hopes that vulnerable readers—especially girls, as usual—wouldn't be harmed by being influenced by the wrong reality.

One Goldilocks, Please, Hold the Bears

The "realism" of the eighteenth- and nineteenth-century western novel was a very careful one, which excluded much of the violent reality of colonization. Scudéry's novels were mostly globe-trotting adventure stories, but the girls in the domestic realist novels that followed usually stayed home.[47] In England, Samuel Richardson's *Pamela; or, Virtue Rewarded* (1740) billed itself as intended "to *instruct* and *improve* the minds of the YOUTH of *both sexes*," a typical marketing statement for books aimed at young readers in this era.[48] The novel ends with a description of the characters, and the moral lessons to be drawn from each, with Pamela herself described as worthy of imitation by young lady readers.[49] She refuses to give up her virginity to a rich jerk until he marries her; in this she's both the ancestress of most romance novels and an ideal conservative heroine. By following the fictional Pamela's example, and having lawful sex with the right man, at the right time, young white girl readers can also do their social reproductive duty. (I want to be clear that I love *Pamela* and am not trying to cancel it—but please don't tell Moms for Liberty about it either.)

Pamela was a big hit: it would also later be considered one of the first "true" novels, or true English novels. As plenty of obviously genuine novels preceded it, including forty years of English epistolary novels in basically the same style, a specious ranking system seems to be in place.[50] It does sort of make sense, however, if one of the key characteristics of a "true" novel is that it has vraisemblance: it depicts the world in a way that instructs and improves. A century later, Gustave Flaubert would be sued by the French government on the grounds that *Madame Bovary* had failed in its moral duty to instruct readers in good behavior; specifically, it was charged with depicting the adulterous affairs of Emma Bovary—who, like the précieuses, has been seduced by novels—too *realistically*.[51] Flaubert got into trouble because he went too far with his realism: he skated right past normativity into honesty, presenting the life, scandalous affairs, and awful death of Emma Bovary in an "impersonal narrative voice," as the prosecutor claimed, a technique that "left the reader with no perspective from which to judge the behavior of Emma Bovary."[52] And without clear judgment and punishment for badly behaved characters, a novel is—dangerously—just a novel: a work of art and not a moral lesson.

Every "representation versus endorsement" debate is an echo

of Flaubert versus the French government. We see it in the on-going debates over *Lolita* and whether Nabokov is representing or endorsing the pedophilic Humbert Humbert (Nabokov, being safely dead, is the kind of white man who can be canceled). Aesthetic questions about, say, whether a male pervert's perspective might be overexposed in literature and boring at this point fall away before the moral anxiety over whether readers will draw the wrong lessons from Humbert Humbert and consider him a hero to emulate. Representation is always endorsement if you assume that readers (always other readers, never you) are fundamentally stupid, incapable of doing anything other than identifying with the protagonist and absorbing their values. And then if readers are stupid, especially young readers, then it isn't safe for novels to depict the real world in all its variety, especially ugly and socially condemned behavior. Fiction, by this logic, should only ever depict a Goldilocks level of realism, one that instructs and improves.

The conservative book banners are very clear on this point: they have demanded that school libraries remove all books about gay and trans characters because they view the whole topic as something that deserves to be socially condemned. It doesn't comport with their normative ideas of realism, a realism that has little to do with what is real or representative of total human experience, but with what they believe ought to be real, which values ought to be centered, how gender ought to be portrayed, and how sex ought to be rewarded or punished. Ultimately, many conservatives (and a distressing number of liberals) think of gay or trans people as some sort of cheat or deception; it's easier to believe that gay and trans children are simply being "groomed" or peer-pressured into changing their gender or sexual identity than accepting that they were always gay or trans in the first place. It's unlikely that Disney movies can "trans" kids, as Ron DeSantis has claimed, or that Monica Brown's son—she of the dog-shit brownies—became gay because he watched *Avengers: Age of Ultron*.[53] (On the other hand, it would be reasonable to pick up on Joss Whedon's misogynist characterization of Black Widow in that movie and decide the entire apparatus of heterosexuality is simply not for you.) It's always more comforting to blame the images in popular fiction—and police its boundaries—than endure the fact that other realities could coexist alongside or in opposition to conservative, normative realism.[54]

Setting the bounds of realism to exclude gay or trans children doesn't make these children un-gay or un-trans, but it works to deprive them of a language, a set of images, to describe how they feel, so that they have no choice but to grow up and enter cis, heterosexual, married life with a sense of indefinable misery—so that they might suffer through "the long littleness of life," in Vivian Gornick's phrase, just as their parents did, and the generations might continue to be reproduced in the exact same way.[55] Conservatives would argue—and they often do—that their aim is to protect children from misery: to keep them from "discomfort, guilt, anguish, or any other form of psychological distress." After all, children can be hurt by too much reality: we already keep them away from certain kinds of media via parental guidance ratings and content warnings, on the basis that too much violence, sex, or fearful images could be dangerous for their delicate minds.

Back in the late nineteenth century, a reverend who supported Comstock's crackdown on obscene material claimed that "even a single bad picture or book could ruin the purity of a child forever."[56] This is the most extreme version of the argument, but most people basically agree that children's minds are fragile and too much of the wrong imagery can cause serious and permanent harm. "I'm glad I waited until well into adulthood to read [Patricia] Highsmith," the *New York Times* book critic Sarah Weinman wrote in 2023, "because danger lurks for anyone who might take life lessons from her memorable male antiheroes."[57] Grown-ups, maybe, can handle

Tom Ripley: impressionable children and teens, however, will presumably go around Europe murdering their best friends on a boat.

Representation, Reparation

How fragile are children and teenagers, really? To what extent are they influenced, for life, by what they read and see? The modern concept of "childhood" is only a few centuries old, as is the concept of a separate "children's literature." The Victorians were especially invested in the innocence of children, mummifying and even eroticizing the image of the pure and faultless child. It's true that we're often affected in strange ways by the fiction we encounter early in our lives, inscribed with lifelong obsessions and nightmares. There have even been a few isolated instances of young people acting out violently based on their misunderstanding of the difference between fiction and reality, such as the 2014 incident in Waukesha, Wisconsin, where two teenage girls tried to murder a classmate as a sacrifice to the fictional character Slenderman. Because Slenderman is a creation of the internet, the internet was blamed for their act: the Waukesha police chief claimed (accurately) that it's "full of dark and wicked things." But plenty of kids have run across Slenderman and other "creepypasta" online and never tried to kill anybody. In her coverage of the case, journalist Abigail Jones noted that murders committed by teenage girls—because of what they read in fiction or for any reason—remain extremely rare. When it comes to the Slenderman killers, "their act is so unusual," she writes, "that it tells us little about our daughters."[58]

Other fictional material has more common, if subtle, effects on our daughters and ourselves. Sexual preferences and paraphilias are often rooted in stories from childhood, including Disney movies, even if the material in question isn't overtly sexual or intentionally "grooming." Many furries trace their adult sexual interest in anthropomorphized animals to Disney's animated *Robin Hood* (1973) and other animal cartoons they watched as children.[59] On the other hand, not every child who watches *Robin Hood* will wind up with a lifetime erotic attachment to cartoon foxes. I watched it when I was five years old, and I've never had a thing for fox-people; I did watch *Beauty and the Beast* around the same time, and ended up with a houseful of books, a pretty teapot, and a shaggy-bearded husband. As a matter of fact, the original Beauty and the Beast fairy tale was supposed to be a "grooming" story, a variant of the "animal groom" motif, theoretically intended to help warm up virginal girls to the idea of sex with their (often old and hairy) husbands.[60] And yet some kids might watch *Beauty and the Beast* and only develop a fetish for women dressed as teapots or a lifelong preference for skinny, dramatic Frenchmen—or have no reaction to any of it whatsoever. The long-term effects of any given story are impossible to predict.

There's at least one storytelling element for which we have reliable data: the matter of representation. A 2007 study by Paul W. Richardson and Jacquelynne S. Eccles closely examined how adolescent readers responded over time to their reading. The effects were varied, and unrelated stressors and social-environmental issues also played a large role in the psychic development of individual children, but Richardson and Eccles did find that, in general, voluntary reading (not assigned classroom reading) "allowed adolescents to explore *possible selves*" and that being able to explore the identities of people like themselves was of special value to Black children in particular.[61] Anecdotally, many marginalized people have reported the special joy of seeing themselves on the page. The Afro-Latino author Torrey Maldonado has said that he didn't encounter a picture book featuring a Black protagonist or a neighborhood like his until the third grade. When he finally read *The Snowy Day* (1962), the first U.S. children's book to feature a Black protagonist, "I thought that book was me! . . . What made that book so precious to me is it took my neighborhood and made me see the magic in it."[62]

The *New York Times* writer Jay Caspian Kang, in a 2022 piece about the new availability of diverse books—and his joy that he could introduce his young daughter to "a healthier understanding of self and culture than I had at her age"—wrote that he was pleased that the books his daughter read "are far more diverse and honest about race than they were back in my day." But he noted that while some of these diverse, anti-racist books are quite good, a lot of them are heavy-handed and pedantic. They're very much meant to instruct and improve, *Pamela* style, with nothing left up to any question of representation versus endorsement, and often using words more suitable for grown-ups than kids, such as "policy," "equity," and "access." He suggests the possibility that these books are more intended for white adults than Black and brown children, or at least they have a dreary assigned-reading feel.[63] It's entirely possible that some of this literature really is intended for white people, aimed more at the misty hope of "increasing empathy" than representing children of color to themselves.

The goal of presenting more diverse characters for the sake of marginalized readers themselves has often been presented in tandem with the goal of deprogramming the dominant classes, as if the two are effectively the same. Ellen Oh, founder of We Need Diverse Books, treated both as basically equal objects in a speech she gave to the 2022 School Library Journal Summit, while also tying them into the matter of the conservative book bans:

> Everyone in this room knows how powerful books are . . . It's why there's so many attempts to ban them, censor them, burn them. Books contain knowledge, books teach empathy, books open us up to new worlds and thoughts and

lives . . . If racism and bigotry [are] not taught in
the classroom, if books about marginalized kids
are censored and unavailable, we risk creating
a generation of kids who have never learned the
true meaning of empathy, that never learned the
true, shameful history of this country and who
will repeat the atrocities of the past. And when
marginalized kids don't see themselves in the literature they read, we teach them that they are not
valued, not wanted, that they are not equal. There
is no greater devastation to a child than to feel that
there is no place for them in the world.[64]

It's worth asking, though, whether the real and important (and
measurably effective) goal of representing marginalized children
to themselves in the literature they read also has the effect of ending bigotry in the hearts and minds of other people who read these
books. When it comes to the power of art to fight bigotry, we return to pumping iron in the empathy gym—and may end up treating racism and misogyny as a fundamental problem of *bad thoughts*,
which can simply be overcome with access to the right books at the
right times.

In *Pamela*, the heroine is only able to prove her humanity to
the rich and terrible Mr. B once he reads enough of her letters: her
verbal pleas don't convince him, only her artistically fluent narrative of trauma and despair. It's quite fucked up, and quite a fantasy,
to imagine that this rich white man, who spends the entire first part
of the book trying to rape Pamela, just needs to see enough written proof of her humanity to understand she's a person and that
raping her is wrong. Misogyny doesn't remain a lingering social
problem simply because certain men have failed to read enough
books by and about women; certain men don't read books by and

about women because they are uninterested in women's lives. Boys don't need books to tell them that girls are people: most boys grow up with mothers, sisters, grandmothers, women teachers, and girl classmates, whom they could choose to see as human beings at any time. Assuming that members of dominant classes are merely ignorant of the humanity of other people and just need a little education presumes an innocence on their part that may not be deserved.

When it comes to matters of race and representation in particular, the Black filmmaker Blair McClendon wrote in June 2020 that "it is flattering to our history and to artistic practice to say the problem resides in an inability to recognize humanity . . . What goes without interrogation is whether a shared humanity was ever the problem to begin with." In McClendon's view, the power of images and storytelling to fight bigotry has been largely overstated, since the problem is not a lack of empathy on the part of white people—a lack of empathy that supposedly could be treated through fiction—but rather their refusal to stop reaping the material benefits of racism. "It is not that people have treated each other this way simply because they do not recognize another person's humanity," he writes, "but that humanity is no shield against untethered power." Too much emphasis on the power of storytelling, he believes, is a political dead end. "My fear is that the storytellers have fooled themselves into believing that it is narratives, image-making, representation that offer a way out. They envision reconciliation before the cessation of hostilities."[65]

If fictional representation is the *first* problem—the most important problem, the one that must be solved before any social progress can be made—then material inequality can be punted into some unknown future, to be dealt with when white people have finally come to their senses. This moves anti-racism almost solely into the sphere of artistic and intellectual control, giving writers a feeling of power and importance, which is about inversely equal to their lack of compensation. It also provides a constant and consistent answer to all remaining inequalities: we simply need more and better representation in fiction, both to provide a safe space for marginalized children in an otherwise horribly bigoted society and to teach the beneficiaries of that horribly bigoted society good and actionable lessons. Therefore, anything done in the name of increasing and improving representation can be justified—even attacking writers in ways that lack empathy, and might be defined as wildly cruel.

The Princess Competition

In 2019, Amelie Wen Zhao, an up-and-coming young writer in the "own voices" YA novel scene, was about to publish her debut novel *Blood Heir*. Zhao, who had found an agent through a Twitter pitching event for marginalized creators, had won a rare six-figure deal for *Blood Heir*, the first volume of an intended fantasy trilogy. But six months before her debut, Zhao "self-canceled" *Blood Heir* after the book was accused of anti-Blackness (among other faults). Much of the criticism came from Black YA novelist L. L. McKinney, who read an advance review copy of the book and claimed on Twitter that Zhao's depiction of slavery was a problematic depiction of Black slavery in America. Zhao, when she pulled the book, said that the indentured servitude in her fantasy story wasn't drawn from U.S. history, or intended to parallel it any way, but was based on "the epidemic of indentured labor and human trafficking prevalent in many industries across Asia," including China, where Zhao grew up.[66] Ultimately, *Blood Heir* was revised and published, as were its sequels, and it's possible the negative attention and notoriety may have resulted in better sales for Zhao.

The YA scene has been ground zero for book cancellations in part because of the presumed delicacy of its largely young and female readership, but also because, at least for a while, it was one of the few parts of the publishing industry where it seemed like there was money to be made. Writing a popular YA novel series could lead to a film or television deal—at least for a small handful of white women novelists. Like all other writers, YA novelists have been competing for an increasingly narrow slice of the publishing pie, and it's no coincidence that the plots of so many YA novels have centered around ferocious competitions for survival and recognition. Much coverage of the *Blood Heir* controversy has centered around the specific nature of McKinney's callout and the age-old question of whether something can be considered "objectively" offensive. But while I don't doubt that McKinney meant her critiques sincerely, the issue is hopelessly muddled by the fact that she and Zhao are competitors in the same field, and there are unmistakable material advantages to knocking out the competition. There are also disadvantages: an industry professional close to the situation told me that McKinney had received death threats for her role in the cancellation of *Blood Heir.*

Many of the book cancellations, in any genre, have been as much about money and access as they have been about problematic content. Myriam Gurba, who led the unsuccessful cancellation attempt against *American Dirt*, was upset about the racist stereotypes she saw in the text but also angry that the writer, Jeanine Cummins, received a seven-figure advance for it in the first place, while Latina writers like Gurba (and most writers) generally get a lot less.[67] Separate problems tend to get lumped together: the publishing industry remains an unequal economic environment, with a few mostly white megastars and an undercompensated everyone else. Still, it's not clear how singling out individual writers—as opposed to publishers—is supposed to address either representation or unequal compensation. Cummins was reportedly devastated by the reaction to her book, but it was still a *New York Times* bestseller for over thirty weeks.[68] Possibly cancellation attempts like these will result in publishers being more thoughtful and careful about what books they choose and how they edit them in the future—but then again, the publishing industry exists to make money, and a bestseller is a bestseller. Negative attention is still attention, and attention moves product.

The book cancellations have often been described as the inevitable process of a given literary community regulating itself, but these events aren't taking place around a conference table or in some utopian city of mutual amity. They're taking place in a brutal capitalist society among highly individualized laborers who are competing against each other. (Screenwriters rarely try to cancel each other like this; screenwriters have a union.) Much of the action is driven on and by social media platforms like Twitter (X, if you're nasty), Goodreads, and TikTok. None of these are healthy places: Twitter, even before it changed ownership, was a corporate forum designed from the ground up to encourage cruelty and harassment.[69] The psychically deforming architecture of these particular tech platforms underlies most of these left-leaning book cancellations and censorship debates; centuries-old rhetoric is buttressed by a technology that is designed to single people out and cause them pain.

The most brutal book cancellation (so far) was issued against a previously unknown and marginalized writer. Isabel Fall, a trans woman writer, debuted her first science fiction short story, "I Sexually Identify as an Attack Helicopter," on the science fiction site *Clarkesworld* in January 2020. The title draws from a transphobic meme (which the story means to undercut) and, for a few days, became a subject of huge controversy on Twitter. The early criticism focused on the actual content of the story itself, which some readers felt had legitimate flaws, and then morphed to being about lack of equity and access—could a trans writer get a short story published *unless* it had a controversial clickbait title? After that, the debate mutated again—horribly—into whether Isabel Fall was a real trans woman or a right-wing troll and, if the latter, whether the story was designed to harm trans people. Major names in the speculative fiction scene weighed in, including N. K. Jemisin and other writers who have been major advocates for greater diversity in publishing.[70] Fall ended up pulling the story—and checking into a psychiatric ward for suicidal ideation. Having her identity questioned as a trans woman not only drove her to thoughts of suicide but also drove Fall back into the closet, and she reportedly detransitioned back to her previous identity.[71]

It's not clear what broader goal of diversity and anti-bigotry was achieved by the broader science fiction/fantasy community rejecting Fall in this way. After the "Attack Helicopter" incident and *American Dirt*, the book cancellation trend appeared to lose some energy, as if the cruelty of the one and the ineffectiveness of the other made the whole prospect less palatable—or possibly because Twitter itself became less usable, and many people shifted over to Goodreads and TikTok. Publishers at this time also moved on to mild censorship of dead white male writers: expurgating Roald Dahl and axing a few racial slurs out of Ian Fleming novels (but notably not removing whole racist characters like Oddjob, or James Bond's legendary misogyny).

The Roald Dahl censorship drive has largely been blamed on "sensitivity readers," though a 2023 *Salon* article claims that the advice to Dahl's publisher came from the organization Inclusive Minds, whose website explicitly states that they are not sensitivity readers but rather "a network of young people with many different lived experiences."[72] If Inclusive Minds really is composed of teenagers, then it would be a highly unusual organization in historical terms. Young people rarely demand their own fragility; they've usually been the imagined others who need to be protected.[73] The existence of this company dovetails, however, with claims that we're beset online these days by a plague of puritanical queer children bent on policing art, though the actual evidence of this movement is mixed at best and could be explained in part as teen rebellion against the hypersexualized culture of the past few decades (whatever the dominant culture may be, the kids always rebel against it).[74] Regardless, the kids these days are often considered uniquely responsible for bad behavior online: they're often first to be blamed for any given cancellation attempt.

In fact, when the "Attack Helicopter" incident happened, I noticed that blame for the attack on Fall was almost immediately placed on "tenderqueers," a theorized internet movement of oversensitive young gay and trans people who attack and harass marginalized creators who make sexually explicit and messy art.[75] "Tender" in the case of tenderqueers doesn't refer so much to the tenderness of human kindness but to the fragility of feelings so soft that the slightest brush may bring out a trauma response. Whether the excessively delicate tenderqueers and puriteens exist as a significant force—as with the précieuses, few if any self-identify with these terms—Fall herself didn't hold the tenderqueers especially accountable for what happened to her. In a later interview, she said that she was most hurt not by the reaction from fellow trans people, but from the established cis women writers who thought they were acting as allies by condemning her in the name of vulnerable young trans people.[76]

Young people often behave stupidly, especially on the internet, and looking back at the ancient days of the précieuses we see that young people who don't conform to established gender roles have always made convenient targets for all the ills that supposedly plague the reading of fiction. (Cishet boys and men are rarely imagined as tenderqueers or puriteens; these names are reserved for the girls and gays.) Still, I think it's fair to see in the contemporary rhetoric of "literary harm," whether it's being wielded by the likely small group of real tenderqueers or by anyone else, that two strains of thought have been synthesized into one: certain populations are frail and must be protected from harm, and those who would do them harm through wicked fictions are dangerous and must be condemned. Boileau and the précieuses have collapsed into one, and sometimes the literary salon joins them too, all in the name of protecting the fragile and the traumatized, who are too delicate not to be harmed by art. Even a single bad picture or book can ruin their psychic purity, forever.

Chilling (In a Good Way)

How much harm can one story do? It's never just one story. No novel debuts in an innocent vacuum: books like *Blood Heir* and *A Birthday Cake for George Washington* were intended to be published in an America where, in many states (thanks in part to Chris Rufo), an entire racist curriculum teaches happy slaves as facts and the founding fathers as heroes. Maybe one bad book doesn't ruin a mind, but an avalanche of them makes a difference, especially if only one version of reality is depicted in fiction while most alternatives are suppressed. If book cancellations create a chilling effect, it's somewhat beneficial: it never hurts fiction writers to be more thoughtful about their work, especially when it comes to matters of race and the often monstrous history of the Americas.

In the face of the far more serious matter of the book bans—and the economic imbalance of the publishing industry—it doesn't seem like a good idea for marginalized writers to pick each other off individually; it would be better to extend to one another the same courtesy usually reserved for living cishet white male writers, who are allowed the artistic grace of having their work criticized as art rather than being sent back like a bad meal. It's also best, I think, to turn away from perceiving young and often feminine readers as fragile fools and toward respecting them as human beings who are capable of discernment and just want to read interesting stories about people like themselves, to see the full complexity of their reality represented at last.

Policing fiction into narrower and narrower visions of reality—and policing writers into narrower and narrower versions of themselves—has historically been a conservative position, and we should leave them to it. There will never be a version of this policing that's enough, no place of absolute safety that can be reached. In 2023, the Houston Independent School District—which has 90 percent minority enrollment—announced that it was going to turn some of its libraries into "Team Centers," or glorified time-out corners for misbehaving students.[77] If books are full of harmful ideas that might cause children to act out if they learned about them, the safest solution will always be to get rid of them entirely.[78] The children can never be made safe (and inert, and nonthreatening) enough. The dead end of harm is no art at all, a reality perfectly protected from stories about it.

Books can harm: they can hurt, upset, demean. But we also survive our reading. Children grow up, we become adults who reckon with what we encountered in our past, however painful and damaging it may have been. We continue on, existing somewhere in the space between fiction and reality. Time passes.

CHAPTER TWO

The Victory of the Nerds

The further fiction gets from reality, the more suspicious it tends to become. This isn't a universal truth but a modern one, in that it literally was ushered in with modernity and the modern novel. *Don Quixote* is often called the first "real" western novel; it could also be called the first salvo in the war against the nerds.[1] The protagonist himself is the ur-typical nerd: a quiet, educated guy (though not young) who goes crazy and starts LARPing as his original character, Don Quixote. Armed with all the chivalric lore in existence, the newly minted Don Quixote takes to the road to seek adventures (and mostly gets the shit kicked out of him). His friends try to help him out by burning his library—after salvaging the best chivalric romances, the well-written sort whose existence they can justify as "improving" literature. But it's too late: Don Quixote has already been ruined by his reading, all those unacceptable non-novels, which convinced him that his fantasy is more real than reality, certainly better than reality. Only after many adventures and defeats does Don Quixote finally go home, and come to his senses, regretting that he doesn't have time to read better books, the kind, he says, "that can be a light to the soul" rather than the silly adventures that only describe a difference between reality and happiness that would drive even the most respectable person insane.[2]

Four hundred years later, heroic adventures are everywhere: the war is over, and the nerds have won. Statistics vary, but about five of the top ten bestselling books of all time are fantasy novels, while eight of the top ten biggest box-office hits can reasonably be classed as science fiction.[3] There's even a level of mainstream critical acceptance: pop culture media properties are commonly reviewed in the handful of serious publications that still exist. Writers of literary fiction increasingly cross over into genre, often with squeaky disclaimers in press interviews about how their writing isn't actually genre fiction, at least not the *bad* kind, those supposedly silly and escapist junk adventure stories.[4] Even "escapism" has lost its conceptual dunce cap: a number of essays in the last few years have touted the psychic value of escapist fiction, because no one wants to live in this world, despite the fact that we all still have to.[5]

This change in the perception of science fiction and fantasy is so recent that I, an ancient hag in my thirties, still remember when it was distinctly *not* okay to publicly enjoy this kind of fiction. When I was growing up in the 1990s, it might have been okay to watch *Star Wars* or read *The Lord of the Rings* (and millions of people did), but to be excited about them, to treat them like *good art*, to get lost in those worlds—that was for dorks alone. Just about everything in the realm of science fiction or fantasy was associated during my childhood with a kind of sad, failed masculinity, unless (particularly in the case of video games) it was a wild, hyperviolent, and uncontrolled masculinity. And if you were a girl who liked these things, forget about it: you must have been socially or sexually unfit yourself, and your male comrades were scornful, thinking that because science fiction and fantasy were for men, then clearly, you were only hanging about because you were hoping to have sex with them. (You were hoping to have sex! With them!!!)

This was the best-case scenario. The worst-case scenario was what N. K. Jemisin described experiencing on early fantasy and sci-fi internet forums such as Asimov: key gathering places for genre fans in the less respectable days. "For a while," she told an interviewer in 2015, "you would go into the Asimov forum and see people openly speculating about the humanity of black people, or women."[6] The science fiction and fantasy publishing sector has slowly diversified since the 1990s and 2000s, to some backlash from a relatively small old guard of bigots in the community.[7] In the mid-2010s, a group of mostly white, mostly male sci-fi writers calling themselves the Sad Puppies—if you're unfamiliar with this story, I am not making this up, they really called themselves *sad puppies*—launched racist attacks against Jemisin and other writers of color and tried to rig the annual Hugo Awards in their favor. The whole effort was a short-lived offshoot of Gamergate, which survives today in the near-daily right-wing reaction to every new remake or sequel in the pop cultural sphere that features just a little diversity. The film and television part of this backlash is a complex phenomenon, and I'll deal with it in depth in a later chapter. But it does make sense that the racists have mostly moved on from books to more popular and lucrative targets. There isn't much money or visibility in book publishing—increasingly less of both—but there's still quite a bit in film and television. When Black sci-fi legend Samuel Delany was asked about the Sad Puppies in 2015, he noted that the pushback is "socio-economic" at its root: a fear that resources are limited and that white, straight men might lose the competitive advantage they've held so far over everyone else.[8]

Resources may be limited, and competition may be fierce, but there's still money to be made, or at least, attention to be gained.

If science fiction and fantasy novels, movies, and television have become increasingly mainstream and culturally acceptable, that's likely because they've become sufficiently profitable—or arguably, there's a point at which "mainstream," "culturally acceptable," and "profitable" all end up meaning the same thing. Of course, science fiction and fantasy was always profitable and popular in its novel form—in 1990, William Gibson used the uncomfortable phrase "the golden ghetto" to describe science fiction's monetary advantages and lack of critical approval.[9] The real change took root about a decade later, with the big-budget (and critically well-regarded) film adaptations of *The Lord of the Rings*, plus the concurrent deluge of superhero films and the corporate consolidation that makes them possible. Again, much of this has to do with money: regardless of their lukewarm quality, these films are big, expensive, shiny tentpole events; they've created a kind of transnational cultural "scene" that can't be ignored, even by aesthetes. Marvel's particular success has had less to do with credible filmmaking and more with terrific casting: they've generally chosen buzzy, charismatic actors, who are effective even when the CGI fails in the background.[10] And once a sufficient number of sexy movie stars appeared in a sufficient number of big-budget adaptations of preexisting popular media, promoted by clickbait coverage and gestures at minority inclusion, surrounded by a constellation of consumer goods orbiting around the white-hot core of the story—well, then it became socially acceptable for everybody to participate, and nearly un-American not to.

But the key element is that this stuff was *already* popular. Superhero comics have long been beloved, and by adults as well as children, despite decades of admonishment that comics are bad, subliterate fiction, escapism for babies at best and mental garbage at worst. In 1972, Umberto Eco wrote that reading repetitive, poorly written fiction like Superman comics and Nero Wolfe detective novels could be understandable as a means of dealing with the stress of reality, but that indulgence in them often went too far and could become self-destructive. It was "natural," Eco suggested, "that the cultured person who in moments of intellectual tension seeks a stimulus in an action painting or a piece of serial music should in moments of relaxation and escape (healthy and indispensable) tend toward triumphant infantile laziness and turn to the consumer product for pacification in an orgy of redundance."[11] It's interesting that the types of media with which a cultured person is supposed to be familiar can shift so completely over fifty years—"action painting" and "serial music" (better known as abstract expressionism and atonal music) are now unfamiliar terms for most people, the ghosts of a midcentury middlebrow education project that was only half effective. And yet, Superman and Nero Wolfe, who are bad for you, are eternal.

Eco makes it clear in his essay that he's very familiar with both Superman and Wolfe, but, as usual, bad fiction is only dangerous for *other people*. And, also as usual, a specific kind—or kinds— of other person is imagined to be at risk. When it comes to the influence of stupid fiction, Eco projects his anxiety onto someone like himself, but not himself: an educated, middle-to-upper-class person, That Cultured Person Over There, a man who is overindulging in pacifying and infantile tastes, fat and lazy as Nero Wolfe himself, destroying himself in an orgy of self-satisfaction. Someone *else*, not Eco, is abandoning his responsibilities: not spending enough time with serious art, the kind that can be a light to the soul, which necessarily means they're putting out that light, for themselves and everyone else. Whether this is a personal anxiety ("I fear I'm not reading enough of the good stuff, and insufficiently improving myself") or a social one ("I fear being squashed and stifled, interpersonally and maybe politically, by the ignorant fools around me") you still find, in the 2020s, a lingering anger and embarrassment over the victory of the nerds. Science fiction and fantasy fans are still often presumed to be merely nostalgic, or immature, or trapped by safe, repetitive delights. And this nostalgia and immaturity benefits only the corporate overlords who want stupid people to escape into other worlds so they don't try to overthrow them in this one; who want people to linger in a permanent childhood, ensuring the continued manufacture of terrible corporate art through their purchasing power, a form of capitalist degredation that you and I are not participating in, because even though whichever blockbuster science fiction and fantasy story we love either openly or secretly happens to also be made by the three to six entities that currently produce media . . . okay, fine, but for us it's *different*. We have taste. We're discerning. We're like Eco, who can enjoy Superman from a spiritual remove; we're like Don Quixote's friends, sorting through his books to pick out the few good ones from the mass of bad, in the silly and embarrassing genre we know as well as Don Quixote does, but it hasn't driven *us* crazy.

One of the great jokes in *Don Quixote*, as Margaret Anne Doody points out, is that *everybody* in it has read the chivalric romances and is fluent with their conventions.[12] Only a handful of characters, like the stuff-shirt canon in the latter chapters of book 1, know that chivalric romances are bad all the way through without having actually read them. Just like a conservative book banner or a Twitter critic, the canon's knowledge comes from excerpts alone: he's glanced at the openings of many chivalric romances before rejecting them as repetitive, unrealistic, and insufficiently educational.[13] There are likely several popular fictions that you simply *know* to be bad, even without trying them; of course there's almost certainly something you're crazy about, some beloved story that has already been bought up and franchised out by a giant corporation like so many highway-exit Burger Kings. I'll have a lot to say, later on, about these corporate powers and their stranglehold on all we hold dear, but for now I think it's best to start with *what* these stories are, why we love them so much, why they've been considered dangerous, and why their imaginative territory has been so fiercely guarded by bigoted gatekeepers, all of which have basically the same answer. Don Quixote's book-burning friends are not—it may be obvious to say—the heroes of the story. The man who loves stories too much is never *other people*: he's us. His fatal attraction to the otherworld of adventure and excitement is our own.[14]

Superhero Origin Story

Defining the boundaries of science fiction and fantasy has always been an idiosyncratic and controversial activity: Delany says that "the overlap is probably so great that worrying about the purity of the genres on any level is even more futile than worrying about the purity of the races."[15] Even defining the differences between "novels" and the fantastical romances that supposedly preceded them is controversial, and every academic (nerd) has their own idiosyncratic opinion. Doody's project in *The True Story of the Novel* is to upend the common wisdom that the western novel burst fully formed out of Cervantes's head: she traces a clear line of inheritance from Greek and Latin prose fiction written in North Africa and the Middle East starting around the second century BCE, and then up through the medieval romance and into the modern novel as we understand it. The critical suppression of the true origin of the novel, Doody argues, has a great deal to do with the development of "race" as a category in the early modern era and hence a growing racist discomfort with the multiethnic origins of prose fiction.[16] It also has to do with the resurgent belief, originating in Plato but aided by Protestantism, that literature could only be justified if it was good for you and healthy for your moral development. This is where we get strange Anglo-centric claims that *Pamela* or

Robinson Crusoe is the first "novel," which has a lot to do with them being English and perceived to be morally upstanding. Cordoning off the first "real" novels from the rest designates all preceding prose fiction as a primitive indulgence, a childish mistake.

Chivalric romances were popular throughout Europe and elsewhere during the medieval period, but by the early seventeenth century they were difficult to justify—even by Cervantes, who loved them almost as much as his famous character did.[17] Knights and enchanters and adventures had no place in capitalist modernity: all the giants were dead, or had never existed, and in any case reading about them couldn't be quantified as *useful*. Literature, like life, had become a matter of ferocious competition: there had to be *best* forms, ideal genres, new literature rising from the ashes of the old. This is why, we're told, Don Quixote had to slay the detestable romance, bringing us all into the sunlight of good, useful, serious novels forever.

Here's my idiosyncratic and controversial opinion: while I don't dispute Doody's evidence of an unbroken chain of influence between the romance and the novel, there's at least a *perceived* difference between the two, and it persists to this day.[18] The romance never died: it's always remained wildly popular, and suspicious. We can trace the path of its development by the destruction it has wreaked on critics; by the consistent pattern of discontent over stories of adventure and magic; and by the excitement that appears alongside Scudéry's novels, gothic novels, the rise of genre fiction in its various forms, comic books, video games, and unknown forms to come. The two forms also follow different internal patterns: the romance (or an epic) tends to be sprawling, serial, multiauthored, and reliant on an established set of myths and images, while the novel is supposed to be discrete, specific, single-authored, seeking individuality both in its characters and itself in relation to other books, trying to be *novel* in the secondary sense of being *new*.[19] You could argue that if anything makes *Don Quixote* the first western novel, it's Cervantes's insistence on total authorship: after another writer published a spurious sequel before he could, Cervantes spent a good chunk of his official sequel making fun of the bootleg version. He even killed off his protagonist at the end, ensuring that, unlike the oft-continuing tales of chivalric romance, these adventures really would be Don Quixote's last.

The distinctions between the romance and the novel may be fundamentally kind of bogus (why do we lump all stories about dragons together as fundamentally similar and derivative, while agreeing that all novels about divorce are discrete and original?), but we can see that these distinctions still map with a decent amount of consistency onto what we currently call "genre fiction" and "literary fiction."[20] Fantasy and science fiction novels often appear in multivolume (and sometimes unfinished) form; obviously comic books, and comic book film franchises, rely on serial and interconnected storytelling with multiple authors at every stage. Even genres that lie outside of science fiction and fantasy, like mysteries, are frequently structured more like traditional heroic romances, as the heroes of detective fiction return to solve new and increasingly baroque murders. The basic material of genre fiction itself is also reused, or shared in common: literary scholar Janice Radway commented in her study of romance novels that while the works in the genre "are technically novels because each purports to tell a 'new' story of unfamiliar characters and as-yet uncompleted events, in fact, they all *retell* a single tale whose final outcome their readers always already know," that is, the romantic couple ends up together. This makes them more like a myth, as Eco himself noted, or a romance in the older sense of the term—the long, interlinked, and repeated story.[21]

There's always been lots of fascinating experimentation in genre fiction, but novelty and invention have often been less relevant concerns for both writers and readers: the tension lies in *why* the couple gets together, *how* the murder was committed, *what* this fantasy story is doing with its dragons, not in *whether* the situation will be resolved in the usual way. There's even been something of a crisis in the romance novel community lately over whether the HEA (happily ever after) is an essential or changeable part of the story: Would a different sort of ending be acceptable, or does it rip the fundamental fabric of the myth?[22] The quality of the prose is also often less important in genre fiction than in a literary novel. Some of this is due to editorial mercantilism and laziness—mistaking "what people will settle for" to mean "what people want." I care a lot about good prose, but I've still muddled through some extremely poorly written science fiction and fantasy because I liked the ideas enough to endure the clumsiness of their execution. On the other hand, I only get excited about realist literary novels if the prose is spectacular: I don't see any appeal to real life written badly. This doesn't mean that genre fiction should be held to a lower standard than literary fiction (or, say, that comic book movies should be held to a lower standard than auteur films), just that certain stories can work for people even if they're terrible, in spite of the fact that they are terrible, because the story successfully draws on enough of the basic ur-mythology of the romance to survive a clumsy rendering. A bad drawing of a dragon is still, after all, a *dragon*.

Genre novels of any sort are not *pure* romances: thanks to copyright laws, they remain singly authored, discretely packaged units, and most readers expect at least some novelty, as well as the interiority and dialogic storytelling established by realist novels. Probably it would be more accurate to say that genre novels are a hybridization of the romance and the novel: a fantasy novel is arguably both a fantasy *and* a novel.[23] You can see this clearly in *The Hobbit* and *The Lord of the Rings*, both of which open as (light) parodies of nineteenth-century domestic novels, with their credulous, tobacco-smoking, waistcoat-wearing English country folk. And then the hobbits, these little English country gentlemen, guide the reader into an older, bigger, wilder form of storytelling. You can even track, halfway through *Return of the King*, the exact moment where J. R. R. Tolkien gets bored with the novel form and fully switches over to the language and manner of the romance. (*The Silmarillion*, Tolkien's unfinished masterpiece, which was completed by his son Christopher and other compilers, is a pure romance from beginning to end.)

The romance seems to be naturally hardy, and takes well to hybridization across multiple mediums. Even the chivalric romance is alive and kicking in hybridized form: one of the most popular contemporary fantasy series, *The Witcher*, can be succinctly described as the adventures of a wandering hero who slays monsters. I've tried and failed to get into the novels, though I do enjoy the TV show (I think it's very funny, though not on purpose). *The Witcher 3* is widely regarded as one of the best video games ever made, but I've never played it, mostly because I'm too busy logging hundreds of hours in the newest—and likewise critically acclaimed—*Legend of Zelda* games. *Zelda* is also basically a chivalric romance, complete with magic and quests and a princess to save. The world of these games is restful and immersive (and by the way, if you're an audiobook person, they pair quite well with *Don Quixote*).[24]

This is about where we stand in the victory of the nerds: the romance is maybe not *quite* fully respectable but very healthy, and video games are the youngest medium under its influence to be absorbed and found socially acceptable after decades of public concern. This is another area where there's been a dramatic cultural shift: As a teenage girl in the 1990s, it would have been deeply uncool, or at least socially loaded, to publicly admit to playing a *Zelda* game. Now, I can play and talk about them free of much, if any, social judgment. Of course with social acceptability, and huge profitability, also came the bigoted backlash of Gamergate—but though you might still hear complaints from the remnants of that crowd about "fake gamer girls" and other imagined frauds and haters, it's largely understood by the broader public that video games can now be played by anyone. Whether they're heroic romance-inflected story games like RPGs, or pattern games like *Candy Crush*, these forms of entertainment are now understood to provide welcome self-care after the monotony and frustrations of the workday.

Public anxiety still lingers, however, over those who go too far and become lost in games, who pass beyond the requisite self-care required to keep the machine going and stop being a machine at all. While occasionally the fretted-about game is something like *Candy Crush*, and the imperiled subjects are imagined as suburban, phone-addicted women, the usual version of this moral panic centers around immersive, unreal, and violent games, and the endangered and dangerous group consists of young white men. Violent adventure games are supposed to desensitize these men into viewing everybody else as unreal ciphers, background pixels that can be smashed without consequence; fascist gamers have even been known to refer to people they consider less enlightened as NPCs, or nonplayable characters.[25] The games are usually blamed for reprogramming the gamers to think this way: they're so immersive, and their fantasy worlds of violence and death so lovingly and gorgeously depicted, that their influence must necessarily be stronger and more dangerous than earlier, less immediate mediums, meaning that young white men will simply have no choice but to behave as if these stories are fundamentally true. (Why young women or young men of color are seemingly less susceptible to seduction by unreality may be predicated on the unspoken knowledge that since popular conceptions of whiteness and masculinity are basically reducible to a collection of power fantasies, young white men may be living halfway in a fantasy world already.)[26]

Though we're past the heyday of the anti-video-game panic, violent games are still sometimes blamed for mass shootings, whether the killer happened to play them or not.[27] There's actually very little evidence that playing violent, immersive video games results in mimetic, real-world violence; in fact, some studies suggest that violence committed by young men may actually *decrease* after the release of a highly anticipated video game.[28] The blame laid on video games is often deceptively framed: a 2014 *New Republic* article cites a study about violent and "risk-glorifying" video games and their supposed inducement to murderous acting-out in young men, but what the study actually finds is a correlation between playing these kinds of games and engaging in "deviant" activities, such as "alcohol use, smoking cigarettes, delinquency and risky sex."[29] Whatever the male deviant behavior may be, it can always be conveniently linked to video games: in 2023, an economist cited in a *New Yorker* article about the supposed "decline of men"—really, the decline in male happiness and employment—suggested that, for young men especially, the problem may lie in "the rapid improvement in video-game quality." Games are just *too fun* and too immersive, and young men are leaving the workforce to play until they drop.[30]

Every time the romance has undergone a transformation or hybridized itself into a new medium, it's been blamed for negative, antisocial behavior. It's possible, this time, that video games—the newest and most absorbing form of Romantic escape that we've invented so far—are indeed responsible for socially deviant behavior, but it's also possible that the causation is, and has always been, exactly backward. Maybe violent games—or distracting and exciting games—do turn young men into delinquent, unhappy, frustrated, or violent dropouts, or maybe there's something about modern life, and modern employment, that makes people of all ages, races, and genders want to lose themselves in games instead. And while this may be true of pattern games and building games, it's especially true of story games: the ones that take place in worlds that are not this one, which are different and dramatic or violent or demonic or—in any case—far away from here.

Satan Is Coming for Your Earning Potential

Before Tipper Gore and other activists went after violent video games in the 1990s (and explicit rock lyrics in the mid-1980s), the moral panic du jour centered around tabletop role-playing games, especially Dungeons and Dragons. These games allowed for imaginative play that lay outside the usual boundaries of "reader" and "writer": they let stories unfold that, by definition, couldn't be read or monitored by parents in advance. Within the rules of the game, kids could invent anything they liked: they could experiment with identity, playing as characters whose gender didn't match their own; they could also fantasize about the strength and power they lacked in real life. The anxiety about fantasy role-playing games spiked right around the troubled turn of the 1980s, and was quickly folded into the larger "Satanic Panic" of the era. Many Christian parents were concerned that art that made reference to the demonic—such as heavy metal music, children's fantasy novels, or Dungeons and Dragons—might be *literally* demonic, and that spells cast inside the realm of a game could actually raise hell in real life.[31] But concerns about the immersive power of Dungeons and Dragons and other fantasy games began elsewhere, outside the specific frame of Christianity and demonic entities; the nerve it touched was nationwide. The whole country was gripped in the late 1970s and early 1980s by "stranger danger": a fear, like something out of a fairy tale, that children might get lost, or stolen away.[32]

In one notable 1979 case, a student at Michigan State University vanished into thin air. James Dallas Egbert III, a sixteen-year-old prodigy, was brilliant, socially awkward, and struggling. According to most accounts, he snuck into the university steam tunnels to commit suicide; when the attempt failed, he hid out at a friend's place while the frantic search for him continued. His family brought in a private investigator named William Dear, who decided that the true culprit must be Dungeons and Dragons; Egbert was a known enthusiast, and Dear claimed that the teenager had been playing a live-action version of the game in the steam tunnels. Worse still, Dear decided that Egbert had begun to *believe* the game was real: he could only still be missing if he'd conflated himself with his character, losing himself in the fantasy. Egbert in fact resurfaced a month later, in Louisiana, but the urban legend lingered, especially once Rona Jaffe published a best-selling novel closely based on Dear's account, *Mazes and Monsters* (1981), which was turned into a TV movie the following year, starring (in his first major role!) a charismatic, baby-faced, twenty-six-year-old Tom Hanks.[33]

Both the book and movie versions of *Mazes and Monsters* (the adaptation stays close to the original, though with a few key alterations), may be clumsy and unsatisfying in aesthetic terms, but they're fascinating as historical documents and worth examining in detail. Jaffe, from the first, tries to present her novel as a true and complete history, a lightly fictionalized version of a real event that would still have been fresh in the public imagination. The book opens with an omniscient third-person account of a brilliant college student who vanished into a cave near the school while playing a live-action version of a game called Mazes and Monsters (Dungeons and Dragons being, of course, copyrighted). In the movie version, a reporter explains the facts of the case, along with the dangers of Mazes and Monsters; he says that "the point of the game is to amass a fortune without being killed."[34] Both book and movie take great pains to emphasize that the missing boy and his friends were *good* kids, nice white children from respectable backgrounds, with bright futures and real fortunes waiting to be amassed. This is the source of the horror. "These players," the book's introduction continues, "could be anybody's kids; bright young college students sent out to prepare for life, given the American dream and rejecting it to live in a fantasy world of invented terrors. Why did they do it? What went wrong?"[35]

Neither the book nor the movie really knows. A lot of time is spent on the families and aspirations of the kids who play Mazes and Monsters: there's Jay Jay, a prodigy who is permanently in a state of rebelling against his high-society parents; Kate, who wants to be a writer; and Daniel, a computer genius who just wants to design games, though his parents want him to put his talents to more immediately lucrative use. "This is a very competitive world," Daniel's mother tells him, "and you're going to have to live in it."[36] Robbie—Tom Hanks's character—has no special talent or destiny. He's sweet and sensitive, maybe too sensitive, hung up over the mysterious disappearance of his brother several years earlier, who might have run away to New York, or might be dead. The other three kids play Mazes and Monsters to escape or work out their problems, but they're able to keep themselves separate from the game; Robbie is the one who falls. Too fragile for reality, he has a psychotic break and believes he really *is* his character, Pardieu the Holy Man, and that his missing brother is reaching out to him. Robbie/Pardieu breaks up with Kate, committing himself to the chastity that Holy Men are supposed to embrace, and runs away—not into the cave system near the college where he and the others played their little game, but to New York City, the phantasmagoric horror landscape of the 1980s.

In New York, Robbie wanders among the homeless through unused subway passages, haunted by smoke he thinks descends from dragons. He thinks he must be in a world of dragons who hoard treasure: the abject poverty and despair all around him seems inexplicable by other means. Robbie encounters homeless men he believes are trolls and prostitutes he believes are fairies—in the fairies' company, a man mistakes him for a prostitute, and Robbie ends up stabbing him. Here the movie diverges from the book: the man who attacks Robbie in the film is only a mugger, with no sexual intent (that would have been a bit much, presumably, for a TV movie in 1982). But that's exactly what can't be said, the actual mess of psychic tunneling that lies under the surface of *Mazes and Monsters*. Is Robbie gay? Was his brother gay? Is "lost in New York in the early 1980s" a metaphor, is being unable to have a successful relationship with a woman and graduate from college and acquire a good job a symbol of something much deeper than a morality play about the dangers of losing yourself in fantasy? James Egbert was gay, at least according to William Dear; his struggle with his sexuality is supposedly part of what drove him to Dungeons and Dragons, and to attempt suicide in the steam tunnels.

Tom Hanks's Robbie also attempts suicide: in the movie version, he tries to jump off one of the towers of the World Trade Center. Viewed after 9/11, the scene is even more disturbing than intended: it reads like an omen. There's something sickly and eerie about *Mazes and Monsters*, something that can't be addressed out loud. *Something is wrong with America*, it says and doesn't say.

By the end of both versions, Robbie has recovered: his friends rescue him from the deadly city and return him to his parents' suburban house. There, however, he slips back into believing he's a magical character, permanently, like a child stolen away by the fairies and replaced by a changeling. The three sane and healthy friends join him for one last sad game of Mazes and Monsters before giving up on games, fantasy, and childhood forever. Jay Jay accepts his class privileges, deciding to become a famous director;

Kate commits herself to writing the story of their experiences, and to marrying Daniel, who in turn has accepted his fate as a future "rich, successful captain of industry."[37] As a group, they pledge themselves to money, to normality, to the American dream. Robbie, eaten up by the underside of that dream, is lost forever. Unable to amass a fortune, he is socially dead. His brother never resurfaces. In real life, James Egbert was lost too: he killed himself in 1980.

In the years to come, Dungeons and Dragons would be linked in the press to several suicides: all were by young, middle-class white men who had played or been interested in role-playing. According to *Dangerous Games*, an excellent history of the subject by Joseph P. Laycock, there was no meaningful connection whatsoever between tabletop role-playing games and these suicides, and in fact the deaths didn't represent any sort of statistical cluster or anomaly. They were just reported on because of the class and racial status of the dead young men, because of the preexisting moral panic over Dungeons and Dragons, and because their grief-stricken parents were desperate for answers.[38]

One of these mothers, a woman named Patricia Pulling, started BADD (Bothered About Dungeons and Dragons), an advocacy organization that succeeded in banning students from playing the game in schools throughout nine states, a sort of miniaturized version of the current book bans.[39] BADD and other organizations claimed that role-playing games were satanic partly because they needed an external reason for the suicides, for the unhappiness and anxiety that they saw in young people growing up in the 1980s. They needed to believe that their children's anxiety and discomfort—especially discomfort with repressive sex norms and the pressures of capitalist competition—could only be the result of an evil force that came from outside. Laycock reports that many of these organizations relied on a particular quote from a gamer named "John": "The more I play D&D," John is supposed to have said, "the more

I want to get away from this world. The whole thing is getting very bad." Clearly, his world was fine, his future was bright, and only Satan could have made him want to run away.[40]

Don't Look in the Box

There's a meme I like very much, in which Don Quixote—wearing a mad troll face—runs about to the commentary of two bland observers: "Look at this fool Don Quixote, he is a raving lunatic!" Don Quixote, armed with a gun, attacks a factory—a classic nineteenth-century dark satanic mill—and they laugh at him: "Does he truly think he fights giants that feast on men?" Quixote runs to assault a smug priest and a rich man in a top hat: "Does he truly believe the most noble of men in our society to be wicked sorcerers that worship demons?!" The final panel shows only the two bland commentators, the respectable bourgeois neighbors, against the backdrop of a smog-choked nineteenth-century factory town and industrial death. "HOW LUCKY WE ARE," they scream, "THAT OUR WORLD IS RULED BY THE SANE AND REASON-ABLE; IMAGINE OUR WORLD IF THERE WERE MORE PSYCHO-PATHS LIKE HIM!"

Academics might take issue with some of the meme's technical inaccuracies, but for a succinct and cogent read of *Don Quixote*, I think it's hard to beat. Don Quixote is at war with modernity, with technology (the famous windmills), with capitalist realism itself. The seventeenth-century Spanish countryside is full of cruelty and misery; in Quixote's view, that's because the public has abandoned chivalry and no one is trying to help or defend the weak. The fact that chivalry never really existed the way it does in medieval romances is irrelevant to him. Quixote needs the world to be beautiful and significant, rather than commonplace and meaningless, and he needs it so badly that he starts to read all reality as if every tiny detail is of great and romantic importance. Without knighthood, without purpose, without meaning, he will die—and he does die as soon as he regains his sanity.[41] In more ways than one, Don Quixote can't live outside a story.

A cheery 2020 Medium article about the usefulness of fictional stories declares that they're not a waste of time for the usual reasons—they build empathy, they're good for you—and then concludes, shockingly, "After all, we need fiction to survive reality."[42] This is an insane thing to say, or rather, what it says about our world is insane. Reality needs to be *survived?* We live through stories, following them like a sugary trail, until we die? Presumably this is a psychic survival, not a physical one; those who are most in need of physical, literal survival are probably not wondering whether it's a waste of time to read books or watch movies. But it's interesting that socially and economically privileged people can admit that this world sucks, but distraction can get us through it—or if not *us*, then at least the unfortunate masses at large, hypnotized and corporatized by popular fantasy escapes. The change in the perception of fantasy and science fiction isn't just that these genres have been proved to make money: there's an understanding now, or an admission, that money itself has ruined everything, but coupled with a shrug, an acceptance of capitalist realism. It's okay to enjoy these stories, since enjoying them is all we can do. The pursuit of pleasure is an endless end, and the only one we have.

A good deal of the academic and critical work on pop culture has endeavored to prove that it isn't just trivial, escapist, and a social soporific; that the descendants of romance are as worthy of serious study as, say, action paintings or serial music. Neil Gaiman said in 2013 that escapist literature can also be of political value: it can "give you knowledge about the world and your predicament, give you weapons, give you armour: real things you can take back into your prison. Skills and knowledge and tools you can use to escape for real."[43] It's a nice image, but makes a somewhat risky demand: What happens when, despite all the moral panics over imaginary worlds, the skills and knowledge gained from experiencing those realms hasn't busted us out of prison? A decade after Gaiman's comment, escapism is more commercially popular and socially acceptable than it's ever been, and yet we're no closer to "escaping" the brutality of capitalist realism, or the climate consequences of four centuries of dark satanic mills. If even escape can be packaged into a product to be sold, an acceptable outlet for a busy and cultured person, it doesn't represent any kind of real escape, but something more like a warden-approved picture of a landscape hanging in a prison cell.

Gaiman was riffing on Tolkien, who in his 1947 essay "On Fairy-Stories" makes a direct comparison between the "escape" of escapism and what he calls "the Escape of the Prisoner"—the longing for a world that lies outside the prison of ordinary reality.[44] *Don Quixote* also makes frequent reference to prisoners and freedom (Don Quixote frees prisoners; he is himself more than once imprisoned or chained), and Cervantes may have come up for the idea for the novel while languishing in a debtor's jail.[45] The history of the western novel is closely tied to the history of educated white people who want to escape—the very people who were supposed to benefit from the broader system of bloody exploitation but find themselves made miserable and trapped, alienated psychically if not physically. Anarchist anthropologist David Graeber has explained that "alienation" is not, as it's often misunderstood, simply a matter of downtrodden people feeling excluded from the capitalist system, "but that even the winners do not really win, because the system itself is ultimately incapable of producing a truly unalienated life for anyone."[46]

The broader genre of "alienated people driven crazy by stories" has almost always been the creation of white novelists writing white characters: obviously Cervantes and Don Quixote, Flaubert and Emma Bovary, plus Rona Jaffe and her college students. There's also Jane Austen's *Northanger Abbey*, a satire of gothic novels, in which the young bourgeois Catherine Morland, misled by her favorite books into believing her life is supposed to be interesting and romantic, opens secret chests and cabinets in a mysterious abbey only to find . . . nothing, just linens and bills, because her whole life, haha, will be little more than linens and bills. Austen is working in the Goldilocks version of realism, and—as in most of her novels—the deeper reality of colonialism remains mostly invisible. *Northanger Abbey* doesn't reference the fact that the fabric in these chests almost certainly came from cotton picked by Black slaves in the American South; it would have been shipped to England to be beaten into cloth by girls in factories who were not as lucky in their class status as Catherine. The actual gothic horror of *Northanger Abbey* is that there's no horror at all: once Catherine realizes her life isn't actually a gothic novel, "the anxieties of common life began soon to succeed to the alarms of romance."[47] Going forward, she'll only ever open her cabinets to find clean white cotton: her whole world is soaked in blood, and she doesn't see it, and never will.

"It's Real"

The great Samuel Delany has sometimes referred to literary fiction like Austen's as "bourgeois fiction" or "mundane fiction."[48] These may be somewhat unfair (and salty) terms, but they do serve to identify certain assumptions about the nature of the "real world" and the political nature of vraisemblance. Delany prefers the term "given world" to "real world," since in his view it better explains the construction and fictionalization of reality: this is just the world we have been *given* to believe in as real.[49] In literary realism, the world operates by certain mundane and unshakeable rules; certain things are possible, and certain things are not; certain fates are both desirable and inevitable (or you'd better desire them, since they are inevitable); certain perspectives tend to be centered while certain people and processes are usually left unseen, and unsaid. Of course, there are an extraordinary number of literary novels that contradict or deliberately attack the rules and assumptions of this reality; Delany is suggesting only that what a genre like science fiction is, and what it necessarily does, is to restructure the given world, to imagine it from outside. And the question of *who* gets to do this restructuring, and therefore the reimagining of "reality" as an agreed-upon public concept, has tended to make certain people very nervous.

Delany has sometimes been called the first Black science fiction writer—he might be, depending on when you start the clock on science fiction and depending on the unknown identities of some of the early pseudonymous pulp writers.[50] Delany, an extraordinary prodigy, published his first novel when he was twenty; he'd won several awards before he submitted the manuscript of his ninth novel, *Nova*, to *Analog* magazine for possible serialization. *Nova*, along with the rest of Delany's early work, has occasionally been criticized for being insufficiently radical: the protagonist of *Nova* is Black, but he lives in a future where racism is over, and he has to tackle different kinds of problems.[51] *Nova* was still too radical, however for *Analog* editor John W. Campbell Jr., who rejected a serialized version of the novel in 1967, telling Delany that while he liked the book, he didn't think that readers "would be able to relate to a Black main character."[52] This sort of rejection is less common now than it once was, but that too is a recent cultural development: Jemisin notes that in the 2000s it was still common wisdom that science fiction and fantasy starring Black protagonists wouldn't sell.[53] Of course, any time a U.S. publisher claims that something won't sell, they're lying. Anything can be sold if you market it properly:

this is America, we have toothpaste for dogs. The claim "it's good but it won't sell" usually means something more like it *shouldn't* sell, or it would be perceived as frightening if it sold, because something about the work troubles the expected assumptions of bourgeois, mundane reality.

Campbell's refusal to publish *Nova* was fictionalized in the 1998 *Star Trek: Deep Space Nine* (*DS9*) episode "Far Beyond the Stars," one of the best episodes of (in my opinion) the best TV show ever made, and an unusually inverted version of the classic warning story about the dangers of storytelling. In *Star Trek*'s utopian twenty-fourth century, racism is a thing of the past (as in the more dystopian *Nova*): Captain Benjamin Sisko, *Trek*'s first Black captain, is aware of racism as a historical matter, but it doesn't form part of his present existence. (He's my favorite captain, and for what it's worth I never found any difficulty relating to him—but it's not lost on me that many of *DS9*'s writers are white and Jewish like me, and "aware of bigotry in the past but not bothered by it right now" sums up many white Jewish experiences in the late twentieth century.) Sisko lives an interesting life with many competing tensions: he spends most of his time running a spaceport and dealing with complicated space problems. By the time of "Far Beyond the Stars" in season six, those space problems have grown wearying, and Sisko is questioning his purpose. He begins to experience a strange phenomenon, a kind of waking hallucination: he imagines himself as a 1950s short story writer named Benny Russell, who is creating the adventures of Captain Sisko.

At first, Benny's editor won't hear of publishing these adventures, for the same reasons Campbell offered in real life: "People won't accept it. It's not believable." ("And men from Mars are?" counters one of the other writers.) The editor offers other excuses, claiming that even if he wanted to run the story, his publisher and distributor wouldn't sell it. And then, finally, he settles on the real answer, the one that Campbell never said out loud: "For all we know, it could cause a race riot." The fictional version of Campbell doesn't clarify how or why a science fiction story about a Black captain could lead to a race riot: we are left to understand that in his view, the mere presence of a story about Black people in the future—living normally and happily in their context—would open up terrifying conceptual possibilities. The contrast between the world of the future and the present would be too dramatic, the necessary tension too violent: whiteness (and maleness) might lose their place as the default, and white men as the main characters of reality, the only ones to worry about.

The writer Benny Russell ends up changing Captain Sisko's story so it's only a dream, being dreamed by a person like himself. The editor finally accepts the piece, but its competing vision of reality is still too much for the publisher, who decides to pulp the entire run of the magazine. Benny gets fired, and he breaks down in the office. "That future, that space station, all those people, they exist, in here," he cries. "In my mind. I created it." Avery Brooks, who both directed the episode and starred in it, positioned the camera directly in front of his face, so there's almost nothing on the screen besides his expression, his breaking voice, and his tears. "The future, I created it, and it's real! Don't you understand? It is *real*! I created it! And it's *real*!"

Some clever internet person once mashed up Benny Russell shouting "It's real!" with a clip from an unrelated *DS9* episode where an angry alien hisses, "It's a fake!" Then this clever person looped the exchange infinitely: "It's real!" "It's a fake!" "It's real!" "It's a fake!" Science fiction (and fantasy) stories are both real and fake: real because they're a way of grasping the real reality, the "might be" or "wish it were," that lies beyond given reality, and fake because, obviously, nothing in them ever happened or could happen right now. But readers and viewers need it to exist, as Benny needed it to exist. In a 1978 speech at the Studio Museum of Harlem, Delany said, "We need images of tomorrow, and our people need them more than most."[54] Mark Dery, the (white) critic who coined the term "Afrofuturism" in an interview with Delany, stressed the risk of what it means that "the unreal estate of the future [is] already owned by the technocrats, futurologists, streamliners, and set designers—white to a man—who have engineered our collective fantasies."[55] The only way to create other kinds of real futures, Dery and many others have suggested, is to imagine them first.

This puts an enormous amount of weight on our collective fantasies. What happens when imagining escape doesn't yield any measurable victories? *DS9* aired in the 1990s to no race riots at all; we are seemingly not much closer to building a *Star Trek* utopia. (Delany himself has called Afrofuturism "a well-intentioned, if confusing marketing tool.")[56] It might be better to say that Afrofuturist stories, and others in the same general register, are demonstrations of imaginative possibilities rather than proximate causes of social change. Without imagining the future, there's no changing the present: but imagination alone doesn't get us very far. What this kind of storytelling does provide, however, is a chance to picture the future: and to feel for a moment that you have a place in it.[57] That you have power and agency, and you are not insane to be unhappy with the present.[58]

The Nightmare

There's another, more troubling side to the way in which science fiction and fantasy can provide a sense of power and agency: a different timeline to be imagined, and a dream to be realized. Elsewhere in the "On Fairy-Stories" essay, Tolkien mentions that "escapism has another and even wickeder face: Reaction."[59] In the context of the essay, he's referring to the idea that people might, thanks to their reading of fantasy stories, become disgusted with industrial capitalism and start smashing it; the context for his own later work is much more disturbing. *The Lord of the Rings* has been beloved by liberals, conservatives, and crunchy eco-socialists alike; it's also a touchstone for many on the extreme far right, including fascists. Giorgia Meloni, the fascist or fascist-adjacent prime minister of Italy, is a big fan: as a child, she attended a "hobbit camp" run by the neo-fascist Italian Youth Front.[60] Though Tolkien fans of other political leanings have made efforts to dismiss the far-right fan base as poor readers of his work, I think the fascists are picking up on clear and omnipresent racial anxieties in the text; their enthusiasm may be limited to *only* those pieces, but they're not imagining what they find. Tolkien wasn't personally a fascist, more of a standard-issue English conservative, but that was still quite bad, and quite racist. The invading dark hordes in *Lord of the Rings* went on to invade the imaginations of many other writers, and have plagued both fantasy and science fiction ever since.[61]

Jemisin has pointed out that, in fantasy, especially of the epic variety, "there is a tendency for it to be quintessentially conservative in that its job is to restore what is perceived to be out of whack."[62] Her own spectacular and award-winning *Broken Earth* series demonstrates how this story can be rewritten: an oppressive present can be ruptured, and history can move toward a different, fairer future. (In her books the rupture takes the form of a gigantic earthquake, which ends a brutal and unequal civilization.) But much of science fiction and fantasy has struggled with how to depict the end of systemic oppression. Most types of genre fiction, including mystery and romance, have had a tendency, if not an exclusive bent, toward the restoration or maintenance of status quo assumptions and values (e.g., police cleverness, monogamous heterosexuality). Nonetheless, whether genre stories uphold conventions or disrupt them, whether escapism is a soporific that makes us sleep through reality or an irritant that wakes us up to it, there's nothing that *it* can do on its own. A story is ultimately just a story. But the fear, or fantasy, that these kinds of stories *can* change the real world—the given world—is enough to make everybody both nervous and excited about what dreams may come.

We can be sure that people will continue to seek out escapism regardless of who's offering it, whether it does or doesn't possess the capacity to change the world, at least until reality stops being quite so awful. The romance—and Romanticism itself—remains a rejection of given reality, of capitalist modernity, even if that rejection is only psychological and not actionable. For the fascist fans of escapism, however, it's not just a fantasy: they've historically been discontented with fiction as fiction and have interpreted it as something closer to a depiction of real reality, trying to implement it in the physical world. Meloni has referred to *The Lord of the Rings* as "our Bible" and, as Luigi Mastrodonato wrote for *Vice*, the Italian Youth Front has used "the story of the humble hobbits and their good-guy allies protecting their idyllic homeland from hordes of orc invaders . . . as a metaphor for the fight against mass immigration."[63] Fascists have often acted much like Don Quixote, unwilling or unable to tell the difference between medieval fantasy and reality. It's notable that Don Quixote doesn't exist until he turns himself into a hero, an aristocrat: until he can believe himself better than other people, not some useless normie NPC. Fascism, like any other descendant of Romanticism, arises from the blurry swamps between reality and fantasy, the catch points where modernity has failed; you could argue it's an attempt to turn the whole world into one huge fantasy story, one flat and evil dream.

CHAPTER THREE

Stop Making Fun of Our Übermenschen!!!

There have been many heroic efforts to define and describe fascism and fascist art, under the apparent belief that if we can just analyze and identify the tendency exactly, we can vaccinate the public against its influence. For the purposes of this chapter, I'm not going to split the differences between fascism, Nazism, and apple-pie American white nationalism—they're alike enough, especially when it comes to their particular and unusual relationship with fiction.[1] Any sort of propaganda can be considered "dangerous," of course, in that it might change minds in a socially undesirable direction, but what makes fascist art uniquely frightening is that fascism itself can be described as a kind of fictionalizing tendency, deliberately co-locating itself inside categories of thinking and feeling more normally reserved for literature and art. Fascism operates at the level of story; it works like a story, with violent heroes and monstrous villains. This may be why white supremacist films like *Birth of a Nation* and novels like *The Turner Diaries* have inspired more direct and murderous action than any other form of fiction. And yet, fascists are uniquely *afraid* of fiction, more so than everybody else. Neo-Nazis commit spree murders based on their reading of fascist novels; they also cry online about Black mermaids in their Disney movies.

Fascists care a lot about the power of art, in any direction. "The logical result of Fascism," Walter Benjamin famously wrote, "is the introduction of aesthetics into political life."[2] Of course politics and aesthetics have never been strangers—the pageantry of kings has ranged from the immortal self-documentation of Egyptian pharaohs to the whole embarrassing show business of contemporary British royalty—but fascism blurs the lines between the imagined and the real in an especially irrational and fictionalizing way, which is part of what makes fascism so difficult to explain in direct and logical terms and yet so easy to *feel*. Fascism isn't a rational or even necessarily coherent ideology: it's often been anti-modern and pro-capitalist, nostalgic for a preindustrial past and enthusiastic about technological control, obsessed with fictional stories and committed to acting them out in dramatic fashion while simultaneously terrified of the influence of the "wrong" narratives.[3] Fascism is also self-aware of its origin and function as a powerful story rather than as a clear and rationally developed political program: the future it offers is one in which stories become real.

Discussions of "the power of art" tend to hold all kinds of art as fundamentally equal in potential, missing the unique character and appeal of fascism as an aesthetic project. And in doing so, these arguments degrade every form of art into a potentially deadly vehicle for propaganda, a mind-virus that can take control of a fragile, infantilized public. Jonathan Gottschall—that's right, we're picking on him again—takes this to an extreme in *The Story Paradox*, where he argues that the true villain of the story of human communication is "story" itself, a category that he defines more broadly than novels or movies to include any kind of method of making sense of reality. We are all victims of narratives—moral automatons acting out a programmed social script—and entirely helpless to resist. This is fine when we're surrounded by good narratives, he claims, but deadly when they're bad. According to Gottschall, the Tree of Life synagogue killer was likely turned into a monster by exposure to the pervasive fiction of antisemitism, while Nazis and Confederate soldiers "just had the moral misfortune of being born in cultures that, we now see, mistakenly defined bad as good."[4] The Nazis and Confederates simply couldn't help it, Gottschall suggests, and neither could any of us. "If we had been born in such circumstances," he insists, "we'd likely have behaved the same way."[5]

His conclusion doesn't stand up to a hot second of scrutiny—the Jews, Roma, gays, communists, and dissidents persecuted by the Nazis were apparently able to disbelieve the dominant narratives of the culture they lived in, as were the slaves, free Black people, and abolitionists in the United States—but Gottschall is simply taking the anti-fiction argument to its logical extreme. If we have limited psychic defenses against the power of narrative, and the most dangerous narratives can turn men into monsters, then any one of us might be taken in by potent mythologies of power and control.

In theory, membership in an identity group despised by fascists is supposed to offer protection against fascist narratives, but in practice that isn't always the case: there are a surprising number of men of color among white nationalist groups like the Proud Boys, as well as white women politicians who hold prominent positions in historically hypermasculine fascist or right-wing parties in Europe and the United States (Giorgia Meloni, Marine Le Pen, and Marjorie Taylor Greene, to name a few).[6] And there's Stephen Miller, who is Jewish—and related to Jewish refugees who were denied entry into the United States in the years before the Holocaust and subsequently murdered—and yet was also the architect of an immigration policy that denied entry to as many immigrants as possible, tearing families apart and deporting thousands of people sometimes to their deaths. (And as of the time of this writing, he aims to do it again, only on a much more hideous scale.)[7] The founder of *The Daily Stormer*, a neo-Nazi website, once wrote of Miller admiringly: "Everything that he does is intended to stop brown people coming in while getting as many as possible out . . . There is nothing I have seen this Jew do that I disagree with."[8]

My parents refer to Miller as "that Jewish Nazi," a hideous contradiction in terms, and many American Jews find him uniquely embarrassing.[9] Jewish fascists aren't unheard of, even as a matter of historical precedent: there's the German Jewish philosopher Leo Strauss, who at least somewhat supported national socialism before leaving Germany ahead of persecution in the 1930s. (A fun story: Strauss once attempted to flirt with a young Hannah Arendt in the Prussian State Library, but she rebuffed his advances and reminded him that however much Strauss liked the Nazis, they would never like him back.[10]) In the decades after the Holocaust, American Jews have remained largely left and liberal (on topics other than Israel); outright American Jewish fascists, especially of the type that *The Daily Stormer* would approve, are still relatively rare and disturbing.[11] Patricia Pulling, the bereft mother who started the BADD campaign against Dungeons and Dragons, was a secular Jew: after her son killed himself, she found Nazi references among his papers, and it's no surprise that she sought an external, demonic explanation for the narratives that had influenced him.[12]

Miller's anti-immigrant racism has often been traced to his affinity for the viciously anti-immigrant novel *The Camp of the Saints;* the journalist Jean Guerrero, who wrote a biography of Miller, names it before any other influence.[13] Blaming a book does feel like a reasonable place to start: when it comes to people who choose fascism against their own history and political interests, it seems like there has to be a source for the disease that they ought to have been inoculated against at birth. As fascists go, I find Miller to be a particularly fascinating and loathsome case—we were born in the same year, coming from the same ethnic group and a somewhat similar socioeconomic background (his family seems to have had more money but less stability). Surely the same pressures, the same social scripts, that went to bear on him also went to bear on me: if Gottschall is correct, then if I'd simply read the wrong book at the wrong time, I might have ended up a fascist too. Gender might be a separating factor, but none of the boys I went to Hebrew school with have ended up as fascists either (you better believe my mom would have told me). There must have been a reason that Miller ended up not just a recipient of the latent white supremacist ideology fed to me and my classmates and all young people in the United States but an out-and-out fascist—and not just a believer but one who actively sought power so that he could harm as many people of color as possible. According to Guerrero, Miller wasn't just influenced by *The Camp of the Saints*; he also promoted it to *Breitbart* reporters and Steve Bannon, attempting to spread its racist message as widely as he could.[14]

The Camp of the Saints is a hideous book. I tend to be relatively libertarian about freedom of speech, and mostly in favor of prison abolition, but when I finished *The Camp of the Saints*, I felt that everyone who read it, including myself, should be in jail. The book is speculative fiction of a sort, imagining a mass wave of immigration from the "Third World" to the "west." Every page crawls with racist imagery: human beings are constantly compared to animals, plants, bodily fluids, a flood, the organic horror of the planet, and the living are little different from the dead. Young immigrants are called "monster children" a total of seventeen times, and the foolish white people who want to defend them are referred to as mindless zealots and "statues."[15] The author, Jean Raspail, wasn't some random crank, as the authors of racist screeds like this usually are. He was a distinguished French travel writer, decorated by the Académie Française, and awarded the Legion of Honor.[16] And his novel, which has spurred more people than just Stephen Miller toward the kind of anti-immigrant politics that condemn people to suffering and death, is an indisputable example of a dangerous book. Even Raspail himself admitted in an interview that his novel was "dangerous"—and refused to make any changes.[17]

The Turner Diaries (1978) is even worse, and the Southern Poverty Law Center has been documenting its influence for decades. "Few works of fiction," the center claims, "have moved readers to action quite like The Turner Diaries."[18] Another violent speculative fiction novel, The Turner Diaries depicts an anti-government uprising and a race war in which white people murder Black people and Jews. Timothy McVeigh was a huge fan, and it at least partially influenced his decision to bomb a government building in Oklahoma City in 1995.[19] In the 1980s, a group of neo-Nazis who took their name from the Order, a white supremacist vigilante group described in the book, proceeded to stalk and murder three people including Alan Berg, a Jewish radio host.[20] In 1998, three white supremacists lynched a Black man named James Byrd Jr.; one of the murderers reportedly claimed to be "starting The Turner Diaries early."[21] And those are only the *most* prominent murders that can be linked to the novel: The Turner Diaries has been cited in over two hundred killings and many armed robberies.[22] Even The Camp of the Saints pales (sorry) in comparison.

"Books represent humanity at its best and its worst," the writer Azar Nafisi has said.[23] What are we to do with the worst, the absolute worst, the ones that have led to the commission of documented crimes, that have aided and abetted murderous fascists? There have been few efforts to ban or proscribe The Turner Diaries—it's not currently available on Amazon or at Barnes & Noble, but it's sold on smaller platforms and quite easy to find as a free PDF. Physical copies of *The Camp of the Saints* are relatively rare and expensive in the United States (they only exist in English at all due to the efforts of anti-immigration activists in the 1990s) but free PDFs—and normal-priced ebooks on both Amazon and at Barnes & Noble— are readily available.[24] Major corporations might choose not to stock *The Turner Diaries*—probably as much to avoid bad press as from real conviction, or else they'd remove *The Camp of the Saints* as well—but we can expect that digital copies will always be made available for free, because these are propaganda novels, intended to push a point of view rather than to make money.

And yet, for all the documented cases of harm, these books don't have power over everyone. *The Camp of the Saints* made me feel physically ill, but I don't think it made me a fascist. The prose is also quite bad: Raspail may be a decorated writer, but *The Camp of the Saints* is simply not a good novel. It lacks characterization, subtlety, or even good pacing; the text is interspersed with dialogue bricks where heroic men make righteous speeches at smug villains. Raspail's sentences are literary, I guess, in the sense that they are long. The rhythm of the clauses resembles that of a serious work of fiction. But it's a bland book, with one intended reading and one direct call to action: restricting the immigration of people of color to the west. It's unimaginable to me that someone could enjoy *The Camp of the Saints* as literature—that is, unless they already agreed with its politics in advance. *The Turner Diaries* too is read for its racism and not for its literary value: it was dashed off quickly by the neo-Nazi William Pierce and is famous for its awkward prose.[25]

But not all fascist or fascist-adjacent novels are so poorly rendered—some are subtle, and even beautiful, and yet at the same time not all their readers are turning into fascists en masse. Samuel Delany has frequently discussed his admiration and respect for science fiction writer Robert A. Heinlein, while acknowledging that much of Heinlein's world view tends toward fascism, and

Farnham's Freehold in particular is an "appallingly fascist" novel.[26] And yet Delany still loves Heinlein—and still hasn't become a fascist. Tolkien fans, as previously mentioned, must grapple with the story's hideously racist formulations about dark invaders and white heroes, and yet not everyone, or even most people, who read *The Lord of the Rings* as a child or an adult will become fascists either. What is it that turns some people into a Giorgia Meloni—or the Italian fascists who ran the "hobbit camp" she attended—while other readers only absorb its racist themes unconsciously, and still others can intentionally recognize, acknowledge, and reject the fascist parts of the text? What comes first: a fascist reader or a fascist book?

The Banality of Hypermasculinity

Guerrero's intensive biography of Stephen Miller details the many early influences on his life and politics. Miller's parents are Southern California conservatives and big fans of right-wing talk radio; the rest of the family is firmly liberal and estranged from Stephen Miller's branch. Since he was a young teenager, Miller has been a vocal conservative activist—he was sought out and mentored by David Horowitz, another Jewish right-winger who founded the Freedom Center (also known as the School for Political Warfare), which seeks to educate young conservatives to become anti-left debating stars. While still an adolescent, Miller was a frequent guest on *The Larry Elder Show*, a local radio program in the Southern California area hosted by the eponymous Larry Elder, a Black conservative who claims racism isn't real. It seems that Miller was sculpted into a right-wing activist thanks to an unusual set of direct political influences, over and above any encounters with dangerous fiction.

In fact, besides *The Camp of the Saints*—which Miller may have encountered as an adult—his adolescent taste in fictional stories appears normal. He was a passionate fan of *Star Trek: The Original Series*; he also loved Martin Scorsese's gangster movies, especially *Goodfellas* and *Casino*. His affinity for these Scorsese films took a somewhat curious turn: in high school he often cosplayed as DeNiro's character from *Casino*, dressing in mobster outfits and a noticeable gold pinkie ring. His classmates thought it was weird, Guerrero reports, but it's still within the normal range of weird for a teenager to act out their favorite characters, and of course adults cosplay at comic cons and other events all the time. What's strange about Miller, however, is that he doesn't seem to have ever stopped cosplaying; his embrace of the mobster antihero appears to have known no contextual boundaries. During the 2016 Trump campaign, Guerrero noticed that Miller was still imitating DeNiro's body language: "The loose hands, the fingertips-on-fingertips, the head tics . . . He'd stand at podiums and conjure the old mobster in himself."[27] This is more than just influence and liking: it seems to approach real imitation, real mimesis. Miller didn't just happen to enjoy some gangster movies, as lots of people do; he seems to have incorporated the mobster mentality into his daily life. As a Republican staffer in the 2010s he was still subtly cosplaying as a mobster, wearing a gold pinkie ring and narrow ties, and bringing the amoral, murderous, us-versus-them attitude of gangster films into real-life immigration policy.[28]

It's normal to be influenced by what we read and see—you might go out and buy a nipped-waist dress because you enjoyed a Sophia Loren movie—but that doesn't necessarily translate into behaving as though you *are* a Sophia Loren character and you believe that her movies are *true* in some mythic sense, depicting the secret real meaning of the world, and that real life should be reordered until it matches her movies. It's true that most people regard themselves as the protagonists of their own reality, the heroes of their own stories (that's just what human perception is like), but not everybody thinks that they are a *literal* protagonist and their life is literally a movie and should obey something like the logic of one. Most people understand, at least intellectually, that movie logic and life logic are quite different, even if it's sometimes comforting to imagine your life through the certainty of a five-act structure.

Fascists, however, as Benjamin and others have noted, tend to conflate life and art more fully than other people: they introduce aesthetics into both public and private life, seeing no difference between the vainglorious story of their own selves and the shaping of real-world politics around that story. Most of us grow up with stories where "the hero gets the girl," and yet many of us manage to date and marry without having to rescue anybody from dragons. But incels—and inceldom is best understood as a fascist tendency—can't tolerate the difference between reality and fiction, the difference between ordinary misery and the heroic identity that fiction "taught" them they should possess. Stories made incels believe (or really, they decided that they wanted to believe) that they were better than other people. When reality suggests something different than this, incels spend their time theorizing about who holds what role in the broader social story, sorting themselves and everyone else into categories of race and gender or their own original social constructions (virgins versus chads, or "alpha" versus "beta"—the latter set of labels was derived from studies of captive wolves that were once mistakenly believed to apply to the whole wolf population.)[29] And then sometimes, based on these imaginary inhuman labels and despair over the difference between stories and reality, incels commit mass murder so that they will become infamous, with the logic that if you can't be a hero, you can at least be an antiheroic protagonist. Incels—and fascists more broadly—really don't regard "other people," however categorized, as human, but they don't even necessarily see themselves as human in the first place.[30] Everybody's just a character in a play.

Hannah Arendt's famous phrase "the banality of evil" doesn't just refer to the fact that Adolf Eichmann was kind of boring, but also to her observation that he could only speak of himself in literary clichés, as if he were indistinguishable from the protagonists of his favorite novels and operas. Eichmann felt he was operated on by outside forces—the victim of terrible luck, just like the star-crossed hero of a tragedy. He seemed to regard himself as a passive character, compelled along by the way his story had been written for him: he seemed incapable of understanding that he had agency in his life and had taken deliberate steps, which had resulted in the massacre of millions of people.[31] His psychic passivity may seem strange, given that fascists tend to valorize the will to power and celebrate violent action, but of course they're also happy to submit to an authoritarian strongman. These may seem like contradictions, but really they're just two different types of fictionalizing. The first is actively writing reality while the second is passively acting out a narrative written by someone else. Eichmann thought of himself as a character in a bureaucratic fiction; he simply had no choice but to send millions of Jews and others to their deaths. Gottschall is slightly right in that people sometimes *decide* they're passive vessels of broader social narratives, that they have no choice but to act out the scripts they have received. The story is reality; it is all of reality.

Gottschall actually takes the argument even further than this: he says that people not only act out whatever stories they encounter, like animatronic puppets, but that all fictional stories are fundamentally about good versus evil, "us" versus "them," and that's why all stories, of any kind, are suspicious reservoirs of dangerous ideologies that might lead to violence. This full claim is easily disprovable by thinking about classic literature for a single minute, but it's true that a fair number of fictional narratives are built around a simple framework of "good versus evil." Toni Morrison has commented on how much the American import of the older European romance forms involves a fear of "boundarylessness": a world without borders, a world where nature runs riot over civilization, and where "darkness" in all its possible manifestations is something to be feared.[32] Fascist ideology represents an extreme form, maybe the *most* extreme form, of this tendency. It's fantastical, in the sense of perceiving the world as something like a fantasy novel with light versus darkness, boundaries versus invasion, but it's not imaginative, in that it can only imagine a single story and a single framework.

There are, of course, religious people who would agree that the world is a battle of good versus evil and all reality can be fitted to that framework, but the key difference between this and the fascist world view is the framing of *established* fictions—created by living people in recent memory—as being meaningfully "true." When Giorgia Meloni calls *The Lord of the Rings* "our Bible," she means that it's real for her, at least mythically real, a myth that is indistinguishable from literal truth. Certain fascist authors also insist on the literal truth of their art.[33] Raspail, who was mostly a nonfiction writer and not a novelist, frames his near-future *Camp of the Saints* as something close to truth: not, he insists, a "wild-eyed dream," as a normal near-future science fiction novel might be, but more like a kind of prophecy, which needs to be acted out before the west is overrun by immigration.[34] The various "trad" accounts on social media sites that mistake 1950s advertisements for actual family life, or video game footage for a vanished medieval era, can be seen as part of this same expression: confusing a created thing, an advertisement or a video game, with a documentary about reality. But it's never truly a *mistake* or an act of confusion; it's always a deliberate attempt to make the unreal into something real. When these trad accounts posit a nostalgic return to a world that only existed in 1950s advertising—or an AI render of a prompt that they themselves dreamed up and fed into the machine—they aren't only doing bad cultural criticism but trying to will that world into actually existing, right now.

The most obvious expression of the collapsed relationship of art and reality under fascism is, of course, Hitler himself—it's nearly cliché at this point to note that he was a failed painter and turned his artistic frustrations toward forcing reality to conform to his visions. Norman Spinrad made great use of this concept in his metafictional novel *The Iron Dream* (1972), which explores what would have happened if a young Adolf Hitler had moved to the United States in the 1920s and become a pulp science fiction writer. If Hitler had only spun out his fantasies as mere fantasies, instead of politics, then they would have resulted in ridiculous—if fervently committed—pulp novels full of stoic violent antiheroes, monstrous villains, and extremely phallic weaponry. Fascist ideas make more sense in the framework of a pulp fantasy universe; if fascist regimes hadn't already existed, they wouldn't be plausible in reality. The "alternative conclusion," declares a fictional critic at the end of *The Iron Dream*, "is to accept the ridiculous notion that an entire nation would throw itself at the feet of a leader simply on the basis of mass displays of public fetishism, orgies of blatant phallic symbolism, and mass rallies enlivened with torchlight and rabid oratory. Obviously, such a mass national psychosis could never occur in the real world."[35] The brutal irony of Spinrad's book is even more relevant when compared to a Trump presidency full of blatant phallic symbolism, rabid oratory, and mass rallies of a crowd warmed up by a gangster-imitating anti-immigration advocate who seems to have been fervently convinced of his own glorified antiheroism.

We still don't have a clear answer as to why this very particular fantasy of antiheroic good versus evil, violence and the conquerable dark other, plus the reestablishment of a romanticized past that never existed has such a potent effect on some imaginations but not all of them. What do some people choose to become anti-immigration demagogues or gun-toting incels, and not everyone? Why is phallic symbolism a joke to some and a literally potent image to others? Klaus Theweleit found in his landmark work *Male Fantasies* (1977), a study of novels and memoirs written by the men of the Freikorps—some of the first and most eager Nazis—that these men were obsessed, to a man, with masculinity. They were disgusted by women, whom they largely erased from their narratives or reimagined in mythic terms as a holy innocence to protect; in any sense, their primary erotic attachment was to violence. Writing fiction and memoir in the immediate aftermath of World War I, they weren't horrified by their experiences but lonely for them. Most of the literary output in the 1920s described the war as a horrific experience (Erich Maria Remarque's novel *All Quiet on the Western Front* is a classic example), but the Freikorps men rhapsodized about the beauty of death. Life was vile to them: life carried the risk of softness and penetration.[36] *The Camp of the Saints* is likewise terrified of life and penetration: it envisions the west being overtaken by "rivers of sperm."[37] The other side of this fear is the fantasy of protecting women and the self from those rivers of sperm, a fantasy that constantly reemerges in fascist writing: of being a hypermasculine hero, safe from penetration, eroticism, change, life, in perfect control of the female body, which—being weak, protected, and contained—can't feminize you in turn.

The fear of penetration is also a fear of outside psychological influence: the fear of encounter with subversive ideas. That's exactly why nobody is—paradoxically—more worried about the impact of stories than fascists. The Nazis burned books by writers they felt were racially unfit or writers who normalized gender and sexuality outside the strictest male-female binary; contemporary fascists ban these books instead. It may be controversial to call the contemporary right-wing book banners fascist, but when it comes to a political ideology's relationship to fiction—both the enthusiastic, reality-crossing embrace of some stories and a rejecting terror of others—fascism is as fascism does. The right-wing book banners don't just want to eliminate certain books from school libraries; many want to prosecute librarians and other professionals who disagree.[38] Monica Brown, our friend the dog-shit-brownie mom, advocated for the arrest of librarians who refused to remove the books she believed were dangerous; as another mother told her in a confrontation outside a school board meeting: "That's fascism. You're a fascist."[39]

"Try Reading Books Instead of Burning Them"

All told, the Nazis burned about eighty to ninety thousand books: many novels but also poetry, medical manuals, and scientific texts. The unironically named German Ministry of Propaganda and Enlightenment oversaw the censorship and destruction of literature as well as film, theater, visual art, and music.[40] The attack on culture was twofold: to destroy "bad" art and promote "good" art, "bad" being defined as that which was decadent, overly intellectual, and weakened the resolve of fighting men, and "good" as that which did the opposite. It was Plato's censorship playbook for a good society, more or less exactly. *All Quiet on the Western Front*, being an anti-war novel, was banned, along with anything that could be denigrated as a carrier of "cultural Bolshevism": a supposed conspiratorial Jewish-communist influence that—so the Nazis imagined—was destroying good German values and leading citizens to question the state.[41]

This fear of pernicious Jewish influence was hardly limited to the Nazis. Around the same time in the United States, Christian organizations were attempting to regulate the film industry, which they viewed as unacceptably Jewish. Several Jewish immigrants had risen to become some of the earliest studio heads, and Christian pro-censorship reformers felt a great degree of anger and anxiety about the prospect of Jewish wealth and possible cultural influence. Much of what would be dictated by the Hays Code—and later watered down into the film ratings system—was organized around then contemporary Christian, and especially Catholic, notions of public morality. As film critic Karina Longworth has noted, film censorship wasn't introduced in response to, say, racist films like *Birth of a Nation* but mostly in response to sexy movies about liberated women, or violent crime dramas that embarrassed the police. Sex, violence, profanity, anything that could be perceived as glorifying criminal behavior or criticizing Christianity—these were pared back by the new rules, which, as Longworth points out, were "basically imbued with the philosophy that the reason for movies to exist is to have a positive moral influence."[42] Controlling the content of movies was essential to the goal of teaching good sociopolitical values as well as deleting bad ones: that is, removing wicked foreign Jewish influence, which might introduce unacceptable ideas. As usual, the actual impact that movies had on the public was less measurable, or less measurably important, than the terror that they might penetrate and change the dominant culture.

Underlying this sentiment is a deeper presumption that *only* an insidious Jewish sensibility could corrupt the "true" white German or American spirit; only a spiritual enemy, a secret virus in the culture, could turn people away from how they should behave. Otherwise, people (at least the "true" people, the *volk*) would be perfectly happy to uphold whiteness, strict gender norms, and heterosexuality in the traditional manner. If the public was turning or had already turned against what they ought to have believed, it could only be because evil stories had planted false ideas in their heads. This strain of antisemitism is still with us today: it can be found in the supposed threat of "cultural Marxism," which is an updated version of "cultural Bolshevism" (and often replaced with fresh metonyms such as "critical race theory," "diversity, equity, and inclusion," and maybe a new one before this book goes to print).[43] The usual pedigree given for cultural Marxism is that it descends from the work of Antonio Gramsci and the Frankfurt School, who were mostly Jewish, but the conspiracy theory has almost nothing to do with anything these philosophers wrote or advocated.[44] (Theodor Adorno once wrote, crankily, that newspaper horoscopes were fascist; he didn't suggest hacking the horoscope to push a secret multicultural agenda.)[45] But in the fascist imagination, there must be a victim to be protected and an invasive enemy on the attack: if young people are adopting beliefs in multiculturalism, gender fluidity, and socialism, then someone *must* be forcing these ideas on their innocence. The name of the enemy virus changes constantly, according to Christopher Rufo's daily whims; say what you like about the Satanic Panic, at least it had a coherent set of devils.

But the very unseriousness and dishonesty of the effort to blame everything on a secret multicultural agenda reveals the inherent fascism that underlies it. Jean-Paul Sartre once noted that fascists often come across as silly, unfocused, and unserious, up until the moment they aren't,[46] while Umberto Eco pointed out that fascism requires a social enemy to rail against that is both strong and weak at the same time.[47] Jews, being a long-established minority, have been useful for centuries as both a strong and weak enemy; "culture" itself has also been useful as a strong and weak enemy; the image of Jews or other marginalized people controlling culture makes for almost the ideal strong and weak enemy. Popular fictional stories are especially useful as areas of fascist cultural anxiety, as fiction has both a powerful influence and an indeterminate one. It's been highly convenient both as villain and victim.[48]

To that end, fascists often go after fictional stories as the initial cultural enemy that has to be destroyed or controlled, and they also tend to fight the first battle of that war on fictional territory itself. William S. Lind—a paleoconservative and one of the more successful proponents of the cultural Marxism conspiracy theory—wrote a *Turner Diaries*-like novel in 2014 called *Victoria* in which heroic knights dressed in crusader outfits murder Dartmouth's cultural Marxist professors. (Lind attended Dartmouth.) "The floor ran deep," he writes, "with the bowels of cultural Marxism."[49] This certainly lands somewhere on the silly-scary spectrum of fascism: it's ridiculous for anybody to be this terrified of a couple of professors, and it's creepy to write about killing them.[50] But the supposedly malign influence of cultural Marxism (or critical race theory, or DEI, or wokeness, or whatever) is considered significant enough—or the creation of a strong-weak enemy convenient enough—for Lind to have written out the imaginative destruction of his foes, which is likely meant to encourage the acting-out of violence in the real world by real fascists (provided they can score those crusader outfits first, I guess). We've already seen with *The Turner Diaries* and *The Camp of the Saints* that fascist terror and imagined violence can easily become real: the fascists are happy to make them real.

It's also possible that fascists, in their unseriousness, have simply chosen a convenient enemy; they aren't necessarily as threatened by stories as they pretend to be. When lifestyle guru and steak advocate Jordan Peterson became upset about *Frozen*, a lightly feminist retelling of the classic fairy tale "The Snow Queen," his tears in defense of masculinity might have been sincere (in that he was literally afraid of a movie) and calculated (in that it is very easy and safe to pick on a movie, a rhetorical choice that will garner lots of attention because everybody loves to talk about movies and debate their meaning and influence).[51] It's silly business until it's useful to be serious about it; the fascists never mean it, until they do. In their classic irrational and contradictory manner, fascists might not consider fiction dangerous as much as understand that cultural products make for excellent enemies. If you want to look tough, and you're not, pick an opponent who can't punch back.

There's an inherent fearfulness and weakness in being afraid of stories—or in pretending to be—as well as an inherent fragility and penetrability in being terrified of penetration and wanting to harm someone before they can harm you. Gottschall compares the power of storytelling to the Force in *Star Wars*, with its light side and its dark side—but he neglects a key part of the image, which is that the Force has a strong influence on the weak-minded.[52] I don't mean this in an insulting way, just a clinical one. Watching a movie and talking about it afterward, refracting your understanding of your life and yourself through its images—that's all perfectly normal, and even psychologically necessary. But watching a movie and then going out and killing somebody is a sign of unusual psychic fragility, proof of being overwhelmed and overmastered by external influence.[53] "[He] has a weak soul," Katherine Burdekin writes of one of the Nazi characters in her eerie 1937 novel *Swastika Night*, "a baby soul."[54] If fascists felt strong to begin with, they wouldn't fear, or invent, or fear-invent the power of evil cultural influence; if they felt like men, they wouldn't try so hard to be manly. The Proud Boys may go around harassing drag queens at children's story hour, but proud *men*, presumably, have something better to do with their time.[55]

"Only a child is afraid of everything," Patrick Nathan wrote in his recent book on art and fascism. "Only a child demands protection from every absurd, imagined fear. Only a child's stories lack complexity."[56] This may be a little unfair to children's stories—many are indeed complex, or at least a bit more complex than fascist narratives, and many children learn to tell the difference between fiction and reality at a fairly young age.[57] But it's true that some people prefer to remain like stereotypical children in an absurd heroic dreamworld, not engaging with it from time to time as an adult cosplayer might but always mistaking it for reality, wishing it was reality, and, if provided enough easily available firepower, physically making it into a violent and horrible truth.

In a video recorded from his car in 2014, Eliot Rodger, the incel killer, filmed himself laughing like a Hollywood bad guy. He was trying his hardest to come across as tough, cool, and dangerous: he only managed to evoke the most banal, cartoonish, B-movie villain imaginable. And yet, silly as he sounded, he then drove out and murdered six people in Isla Vista, California, wounding fourteen others before killing himself. He doesn't appear to have been acting out a character from any specific movie or even a fascist propaganda novel: he was just giving a general cinematic impression of what a tough, murderous sociopath might look and sound like. The twenty-two-year-old Rodger seems to have been largely motivated by his hatred of women: he was a virgin and had grown up in an American culture that emphasizes a man is only a man if he has power over women.[58] Much of this cultural imagery is filtered through fictional stories—not just one movie or video game or book or TV show, but many of them, even most of them. This kind of persistent, subtle, nonspecific, and nondirected force can have a very powerful effect on a particularly fragile sort of ego—and the extent of its influence is difficult to grasp and account for, even by those who are really paying attention.

Magneto Was Right

If fascists are so weak and so susceptible, and prone to physical violence based on their reading of aggressively propagandistic—or subtle and indirect—fictional stories about hypermasculinity and

DANGEROUS FICTIONS   83

violence, then you could argue it's the responsibility of the culture industry to create anti-fascist art. We do have the satisfying genre of Nazi-punching movies (*Inglourious Basterds, Indiana Jones* installments 1 and 3, let us never speak of any others), along with works that parody fascism or seek to expose and condemn toxic masculinity and violence at their root. *Fight Club* is a solid example of this latter type: both book and movie are meant, in their obvious surface reading, as anti-fascist works. *Breaking Bad*, even more blatantly, explores the horror unleashed when a seemingly mild-mannered family man finds a way to act out his most dangerous hypermasculine fantasies. The clear and obvious reading of Scorsese's gangster films—so beloved by Stephen Miller—is that they're about the weakness of masculine self-image and the physical and psychic damage wreaked by the so-called tough guys on the people around them. And yet all these popular and critically acclaimed stories (and too many others to list) have often been read by the far right—or even the more ordinary center right—as celebrating what they're meant to condemn. Kyle Smith, a conservative film critic, has asserted that *Goodfellas* depicts a male fantasy, but an entirely positive one. Women viewers, he says, might not understand *Goodfellas*, but men understand that the gangsters are "heroes" who "rule the roost."[59]

Is Smith simply a bad reader (and a bad critic), or should these sorts of stories work harder to establish their ideological position? It would have been difficult for the *Breaking Bad* showrunners to have made Walter White's arc more obvious: he enters the story looking absolutely ridiculous, driving naked except for his tighty-whities, and exits to a song with the lyrics "Guess I got what I deserved" playing above his corpse. And yet, many far-right viewers have admired White as a positive symbol of male antiheroic whiteness against the framing of the narrative choices, including the very deliberate choice of his name. Whether the "intended" reading of any given text matters at all is an open question: stories can be read multiple ways, and any reader can imagine or twist a reading to suit their needs (you could call any sort of creative reading, even the fascist kind, a "queered" reading, if you wanted to start a fight). That being said, some fascist readings may be fairer than others—a few left-leaning critics have argued that *Breaking Bad* really does promote white hypermasculinity as virtuous and necessary, and for all that the *Fight Club* movie may intend to be read as an anti-fascist text, its casting and narrative choices make fascism look awfully sexy and powerful.[60] But regardless of how justified these readings may or may not be, we're faced with the problem that fascists will happily interpret even intentional criticism and satire of themselves as barefaced unironic approval.

For all that they are terrified—or act terrified—of external influence, fascists can often be remarkably resistant to any art that doesn't already comport with their world view. This is another of the essential ironic contradictions of fascism: both weak enough to be influenced and strongly insistent on their readings whether they are justified or not. Fascists read every text as proof of who they are. They might be further radicalized by what they read, even into murderous violence, but whether they can be *de*radicalized by criticism or alternatives—or even perceive the existence of such—is another matter entirely.

A better route toward creating anti-fascist narratives may lie in simply not centering so many stories around violent white male antiheroes in the first place. Emphasizing different kinds of characters often leads to interesting and creative aesthetic places—if publishers and producers will allow it, which they often don't. But any depiction of violence can be fascistic, even if the violence is committed by someone who isn't a white man. Many of the most popular recent TV shows about heroic American intelligence agencies (such as *FBI* and its spin-offs) have featured diverse casts fighting sinister internal or external enemies in classic fascist style. Maybe we should avoid creating stories that center violence or monstrous enemies at all—but then again, many Americans love violence, including me.[61] Honestly, I will show up for just about anything with monsters and explosions. Sometimes, as in my favorite kind of story, it's the monster characters who are coded as heroic or just complex and interesting—this, arguably, is a way of unwriting the usual fascist expectations around alien outsiders. But it's worth asking whether even these stories manage to "unwrite" fascism or, at least, defy fascist readings.

Efforts to write anti-fascist or simply more diverse pop culture narratives have frequently been met with angry opposition from fascist readers. Comicsgate, a sort of miniature version of Gamergate, erupted in 2018 largely in reaction to Marvel's "All-New, All-Different" lineup, which temporarily replaced classic white and/or male characters with non-white and often female versions. A white woman Thor stepped in for the classic white male Thor, a Black female heroine stepped in for Iron Man, etc. The virulent response to this from a small but vocal number of white male comics fans showed considerable ignorance of comic history—these sorts of character reinventions and replacements are commonplace and had happened before—and gave Marvel more credit for progressive action than it really deserved.[62]

Some critics noted the irony that, as Elaine Castillo put it, the "home of the *X-Men*, that supposed bastion of civil rights metaphors," could have found itself "at the crux of such right-wing, misogynist, racist, homophobic fervor."[63] Comicsgate had little connection to the X-Men—Wolverine was among the characters swapped out for new versions, but comic book universes like Marvel's and DC's are enormous, and fans often have preferences for one character or family within it. Just because a white male reader flew into a foaming rage over the idea of a lady Thor doesn't mean he reads or cares about the X-Men at all. Still, Castillo concluded in her book about bad readers that the fascist pushback against Marvel happened because the X-Men and other narratives like it are incomplete in their commitments: "lifting from the historical struggle of racial, sexual, and economic minorities, and replacing those bodies with white, cis, straight characters."[64] If the stories were sufficiently anti-fascist in the first place, and centered on minority perspectives, Castillo suggests, they would have no fascist fans, and the comics could not be misread as being about anything other than racial oppression.

Variations on this opinion have become relatively popular in the last few years: it's often referred to simply as "the X-Men problem," an inherent flaw by which a story has failed in its moral duty to represent oppression accurately and therefore fight fascism.[65] But the question of what the X-Men "represent" and what their political and ethical responsibilities would therefore be, is somewhat less clear. Stan Lee and Jack Kirby, who created the X-Men in 1963, claimed they intended the story to have subtle political overtones related to civil rights—though Lee said the mutants were deliberately not meant to function as a direct allegory for any particular movement.[66] You may have heard that Professor X was written to represent Dr. Martin Luther King Jr., while his more aggressive opponent Magneto is supposed to represent Malcolm X—this would indeed have been a very clumsy and ineffective allegory, so it's fortunate that this assumption is based on an unfounded internet myth. X-Men writer Chris Claremont, who relaunched and reinvented the series, has stated that he had something more like Israeli prime ministers David Ben-Gurion and Menachem Begin in mind, respectively.[67] But even then, these comic book characters were only *influenced* by political figures: they weren't intended and don't make legible sense as literal stand-ins or allegories.

Despite the current popularity of analyzing fiction—especially science fiction and fantasy—as political allegories for real-life events or social struggles, true allegory is rare. Most science fiction and fantasy stories work on the terrain of imagery or metaphor instead: X character doesn't equal Y real thing, but only suggests it, glancing at it from the side. As members of an oppressed minority who generally come into their power and difference as teenagers, the X-Men work as a metaphor (but never effectively as an allegory) for many different kinds of oppression: racism, antisemitism, homophobia, transphobia, and ableism. Under the direction of Claremont, who revived the series in the 1970s and introduced a more international and increasingly multiethnic cast of characters, the X-Men became increasingly diverse and eventually more openly queer.[68] But of course there are still some cis, straight, and white characters among the X-Men: they represent many different types of identity and axes of oppression, and none specifically.[69]

The X-Men can also be read fascistically, as actual fascists, if you like; mutants call themselves "homo superior" and some consider themselves a literally superior race. Magneto has historically been the leader of the master race faction; his fevered defense of mutants is supposed to be the result of his traumatic history as a Jewish survivor of the Holocaust. The fact that Jewish writers (Lee, Kirby, and Claremont are all Jewish) would choose to explore and indict fascism (and Israeli politics) through the lens of a Jewish Holocaust survivor villain/antihero is a fascinating move both politically and aesthetically.[70] Magneto is also occasionally depicted as a hero, both in the comics and in movie adaptations—does this make the X-Men pro-fascist? Against it? The reading is not so simple. It raises questions rather than answering them; it doesn't fall neatly into binaries of good and evil, or provide obvious takeaway messages of right and wrong. Art—especially popular, enduring art—is rarely reducible to a single interpretation.

Two years before Comicsgate, Marvel was subject to criticism from the opposite direction: left and liberal fans were upset at the announcement that Captain America was going to be revealed as a secret agent of Hydra (i.e., a kind of Nazi) all along. The backlash was again the result of internet ignorance—superhero backgrounds are retconned and re-imagined in comic book universes all the time. But there was also a degree of anxiety over whether this plotline was antisemitic (Captain America having also been created by Jewish writers, and Hydra being a fascist organization) and a boon to potentially fascist readers. I happened to be working at Marvel while this happened and read an early release of the first issue; it was clear that the story arc was going to explore "what if this blond superhuman symbol of America was an evil fascist all along," an impulse that seemed obviously, even pedantically, aligned with left-liberal politics (not to mention the complicated historical interplay between European and American versions of fascism and pre-fascism). Around this time, I ran into a friend of a friend who was also a comics fan, and also Jewish. She informed me, without having read the comic, that it was antisemitic; I told her I'd already read it and thought it was aiming at critique of fascism rather than endorsement. She replied that she still thought it was antisemitic and pro-fascist and shouldn't have been written in the first place. She essentially read the comic (or didn't, since she never actually *read* it) in the way a fascist traditionally would: as something too dangerous to be allowed, which might carry an evil influence that certain readers—the Stephen Millers of the world—would be too fragile to withstand.

Ultimately, I found the full "Hydra Cap" storyline disappointing—the Marvel comics universe generally returns all new ideas to the status quo, forbidding real change and exploration—but I've never forgotten the certainty with which this other fan decided that a comic she hadn't read was both dangerous to our people and a boon to the fascist cause. To avoid radicalizing more helpless young white boys like Stephen Miller into fascism, Captain America, the white Übermensch symbol of America—who entered the comics universe in 1941 punching Hitler in the face—ought to remain unchanged and unquestioned. That the story was meant to be a commentary on fascism and America was irrelevant; that it was aiming for complexity made it suspicious, and too dangerous to read.

Holding Up Art as Mirrors to Themselves

We can, if we like, try to idiot-proof all art so it can't co-opted by fascists, but in many cases they've already decided on the radicalizing direction in which they'll read it, based on whatever narrative they believe will be most successful in rewriting reality to meet their needs. They're influenced as far as they want to be; they may be weak to external influence, but ultimately they're only pretending not to choose. If a person is already looking for validation of their belief that they deserve power over others, then fascism is simply the purest, though not quite exclusive, political and aesthetic expression of that need. (Art is also hardly required for political cruelty: there's no documented rash of *Camp of the Saints* fans in the Biden administration, and yet their immigration policies have done plenty of harm to asylum seekers and other desperate people.)[71]

Anti-fascist art, then, doesn't make much difference to the converted; it can only impact, possibly, those who haven't yet made any commitments. If those commitments, however, are ultimately a matter of choice, then we can still have complex and interesting art; we can have metaphors rather than pedantic one-to-one allegories. We can have complicated art that interrogates evil without worrying it will be read as an endorsement of it, except by those who want it to do the endorsing. Whatever the text actually says, fascists will read the messages that they want to read in it. What people so often find in fiction is themselves.

But even the idea of "complicated" art that doesn't endorse an obvious political position is itself complicated. It's time for me to pull you into an alley and whisper that the very idea of "artistic complexity" and politics being naturally at odds with each other may have been implanted in our brains by the CIA. I'm joking, of course (there's no alley), but it's true that our ideas about what makes a "political" story and what makes a "not political" story are themselves politicized and not rooted in neutral territory. After (as well as somewhat before and during) World War II, a great deal of American money and manpower went toward combatting danger-ous stories—though not fascist ones, which have generally been tolerated in the United States—and propping up certain realities located between extremes of narrative possibility as normal, and just right.

CHAPTER FOUR

Fear of a Red Literature

A famous Cold War joke: An American student and a Russian student meet up for a friendly conversation. The Russian tells the American that he's studying the kind of propaganda perpetuated by the U.S. government. The American says, "What propaganda?" The Russian says, "Exactly."

You may have heard that during the Cold War, the CIA and other elements of the U.S. government helped shape the kinds of stories that were (and to a degree still are) written, funded, distributed, and lauded throughout the world. And you might think that sounds crazy; you might look for my corkboard full of pushpins and yarn. But it's a matter of public record that the CIA was involved with the international production of world culture during the Cold War, founding influential magazines and international literary festivals, feeding money through front groups and nonprofit foundations to a slew of writers including Saul Bellow, Wole Soyinka, Jorge Luis Borges, and Hannah Arendt whether they knew it or not.[1] Against Soviet realism (in novels, movies, and other forms of art), the CIA promoted modernism, individualism, and freedom of expression. You might think: those are all good words, I like the products of those words. But all that modernity and individualism and freedom came bundled together with the twin goals of empire and capitalism. The CIA didn't fund all that freedom of expression for free; they had subtle propagandistic goals in mind.

We tend to assume, if we think about it at all, that these propaganda efforts were ineffective, especially after all these years—that they only out-competed bad Soviet-style realism, or that only *other people*, foolish people, were ever hoodwinked by pro-capitalist messaging. But if our perceptions were indeed altered thanks to art that still bears the marks of CIA influence, even decades later, then it would be difficult to know it. And this is a scary prospect, maybe the worst of fiction's many proposed dangers: that it has already shaped our imagination in ways that we can't even perceive.

So much anxiety about fiction is related to *new* ideas leaking in, but if these ideas are already here, and solidified into our dominant cultural patterns, then their power over us would be much harder to identify. Correctly sorting out the kinds of assumptions that make up our current "given reality" is always a squishy art at best, but I'll attempt to tease out what I see as the lingering influence of what we might call "CIA bullshit" in U.S. literary fiction and the institutions around it, because I think while the larger conspiracy is very dead, pieces of it remain embedded in the structural framework of writing and our critical assumptions about it, unleashing a process that has shaped the idea of "individual freedom to write" and limits the kinds of stories that tend to be published without us even realizing it.

I'm not remotely the first person to bring up the connections between the CIA and the construction of literary possibility as we understand it. But knowledge of the CIA's historical involvement in world culture—or the Pentagon's continued relationship with Hollywood action movies—has a tendency to disappear and reappear in the public consciousness every few years.[2] The facts of the case don't stick in the mind; they feel made up, like a movie. This is a paradox that's long been recognized by left intellectuals: sometimes true events that really happened feel improbable, cinematic, hysterical, and unreal, while tidy but false narratives make up the constructed reality that we accept as true every day.[3] Describing our constructed reality—our "given reality"—is always a challenge: How do you describe the air, especially if it's motionless? You can describe smog or wind: obvious artificiality or disturbance. But it's hard to name something that refuses to admit it exists, even as it presses down on you. It's easier to say that the air around you is perfectly clean, unmarked, and has no qualities.

When it comes to questioning our "given reality," and how it's been constructed by fiction and the institutional resources put into fiction, there's an additional danger of losing yourself in a vague distrust of everything. Conspiratorial thinking can provide its own false certainty: convincing yourself that every piece of art is propaganda and every piece of received wisdom is fake is how you end up believing in the Flat Earth theory. The basic facts of how the CIA once influenced world culture are, however, well established. In *Who Paid the Piper? The CIA and the Cultural Cold War*, historian Frances Stonor Saunders demonstrates how the CIA provided patronage for writers and other artists mostly through a front organization called the Congress for Cultural Freedom (CCF), which billed itself as a free speech organization with a neutral interest in supporting freedom against totalitarian censorship worldwide.[4] The CCF was exposed as a CIA front by investigative journalists in 1967 and folded soon after that.[5] Still, for the nearly twenty years of its influential life, the CCF's patronage often made the difference when it came to who could afford to write and what kinds of writing were regarded as serious and aesthetically valuable in the first place. The fallout from those decisions lingers today.

In any capitalist system, writing only has aesthetic value if it has literal value: that is, if it can be turned into a product that can be sold on the open market to a desirable demographic. In this way it's always been very easy for capitalism to co-opt and sell ostensibly "radical" literature. Many of the writers who received financial and critical support from the postwar CCF were leftists, and even socialists—but usually non-communist, or at least writing in a style that was divorced from the doctrinaire socialist realism of the Soviet Union. Financially supporting leftist "free expression" worldwide was a neat way of making sure that unequivocally far-left writing never saw the light of day; it also proved the superiority of the American way of life, the subtle ideology of money. Any idea under the U.S. capitalist umbrella could be freely expressed, provided it had a buyer; the mere fact that it *had* a buyer proved the worthiness of its expression.

The strangest recipient of CIA literary funding is probably Gabriel García Márquez. A committed leftist thinker and writer, Márquez was legally forbidden to enter the United States on the grounds of his politics. Still, a magazine called *Mundo Nuevo*—a CCF outfit openly rumored at the time to be funded by "gringo spy money"—ran promotional excerpts of *One Hundred Years of Solitude*.[6] Márquez's famous novel is political in its way, in that it references political events, but it couldn't be called, stylistically, a communist or social realist novel. The lack of overt left propaganda and Márquez's exquisite prose style were useful to the CCF's project; while the CCF did promote some mediocre writers, geniuses were highly valuable to them, because the very existence of individual, experimental geniuses rising out of capitalist societies proved the power of individual talent unfettered by the state. Mid-century literature was so good in part because the CIA paid for it, and because it deliberately leveraged this literature to demonstrate the superiority of the American-led, capitalist, rugged individualist way of life.

It's typical in the twenty-first century, where capitalism is so ubiquitous and omnipresent, to assume that genius is always self-evident and that *One Hundred Years of Solitude* would naturally have received praise and literary coverage simply by existing. But that requires a complete and frankly pathetic degree of faith in the literary free market to decide what constitutes great art and what doesn't. The CIA itself never had such faith in the free market and in individual actors to make their own decisions: if noncommunist, nonthreatening literature was so obviously superior, then it wouldn't have needed a secret directional boost, a multipronged cultural ad campaign. The invisible hand of the market was, for many years, the CIA's own. The fact that we still believe so thoroughly in the objective power of the market—and in the taste-making powers of a publishing industry and literary culture that still, after all, operates for profit—is a pretty good example of just how successful these efforts have been.

The CIA, of course, isn't solely responsible for the promotion of capitalism and the free market, especially inside the United States. When it comes to its direct activities, the CIA may have meddled with the cultural output of other countries (messing with other countries is, after all, literally their job), but the CIA's remit technically forbids the organization to practice spy craft in the United States, and occasionally, the CIA even respected their own rules. It's true that the CIA did help fund important domestic literary magazines such as the *Kenyon Review*, but when it comes to the persistent rumor that it funded writing programs throughout the United States, including the Iowa Writers' Workshop (IWW), the agency was relatively hands-off.[7] English professor Eric Bennett—who wrote a companion book to Stonor Saunders's about the ideological and monetary underpinnings of U.S. writing workshops—says that in 1967 the CIA gave about seven thousand dollars to the IWW through the Farfield Foundation, a known front organization, and nothing after that.[8] Much more funding for the IWW over the years came in through a complicated tangle of State Department interests, local businessmen, and private philanthropic organizations such as the Ford and Rockefeller Foundations. (Bennett notes that these foundations were formed as tax dodges by the Ford Motor Company and Standard Oil, respectively, and that the revolving door of employees and board members between the Ford and Rockefeller Foundations and the State Department made these organizations basically "the privatized face of American foreign policy.")[9] So the short answer to "Did the CIA fund American MFA programs and therefore literary fiction?" is "not really." But the long answer—if you interpret "CIA" as a metonym for U.S. state power and interests—is "and how."

Even so, when the CIA, the State Department, and various philanthropic foundations led by a wealthy interchange of businessmen funded arts and culture programs, they did so under the banner of a supposedly free and neutral literature. The U.S. government downplayed and defunded communist art and social realism to be sure, but officially, it promoted all other forms of freedom of expression. The McCarthy hearings and the House Un-American Activities Committee (HUAC) disciplined novelists, playwrights, and screenwriters in the 1950s, and that did have a chilling effect on artistic production, especially when it came to representing labor and anything that might be classed as "social issues."[10] But once the blacklists were over, technically anything could be written and said, including a decent amount of fiction that represented the U.S. government in a critical light. The mega-conglomerate control of popular culture has certainly led to an increased sameness and propagandistic quality in American movies and network TV (a matter that will be addressed in later chapters). But in other areas of media—in prestige TV and literature, especially—don't we still have tremendous variety, and complex, compelling storytelling of all kinds?

This is where discussions of CIA or other propagandistic influence on fiction tend to break down. Every kind of subject is, supposedly, allowed in literary novel-writing these days, which means that nothing is openly forbidden: there's no coercion and no state standards. Literary fiction, in the United States and elsewhere, is home to a tremendous variety of mini-genres: autofiction, magical realism, surreal experimentation, sprawling historical novels, even a hybrid literary-genre form. Literature these days is like a well-stocked supermarket: we have every flavor of chip. But in this profusion of options and combinations, it may feel at times that something is missing: something about the packaging, the ingredients, the requirement to be sold, that reveals a concealment, that breeds—like the rest of capitalism—a gnawing feeling of absence and anomie rather than pleasure in abundance. There's something about the way we tell stories, and our implicit assumptions about what's desirable and what isn't, that we rarely question, because we've been led to believe there are no options besides a neatly stacked array of options.

The dynamics of consumption and emptiness are often fairly obvious when it comes to movies and TV; however, they remain true of less obviously profitable enterprises like literary fiction as well. In any context, it's easier to imagine the end of the world than the end of capitalism, easier to imagine that we already have everything we need, that all possible forms of art are already available to us, and nothing needs to ever change.[11] But to understand how the total financial enclosure of art in the name of freedom has affected serious fiction, I want to try to get outside the framework of what has been established as artistic reality, our given reality,

and identify the limits of our expectations.[12] What does our literature—our high and very serious literature—tell us about who we
have to be, what matters, and what's possible? And if we *are* limited, what does that mean? What kinds of stories are we lacking,
and what would it mean if we had them?

"You Do Want to Express Yourself, Don't You?"

In a 2014 article in *The Chronicle of Higher Education*—which went
viral online and is still shared and yelled at from time to time—Eric
Bennett describes his own unpleasant experience at the IWW in
the 1990s. He struggles to define exactly what was wrong in concrete terms: he didn't experience oppression or censorship in any
sense, more of a feeling of a low-key, anti-intellectual conformity
that foreclosed real literary experimentation and prevented students
from attempting big and ambitious novels. "The workshop was like
a muffin tin you poured the batter of your dreams into," Bennett
says. "You entered with something undefined and tantalizingly protean and left with muffins."[13] Muffins—even the best muffins—are
a product that can be quickly consumed, leaving nothing behind.
The true product of writing workshops has been, overwhelmingly,
the writer themselves: their life experience or something like it, fictionalized or something like it. As critic Mark McGurl writes in *The
Program Era*, a more sympathetic look at the history of American
writing than Bennett's, the products of these workshops have often
been "portrait[s] of the artist," as young writers are taught to write
themselves into being—and not much else.[14] Writers attend these
programs to sing the song of themselves, or, more cynically, to sell
the muffin of themselves.

Experiences vary, and many graduates of the IWW and other
workshops speak lovingly of the time they spent there. The doctrine of individualism and personal expression—"finding your

voice," learning how to tell your own story—can be freeing for many writers, especially those from marginalized backgrounds or abusive situations. This kind of speech can have tremendous personal-social value as well: McGurl notes that "the appeal of *speaking for oneself*, or of *having one's voice heard*, is obvious when it is considered as an act primarily of political self-representation."[15] Still, it isn't just white men like Eric Bennett who have found the program experience dissatisfying. Sandra Cisneros says that when she attended the IWW in the 1970s, she would dutifully "inges[t] the class readings" every week and then write "the opposite."[16] What Cisneros ended up writing in opposition to the staid white realism taught in her classes was *The House on Mango Street*, a stylistically experimental and gorgeous exploration of Chicana life in the United States. For McGurl, *The House on Mango Street* is evidence of the strength of institutionalized creative writing rather than an indictment of it: in his view, Cisneros's work demonstrates that the program has enough variety and flexibility to engender its opposites, allowing for dialectical growth and change.[17] There is no individual so marginalized that a writing program can't teach them to speak for themselves and their community, no real-life experience that can't be transfigured into high literature (and then sold for at least some small profit). Unlike the more rigid art movements of the European past, any sort of content can and will be allowed; meaning, incidentally, that there's no need for students to engage in anything like Romanticism or Dadaism or any other unified artistic rebellion. Everything is freely available, the free individual freely expressing themselves, forever, at the end of literary history.

Since the individual is the most important subject, and personal experience the font of truth, I can say that I, individually and personally, hated the undergraduate creative writing program I attended (at Oberlin College, in the mid-2000s). Despite the program's excellent reputation and Oberlin's purported far-left freedoms, I found the whole thing stifling, in a kind of sneering and passive-aggressive way that could never quite admit to its premises. I took a particularly depressing fiction workshop my sophomore year: a magnolia tree grew outside the classroom, and I would take a petal into class with me, slowly destroying it as the hours dragged along. The problem was exactly that petal, and how it felt in my fingers: I was supposed to write about my immediate sensory experiences, my social mistakes and my small depressions, to imagine nothing outside myself and my feelings. Our teachers (who were mostly white women, teaching classes mostly composed of young white women) encouraged us to write what we knew, and we were supposed to know as little as possible. We were supposed to shrink down, as small as that crushed petal, and offer ourselves like dead flowers.[18]

Even writing about my experience just like that—in the first person, foregrounding personal feelings and small details like the magnolia petal—may grant this narrative a particular feeling of authenticity. We've come to expect writers, and especially women writers, to justify their thoughts and their art-making not through research or aesthetic endeavor but through personal experience. And paradoxically, when women writers do break out of this expectation, it's often praised as an achievement against the usual weepy, silly, skinny-girl stuff—a 1999 *New Yorker* review of Zadie Smith's debut novel, *White Teeth*, praises her for "break[ing] the iron rule that first fictions should be thin slices of autobiography, served dripping with self-pity."[19] This is only an iron rule because it's been enforced as such for decades—not because young women are naturally devoted to writing about themselves or because first novels necessarily need to be thin slices of autobiography (or "wan little husks of autofiction," in Joyce Carol Oates's devastating phrase).[20] It happens because it's expected to happen, because women have been encouraged in writing workshops and through the conglomeration of literary fiction to commodify themselves and their experiences into a marketable product, a fact that few people seem to consider especially remarkable or strange.[21]

Again, I don't want to dismiss the experiences of the people who find autofiction or other forms of autobiographical-ish writing aesthetically interesting and even liberating; the "own personal voice" writing taught in most workshops can be viewed as a performance of the self, the profound saying of "I am."[22] But fiction is and has always been stories about other people: not "I am" but "they are." Twenty years after her debut, Zadie Smith wrote a lengthy defense of fiction in *The New York Review of Books*; fiction, it seems, now needs to be defended against the seeming embarrassment and temerity of making stuff up about other people.[23] This isn't a coincidence, and it isn't just that writing about yourself or someone very like yourself happens to be a currently popular artistic mode: the dead end of capitalist individuality is the declaration of "I" alone, forever.

Of course, there are still plenty of literary novels about *other people*, a whole supermarket's worth of stories, and autofiction in particular is just one wee little snack among many. But highly personal writing remains a form that marginalized writers—of any kind—are often expected to choose and a neat way of keeping them from more expansive and experimental forms that could theoretically be deemed more politically challenging. In reviewing *The Late Americans*, a novel by Black and gay writer Brandon Taylor, the white critic Laura Miller complained that Taylor's book was insufficiently personal: it didn't resemble his Twitter feed and his Substack newsletter, which are funny and chatty and intimate.[24] The novel is, incidentally, about a group of people living in Iowa City, where Taylor attended the IWW. But it's a *novel* based on these experiences: not autofiction, a memoir, or a tweet. There's something inherently demeaning in assuming that a novelist, especially one from a marginalized background, must be consigned to tweets and personal opinions—amusement and entertainment—rather than taken seriously on the grounds of his stated project. Taylor has never been vague about his literary intentions and influences; regular followers of his social media or his newsletter know about his love for nineteenth-century European novels. He's also personally dismissed much autofiction as "catalogue fiction," every bit as vague and formless as an IKEA catalog.[25] The only reason to read one of Taylor's novels and expect something highly personal like autofiction is if you believe *certain kinds* of writers should speak in a certain register, about certain topics, in their own personal voice— but *only* their own personal voice, their personal brand under capitalism (and also if you remain unaware that the voice a writer uses online or in autofiction is still a created character, and never an authentic "self" at all).

Further homogeneity has crept into workshop fiction thanks to the fact that, as with higher education, you generally need to come from the middle class or higher to access it in the first place. McGurl emphasizes that these institutionally funded writers' workshops are a triumph of "mass" higher education, but there's never really been anything "mass" about them, especially with the rise in the cost of tuition over the last few decades.[26] Class remains the hidden dimension of writing, the intersection that dare not speak its name: Brandon Taylor is a rare example of a writer of any race who comes from an impoverished background. Bertrand Cooper—a critic and another rare example of a Black writer who grew up in poverty—wrote a viral article in 2021 demonstrating that when it comes to Black novels, movies, and TV shows, most of these narratives are created by the college-attending Black middle class even if the characters are (and they usually are) based on the Black poor.[27] The matter of "who gets to write" is, invariably, a matter of money:

who has time to write, who gets to attend MFA programs and other career-advancing structures, and who has access to support networks once they're ready to publish.

The real difference between the CIA-funded midcentury and the present day is funding: writers are living in the detritus of a culture that still believes in the lingering ghost of self-expression but no longer pays people enough to perform it. We've retained all the rugged individualism and the pressure to express yourself— just like everyone else—but none of the institutional support. And therefore, whether they're expressing themselves through autofiction or historical novels or science fiction or anything else, writers have no choice but to sell themselves like products: to promote their personal brands (a really disturbing phrase that we've all decided to accept as part of our given reality). And that means there's no room, as the short story writer Madeline Cash told *Nylon* magazine, for any writer to act as a "hermetic enigmatic Salinger Pynchon type anymore."[28] The writer—as feminized in literary fiction as she is in the YA and genre scene—now has to be available to everyone. And all of her experiences (often traumatic ones) have to be made legible: her experience being all she is, and all she has.

All this pressure to produce art in "your own personal voice" based mainly on your own personal experiences has tended to inspire work that's more conformist and unindividuated rather than less, especially when most writers come from the same kinds of class backgrounds. As such, the experience of reading literary fiction these days often feels like being at a party where everybody just wants to talk about themselves: everyone is self-interested— and trying desperately to package and sell that self-interest—in the exact same way.[29] The image of the writer as a truly independent voice is dead: it was slowly strangled to promote a particular set of values that no one wants to pay for anymore.

Just a Good Man Who Sometimes Does Bad Things

The first recruits to the IWW were mostly white male World War II veterans. They were encouraged to write about themselves and their own personal experiences partly as a therapeutic exercise, but also for the sake of engendering a specific set of values in a new class of writer. Before the war, many U.S. writers were openly communist or otherwise left-leaning, often poor bohemians living in cities. While some were eventually employed by the New Deal–era Works Progress Administration (including Zora Neale Hurston, Richard Wright, John Cheever, and Saul Bellow) collecting folklore and writing travel guides, many lacked any institutional affiliation or support.[30] The idea of any affiliation between creative writers and academic institutions in the first place, McGurl explains, was largely an invention of the postwar era: we take it for granted now that obviously budding literary novelists would want to sign up for academic creative writing programs, but these are a relatively new historical development.[31] In fact, the programs were intended, partly, as a kind of institutional capture: gather up the writers, who might theoretically otherwise have become bohemian radicals, and train them up in the heartland instead.[32] "Bring the writers to middle America," writes Bennett in *Workshops of Empire*, "where the odor of hogs and no whiff of Marxism filled the air."[33]

Iowa was, in particular, just about as hoggish and far away from the dangerously bohemian Marxist metropolises as you could get: a good spot to teach these newly arrived gentleman soldier-poets and novelists, who at first were largely white, Christian, heterosexual, and often married.[34] Bennett unearths a telling 1955 *Life* magazine op-ed on the subject (*Life* was owned by Henry Luce at the time, who was cozy with the CIA and the various affiliated foundations who were funding cultural influence).[35] The op-ed, titled "Wanted: An American Novel," demands new, more properly red-blooded American books, not those that smacked of being "written by an unemployed homosexual living in a packing-box shanty on the city dump while awaiting admission to the county poorhouse."[36] The era of the impoverished and potentially gay bohemian novelist was over: the United States portrayed in *Life* magazine needed a new wave of respectable, academically affiliated novelists to act as good ambassadors for American values.

"Values" is a word that pops up a lot in Bennett's study of the period: for the founders and backers of creative writing workshops, "values" seems to have been a cute way of not saying "politics." Soviet realism was of course political, and social realism of the type previously popular in the United States was political, but novels about regional slices of life or small experiences (or even big historical experiences, depending on their presentation) could be marketed as being about "values" instead.[37] If novels showed some values as good while others were portrayed as bad, this was still apolitical: "values" were treated as something closer to "morals," though not quite as stuffy and with no political resonance. The lingering presumption of a supposedly neutral and apolitical white male perspective is closely related to this supposedly neutral and apolitical postwar American perspective. Of course, there was never anything "neutral" about this values-based ideology, and it was never neutrally encouraged. Paul Engle, the founder of the IWW, encouraged the import of foreign writers to be trained up at U.S. workshops and sent back to their home countries in an effort to inculcate and colonize their supposedly "cloudy minds" with the right values, and lead them away from communism.[38]

What were these "right" values? Literary novels were supposed to be concrete and full of specific detail, like that magnolia petal. They were also supposed to be politically ambivalent with complex, ambivalent characters, a supposed antidote to totalitarian thinking. Intimate relationships, even sex, made for appropriate subject matter: in a postwar American novel, you could write about adulterous heterosexual affairs without the government banging down your door to find out if you were representing or endorsing the behavior of your adulteress. Still, purges of communist or suspected communist writers during the McCarthy years had a chilling effect on novels, as they did on films, especially affecting the kinds of stories written for popular consumption. Paperback novels—usually meaning pulp or genre novels but sometimes cheap reproductions of older classics—came under suspicion in the 1950s for promoting homosexuality or communism (the two were linked in the public mind as furtive and unruly acts).[39] Many writers in any medium were blacklisted, but others happily collaborated with authorities. Directors and actors such as John Ford, John Wayne, and Cecil B. DeMille secretly assisted CIA-led efforts to make movies centered around "freedom" and what the Pentagon called "militant liberty."[40] Thanks to the loud crackdown on some writers, and the quiet support of others, the broader culture in the immediate postwar period was washed clean of the taint of possible subversion.

But censorship of more openly political art was never total; or at least, it took subtler forms. Rod Serling, who took an allegorical approach to U.S. social issues in *The Twilight Zone* (1959–1964), maintained a 1930s-era socialist view of the relationship between politics and art. "The writer's role," he once said, "is to be a menacer of the public's conscience . . . He must see the arts as a vehicle of social criticism and he must focus the issues of his time."[41] In 1957, before the days of *The Twilight Zone*, Serling tried to write a teleplay allegorizing Emmett Till's recent murder, presumably hoping to trouble and menace the U.S. public conscience. But he was met with censorship and difficulty on the production side—the teleplay was written for *The United States Steel Hour*, a program unsubtly sponsored by U.S. Steel—and the corporation worried about the loss of advertising dollars. In the end, Serling's script was bowdlerized to the point where it was set in the North and not the South, and instead of the entire town being implicated in the murder of an outsider (as Serling had originally intended), the killer became "a good, decent, American boy momentarily gone wrong."[42] It wasn't a deliberately calculated and heinous crime, like the real-life murder of Till had been, but a mistake. Evil was just a confusion of manners, a forgivable misunderstanding.

"Understanding" is one of the key values that was supposed to be communicated by the approved novels and popular culture of this period. Engle, in his appeals for funding for the IWW, promoted a sense of global "mutual understanding," which would bring about peace through the international exchange of high literary novels.[43] "Peace" and "understanding" were contrasted with the communist or more broadly totalitarian world view that was characterized as being intolerant of dissent and saw the world as a collection of evil systems. From the healthy liberal capitalist point of view, systems and structures could never be classed as the problem: there was only individual miscommunication, misunderstanding, and the inability to transcend cultural differences. The apotheosis of this point of view may be the ending of *Rocky IV* (1985), in which the scrappy independent American boxer, victorious over his enormous machine-trained Russian opponent, makes a speech about peace and change and getting along. The Soviet crowd goes wild.

All right, then, what's so wrong with peace, love, and understanding? Nothing, of course. The Cold War–era "Can't we all just get along?" lessons are highly preferable, in retrospect, to the post-9/11 penchant for ideological villains who love violence and hate freedom. The problem here is solely what counts as "political," and what's considered simply normal, acceptable, and *good* writing. If you were to represent the problems between (and within) nations as a matter of confusion and lack of empathetic understanding, then that would be apolitical; if those problems were a question of material conditions, unfairly leveraged economic power, and unhealed historical wounds, then that would be very political, and a failure to empathize with all sides. The specific image of novels and movies as empathy machines or gyms might arise from this Cold War belief in "understanding" as the only pathway to peace rather than any change in policy or social structure. Having empathy meant not writing like a communist or a political activist. A communist had insufficient empathy for the boss; an anti-colonialist freedom fighter had insufficient empathy for the colonizer. The moral complexity of the individual protagonist was a microcosm for the national complexity of the United States during America's various wars on other nations to "free" them from communism. The whole country was just a good man who sometimes did bad things.

Your Honor, My Client

Morally complex literary novels about ambiguous individuals may not be quite as neutral and apolitical as they seem, and we might indeed have been subtly propagandized into individualistic capitalist American values by our reading of them—but even so, the opposite of "ambiguity" and "complexity" tends to be flatness and simplicity. The plain fact is that a lot of communist and social realist novels are genuinely terrible, not even attempting to create vraisemblance to people in real life. Soviet realism is famous for its villainous landlords and angelic worker-heroes, and most people who are interested in Russian literature (including Russians) tend to skip over the official literature of the Soviet period. Most overtly political art is, let's be real, a disaster on an aesthetic level. Artistic subtlety may be dangerous, in that it can be harder to appreciate when we're imbibing propaganda, but it still makes for a more pleasurable experience. Even when we agree with the political intent of a work of art, not all of us enjoy being hit in the face with it; or at any rate, we're hoping for something to enjoy besides the punch.

And lack of subtlety can be damaging in its own way. In his famous essay "Everybody's Protest Novel," James Baldwin criticizes political novels such as *Uncle Tom's Cabin* for representing human beings as less than who they really are. Yes, *Uncle Tom's Cabin* is one of the most effective works of agitprop in history, having successfully enlisted many formerly apathetic white northerners into the abolitionist cause, but it still depicts Black characters in a flat and racist way. The danger of *Uncle Tom's Cabin*, and of all overtly political or "protest" novels, is that even if you agree with the cause and the intent of the protest, and even if it actually manages to "work" in the sense of having a direct and positive political impact, the novel usually fails to represent human beings as human, representing them instead as categories and moral lessons.[44] And that's damaging, Baldwin explains, to our sense of ourselves and one another: it's dangerous to imagine human beings as less than human, especially when their oppression arises from already being perceived as less than human in the first place. A flat character is more than an aesthetic mistake: it's a political error too, even if placed in the service of good politics.

But then, neither "flatness" nor "complexity" make for objective or apolitical categories either. We don't always agree on what makes a character detailed enough not to be dangerous, or how much peace, love, and understanding is required in the writing of fictional characters to pass them off as sufficiently human. While praising the moral complexity of postwar American writing, McGurl mentions, in passing, that Toni Morrison's *Beloved* still features, despite the usual literary standards, "a textbook example of . . . a 'flat' character"—the villainous slave owner referred to only as "schoolteacher." McGurl is puzzled by schoolteacher's inclusion; this character seems, to him, out of step with contemporary realism. In the end, McGurl settles on something closer to a medieval explanation: the slave-owning schoolteacher is "all but allegorical, a token not of the complexity of human motives, but of an abstract set of values tending toward pure evil."[45]

Slave owners like schoolteacher, however, were real people; sometimes human beings, and the characters based on them, behave in a way that can only be described as evil. In 2014, *The Economist* published a review of a nonfiction book about slavery— Edward Baptist's *The Half Has Never Been Told: Slavery and the Making of American Capitalism*—which complained that Baptist's work wasn't "an objective history of slavery. Almost all the blacks in his book are victims, almost all the whites villains." The review was swiftly retracted after public outcry: readers pointed out that depicting slavery as a matter of victims and villains is just plain old accurate historiography.[46] But that puts interesting demands on novelists who are trying to write about a subject like slavery, especially contemporary novelists who are supposed to avoid overtly polemical writing and psychological simplicity, and who are sworn to the aesthetic demand for "the complexity of human motives." What is good, morally complex literary fiction supposed to do when history—actual reality—has villains in it?

McGurl isn't totally wrong, I think, to notice that Morrison's "schoolteacher" is in certain respects lacking in complexity, or complexity as we've been trained to see and understand it. "School-teacher" is so named because he's developed a strict, rationalized, and teachable world view: he's turned racism into a kind of cold-blooded science. The fact that the "lessons" he imparts to his "students" are bizarre and insane is exactly the point—when he instructs his nephews to hold down the teenage Sethe and suckle at her breasts in an empty ritual of lust and dominance, there's nothing scientific to it and no data to be gained. Schoolteacher only *thinks* he's a rational man, a wise administrator of people and resources (and people who are resources). Morrison, however, gives us small hints of his crudity, insecurity, and private sense of his own incomplete power. After a sheriff speaks dismissively to school-teacher, he "beat his hat against his thigh and spit."[47] The cues are subtle, but schoolteacher is really a perfectly round character: you know who he is and what he thinks. You can turn him around and look at him from all the angles. Morrison just presents him without pity, which is fitting, because he lacks it. And that's what's made him, by his own choice, a little less than human.

Morrison's narrative also doesn't forgive him. *Beloved* doesn't offer us any exculpatory evidence for schoolteacher's behavior, some kind of trauma or backstory that might explain how he became who he is, and ask the reader for clemency on his behalf. McGurl is looking for that exculpatory evidence even if he doesn't realize it: he concludes that schoolteacher's role in the novel is to act as the trauma that sets up Sethe for her later act of infanticide, "lending to this work the disturbing ethical undecidability and inexhaustible re-readability we associate with high narrative art."[48] McGurl's implication is that we love novels in part for that ethical undecidability itself: we read *Beloved* over and over again to determine the indeterminable question of whether Sethe is guilty. But that positions the reader not as a reader—Sethe is being haunted by the ghost of her daughter, we already know how *she* feels about her guilt—but as a juror. Was Sethe's murder of her daughter a crime or not?

The question is a perfectly reasonable one to ask in, say, a high school English class, but demanding it of adults, fully educated readers, leans on one of those subtle and unconsciously propagandized beliefs about what American literature does for us and what values it's supposed to uphold. McGurl spends a great deal of his book dissecting the difficult reconciliation between the writer as an individual who belongs to a bureaucratic academic institution, but he misses another U.S. institution which has been unconsciously mixed up with how we are taught to perceive writing: the criminal justice system. If American (and Americanized) writing has been predicated on "values," it's also been highly interested in the judgment of those values: in adjudicating what is "bad" and what is "good" in a legalistic sense. This sense of literature as a theater of judgment didn't originate with postwar writing—see again the nineteenth-century French government's obsession with whether the public was supposed to judge Madame Bovary as good or bad—but it forms an unconscious part of how we understand storytelling. As part of our training in novels as a source and guide to civic values, we are taught to judge literature as judges.

A lot of contemporary critics treat the judgmental reader as an entirely new phenomenon, the result of a contemporary moralizing puritanism. The novelist and professor Garth Greenwell made this argument in a 2023 *Yale Review* essay, saying that his students' "primary mode of engagement with a text often seems to be a particular kind of moral judgment, as though before they can see anything else in stories or poems they have to sort them into piles of the righteous and the problematic."[49] I don't doubt that Greenwell's personal experience here is accurate—other professors have made similar observations about the rigidity and fragility of their students these days.[50] And although it's anecdotal and not reliable evidence, we've all seen some people on the internet—including actual paid critics and writers—sentencing art to death for its problematic qualities. The court is in session, and everyone is a prosecutor.

But the impulse, I think, is older than we realize: it's only an inverted version of the old set of CIA-descended American literary values. Greenwell frames his approach to art as being opposed to the legalizing fashion so common in readers and joyless social media posters. The job of the novelist, he says, "is actively to resist coming to such judgment. Plausibly adequate verdicts may be a necessary feature of the real world, but they are never necessary in matters of art." But for his example of a piece of great art that supposedly resists this kind of judgment, Greenwell makes an interesting choice: Philip Roth's novel *Sabbath's Theater*. Roth has long been stereotyped as one of the "lit bro" white male midcentury novelists; this is largely undeserved, especially as Roth wasn't perceived in his own context as an unmarked white man, facing both antisemitism from the literary world and censure from the Jewish community for his portrayals of neurotic and often grotesque Jewish characters. But the "lit bro" shoe does slightly fit: Roth wrote white male antiheroes who were often based on himself, with intense sexual obsessions and a usually misogynist view of women. Whether this misogyny is better addressed in some novels than others is subject to debate.

What's not debatable, however, is that even being able to critically describe Roth's writing as misogynist is a new development. I remember the ancient days of the 1990s and 2000s, when offering even the gentlest critique of a famous white male writer was usually met with an accusation of failing to understand his genius. We may live in a state of prosecutorial overcorrection, but I think it's a dialectical response to the fact that the default position for a certain kind of white male writer and their self-absorbed antiheroes has usually been ferocious, uncritical defense. We have always been in the courtroom, just on the other side of the aisle; the writer—and the literary critic—have normally worked as defense attorneys. The statement "I think this writing is misogynist" was perceived even before the days of social media as a criminal accusation, a presumption that you were putting the writer and his characters on trial, as well as any of his loving readers as codefendants. It's a very American sequence of ideas, really: to jump straight from a simple statement of critical opinion to the presumption of trials and witch burnings. If a book does *not* have good values, then it must have bad ones; and if it's bad, then it—and anybody who likes it—needs to go to jail.

Greenwell says that Roth's novels, at their best, transcend the simplistic criminal judgment so common to American life: the complicated and messy antihero of *Sabbath's Theater* in particular shows us "that the human is ample and impure beyond all codes of conduct, and in its challenge not to reject or unmake that humanity, but instead to acknowledge it ours." It's a lovely sentiment . . . but it still smacks of the defense attorney.[51] We're in the courthouse, only we're supposed to vote to acquit on the grounds of peace, love, and understanding and that we're all sinners in our way. "Don't judge" is still a lesson about judgment, even if that lesson is nice. If the major reason that characters exist in a fictional story is to make a moral point, or serve as an exemplar, you'll always be defending or prosecuting them; if they only exist to serve as moral teachers, then you always need to justify your relationship with them. Their primary importance then becomes how they exist in relation to *you*, the reader: once again it's *I am*, not *they are*. And that forecloses on more interesting modes of exploration for Roth and Morrison and everyone else, such as the relationships between men and women, the interplay between haunting and grief, and what it means when someone has abrogated their humanity through cruelty or simply failed to see the humanity in others.

And if human complexity only ever equals moral ambiguity, if the purpose of literature is to exonerate everyone on the grounds of their humanity, then you could never really represent human wickedness as wicked—that would only ever be prosecutorial and punishing. Learning to accept each other as messy human beings works fine when the messiness in question fits into the categories of behavior that have been (maybe unfairly) marked out as "apolitical"—such as our ordinary interpersonal ability to not get along, and our failures to understand each other as individuals. It's trickier, though, when our problems don't boil down to peace, love, and understanding but to something far more systemic and implacable, like the material advantages of being at the top of a racist or misogynist hierarchy. Sometimes what's wrong with reality is deeper than individual moral failings; sometimes our problems are greater than an inability to see each other's point of view. And boiling everything down to a failure of individual understanding can work as a neat and deliberate deflection away from those problems. There's a reason that the famous line from *Cool Hand Luke* ("What we've got here is failure to communicate") is spoken by a prison guard who may also be the devil.

The Invisible Hand Loves All His Children Equally

Even if there's a remaining critical preference for certain kinds of storytelling—a particular kind of individual complexity that disallows social complexity—you could argue that none of that really prevents other kinds of stories from being written. If anything, critics these days tend to complain that contemporary writing is *too* political, too flatly good or bad, with characters standing in for the author and anxious to display good behavior for the waiting jury.[52] Regardless, these books sell, or well enough anyway: what both "messy" and didactic art have in common under capitalism is that they can be marketed into something that can turn a profit, and the mere fact of profit remains proof of value and merit. As such, there are no excuses for failure; anyone who can't get their book published or edited through official channels can only be a throwback Romantic, a talentless wannabe bohemian: discontented, adolescent, insufficiently creative. Bennett touches on this in his *Chronicle* article, where he wonders whether his dislike of IWW and his frustrated desire for big "systems" novels (about ideas and structures rather than just individuals) is simply proof that he's a frustrated novelist. This kind of conclusion is easy, the Occam's razor that our system holds to everybody's throat: This is a free society where anything goes and all dreams are achievable, so if you're struggling, could it be that you just don't deserve it?

Let's assume for a moment that every kind of writing is indeed allowed: outside of lingering expectations about personal voices and character complexity and novels as theaters of judgment, literary fiction is open and free, and no type of novel is forbidden or discouraged from mainstream publication—provided that the writing is of sufficient quality, of course. If this is the case, then one of two things must be true. Either the free market really does choose only the worthy, pumping out all the good writing that could ever exist, excluding the undeserving alone. Or, alternatively, while market pressures may affect more popular forms of culture—genre fiction, television, and movies—places like MFA programs and literary publishing imprints remain immune from capitalism, safe from its pressures, above its temptations, developing art maybe not quite for art's sake but at least above the pressure to bend to ideology or an excessive amount of profit. Either the free market naturally selects the best individual writers, or the cognoscenti, above such market pressures, choose the best novels with apolitical aesthetic detachment. Publishing—a lopsided, poorly paid, and highly dysfunctional industry, which is still tough to break into without family money and connections, just so happens to pick the winners, every time.

This alternating faith and total atheism about the free market is, notably, the exact cognitive dissonance that was intended by Cold War-era institutions: the doctrine of "neutral" and "apolitical" market forces metabolized into a totalizing sense of reality. If the United States' Cold War propaganda efforts have receded so far into the past as to be meaningless to us today, then it remains remarkable that we still believe basically everything they said.

It's worth asking, against the recent flood of supposedly "political" and didactically judgmental novels, if there's anything really left out, any sort of story that's genuinely forbidden. Capitalism can successfully digest just about anything, even dissent: it may be less that certain kinds of writing are "forbidden" and more that they are rare. I think we can find traces of what's still missing by looking at what does get published, and by examining the places where even the best writers' imaginations tend to stop. You can catch a glimpse of it at the end of Thomas Pynchon's *The Crying of Lot 49*, which leaves the heroine Oedipa Maas unsure if there's a vast secret society of dispossessed people spread throughout the world, or if her rich dead ex-boyfriend has only been pranking her into believing they exist. If the dispossessed of the earth are everywhere, then what would happen if Oedipa, the executor of her ex's will, gave away his money to them? She immediately realizes this wouldn't work: the probate judge would "be on her ass in a microsecond, revoke her letters testamentary. They'd call her names, proclaim her through all Orange County as a redistributionist and pinko."[53] She gives up on the idea. The mystery of the dispossessed people remains unsolved: the United States will continue being weird and inexplicable, riddled with half-understood conspiracies, and those funds will never be distributed. If Oedipa Maas had given the money away, then both she and *The Crying of Lot 49* would have resolved from ambiguity into pinkos: the book would have been a "political" novel, rather than one that simply hints at politics.

The Crying of Lot 49 was published back in the mid-1960s; characters in the 2010s and 2020s are somewhat less afraid to come across as pinko redistributionists. Novels, whether they're anxious to be politically "good" or not, are now able to depict communists in positive ways or openly criticize capitalism without being automatically dismissed or blacklisted; by being profitable under capitalism, they prove capitalism's eternal power. Sally Rooney, the bestselling Irish novelist, has become wealthy and famous for her dilettante Marxist characters. In her third novel—*Beautiful World, Where Are You*—her heroines send each other long emails about their unhappiness with capitalism, their feelings about the fall of the Soviet Union, and their frustration with the literary world and its pretense of political action. They don't engage in any sort of political action themselves, and at the end, they're heterosexually paired off with men in classic romance novel fashion. With every new Sally Rooney novel, critics go crazy over the question of whether her novels count as "political" or "Marxist" because her characters are Marxists who discuss politics.[54] Personally, I think she's just writing about horny unhappy young leftists, not trying to write any kind of structurally Marxist novel. But that raises the question of what this forbidden Marxist novel would look like: Would it just be simplistic social realism with flat characters? What would have to happen in a Sally Rooney novel that isn't happening? What kinds of situations would she have to depict that she isn't?

The answer is a bit clearer, I think, if we look at a different novelist: Frances Cha, and her book *If I Had Your Face*, which came out in 2020. Cha has dual citizenship in the United States and South Korea; she explains her novel as "a Korean book that happens to have been written in English and published by an American publishing house."[55] South Korean art is often more willing than American art to display openly anti-capitalist attitudes, sometimes to international success: the movie *Parasite* (2019) and the TV show *Squid Game* (2021) are probably the best-known examples. Cha's *If I Had Your Face* is likewise critical of capitalism, following the lives of four young women as they endure working life and misogynist exploitation in contemporary South Korea. But what the novel is missing—and to be clear, I really loved it—is any possibility of political change. The characters complain about the impact of capitalism on their lives, and by the end they've grown as individuals and formed bonds of solidarity with one another, but their world itself can't ever be anything other than what it is right now. South Korea had massive street protests in the late 2010s, but if Cha had chosen to depict them in detail, or a fictional version of them, it could only have been as they'd already happened. She couldn't depict a more extreme version of these protests, even if they're plausible and end up happening in the very near future; she certainly couldn't depict a revolution.

"Revolutions," says literary critic David Shumway, "are, except in Marxist theory, by definition implausible." Cha or Rooney can write Marxist or anti-capitalist characters all day, but they can't depict Marxist protests or revolutions in their plotting in any unironic detail. If they did, their books would suddenly switch genres. "To describe a world different from the present one," Shumway continues, "would make a novel utopian and, hence, not realist."[56]

This is one of the real forbidden territories, as well as one of the lingering differences between literary and genre fiction: only in genre fiction could we see anything like a revolution if it hasn't already happened in the historic past. Only outside the "given reality" are characters allowed to alter the fabric of daily life rather than just learn to cope with it. This isn't to say that genre fiction always depicts real change, or does so in interesting ways, but that it technically *can* go there in a way that literary fiction mostly can't. Literary fiction has lately escaped its former realist boundaries, and yet if we look at contemporary literary/genre crossovers, we can often see how the ideas implicit in postwar serious fiction still limit possibility. Some literary/genre crossovers are no more than beautifully written science fiction, classed as "literary" for the sake of prose style rather than plotting, but others, especially those written by established literary novelists, tend to combine the imagery and settings of science fiction or fantasy with the inertia of realism. Kazuo Ishiguro, probably the best known of these novelists, writes gorgeously and elegiacally from the near-future point of view of clones and robots: they live quiet lives and die quietly too, against the backdrop of crumbling dystopian realities that can't be changed or altered. These aren't bad novels; in many ways, they're very good ones. But they embody a kind of political helplessness, a sigh before the lights go out. In the serious literary novel, it generally remains easier to imagine the end of the world than the end of capitalism.

That being said, if someone did publish a serious literary novel about an anti-capitalist revolution, it would just be a novel: it wouldn't affect capitalism one way or another. Its characters could be flat or round; it could beckon judgment or forbid it. But either way, it would probably just be co-opted like everything else. *Squid Game*, a proudly anti-capitalist allegory, was internationally popular and critically acclaimed. Netflix claimed that the show was its most popular offering in 2022, with 1.7 billion hours streamed worldwide, beating out the Cold War nostalgia epic *Stranger Things*.[57] Today, you can buy *Squid Game* costumes for about fifty bucks a pop, with the freedom to choose either participants or guards.[58] Netflix also made a popular reality show based on *Squid Game*, with the life-or-death challenges replaced by fun competitions; the filming was a disaster, with players collapsing due to "inhumane" conditions.[59] The brutality of capitalism, however it may be subtly hidden or openly criticized in art, continues to be an unavoidable reality.

"Late capitalism" feels like an optimistic term these days; "the total victory of money" might be more accurate. While it remains theoretically possible that some popular book or show or movie could spark some kind of revolution or assist one, it's far more likely that anything good—or even technically bad but politically useful like *Uncle Tom's Cabin*—will only be co-opted by the fast-moving capitalist machine.

The long legacy of American cultural influence is still probably less about the foreclosing of a literal revolutionary possibility and more about the imaginative limits placed on both writers and readers. Would more anti-capitalist stories really help, if the only way they can be popularized is to be sold by the same system they're critiquing? The absolute dominance of the market isn't solely an ideological problem: it's also a practical, material impediment to storytelling, including the kind of stories that might be dangerous in a good way, or at least aesthetically interesting and worth having around. All we have is what the market gives us; all the art we enjoy was determined at some level to be profitable, or profitable enough. There's a complicated relationship between popular art and "high" art, between what the majority of consumers enjoy and what is supposed to be fastidiously appreciated by a small intelligentsia without money acting as any sort of middleman. But the money is all around us, whether in the low theater of pop culture movies or the high art of serious literary novels. We are swimming in it. It's the airless air we breathe.

CHAPTER FIVE

The Gentleman's Club Effect

A few years ago, I had a conversation with a publishing industry professional that I still think about all the time. We were discussing some of my favorite subjects: literary and genre fiction, and the remaining divisions between them. It's true that both literary and genre novelists can now write books about time travel, robots, magic, and ghosts, but they still attend different writing programs, go to different conferences, and compete for different prizes. The difference lies partly in writing style, partly in political-historical possibilities (i.e., what can happen in the plot and what can't), and partly in marketing: a literary novel is supposed to be artful, intelligent, and intended for a smaller, more highbrow crowd, while genre fiction is supposed to be an easier read, more reliant on established conventions, and more popular with "ordinary" people. But there's plenty of crossover, and in this conversation I brought up Ursula K. Le Guin and N. K. Jemisin, smart writers with a literary sensibility who are also solidly in the genre fiction camp. The man I was talking to conceded that Le Guin and Jemisin are indeed real novelists, and added Octavia

Butler to the mix. But then he looked at me squarely, and said that writing like theirs is dying out, because "the population of intelligent American readers is vanishingly small."

This was a real "wit of the staircase" moment for me: I was too stunned to remind him of the obvious fact that, in the case of these three particular writers, he was just empirically wrong. Le Guin and Butler remain widely read and beloved years after their deaths—an unusual fate for any writer, let alone women writers of science fiction, or (in Butler's case) women writers of color, who have historically been erased from the record.[1] Jemisin is in the middle of her career, after the triple Hugo Award–winning heights of the *Broken Earth* series, and she still publishes a regular cadence of novels that have been both popular and critically well regarded. "Who's reading all these books then? Morons?????"—is what I should have said to this guy. Let's pretend I said it.

But really, I shouldn't have been as surprised as I was. This guy's argument was a conventional one, based (whether he knew it or not) on a dusty set of beliefs about the relationships between taste and readership, aesthetics and commodities, and "high" art and "low" art as well as class, race, and gender. Government-based and other politically motivated types of censorship aren't the only means by which theoretically dangerous forms of media are embattled, partitioned, or controlled; another is the common classist presumption that the public at large can only enjoy easy, stupid art that has a narcotizing effect. If there's a smart book by a smart writer, then per the terms of this argument, it *must* be unpopular with the masses, since intelligent readers are always a vanishingly small part of the population, awake and alone among a sleepy sea of idiots. Whole genres and mediums have been singled out for special blame: the low forms of popular storytelling at any given time (take your historical pick: penny dreadfuls, movies, comic books, paperback pulp fiction, TV, video games) have frequently been railed against as the reason we can't have quality art, not to mention the reason we have social problems: usually crime, illicit sex, social unrest. (A currently popular leftist strain of thought holds that popular culture's *lack* of crime, illicit sex, and social unrest is the reason we don't have revolution or sufficient class consciousness. Probably popular culture is less to blame for our current lack of revolution than classist presumptions about the stupidity of the masses, a group from whom these kinds of thinkers always consider themselves separate and exempt.)

Whatever the hated popular medium or genre of the day may be—the one that will destroy good art and the cultural-political fabric by making the democratic public too stupid to exist—it usually becomes culturally acceptable eventually, while sometimes the "high" forms lose their cultural capital or fade into irrelevance. Thanks to the late capitalist corporatization of everything, however, we have very little designated "high" art—most everything is now "pop" culture in one way or another, massed and commodified. There are two general responses to this, one despairing and one celebratory. From the despairing point of view (sometimes called "rockism" or "anti-poptimism"), the nerds won and now everything is *stupid*. From the point of view of the celebratory poptimists, the nerds won and everything is *great*, every kind of art is equally valid as long as it's popular, and in fact its validity can be charted exactly along the ever-increasing line of popularity and profitability, here in the best of all possible worlds.

Personally, I'm not fully on Team Poptimism or Team Anti-poptimism. The anti-poptimists make some excellent points (which I'll discuss later), but by taste and inclination, and a mortal dislike of class snobbery, I lean somewhat more toward poptimism. I think most people sincerely like what they like, whether it's "smart" or "stupid," whether it's good for them or bad for them or anything else. (Also, much great art does end up being *popular* in the sense that it sticks around across the generations, as new readers find new points of entry and appreciation.) Taste in fictional stories is personal, idiosyncratic, and never objective—except that other people objectively have bad taste, while mine is flawless. I'm joking, of course, but just about everybody believes that their own taste is good, or at least honest, while other people are either stupid or pretentious. No matter what, it's always *other people* who have misjudged a piece of art, other people who have bad taste, and this is, in turn, often regarded as a civilization-destroying concern rather than a simple difference of informed opinion.

Taste is never just taste: it's a very serious business. It may seem far removed from the use of fiction as a political, reality-shaping force, but it's as political as anything else and often regarded as just as dangerous. And I think there's a genuine element of risk here, which is that while arguments about taste can be fun, they're ultimately distractions from more important questions of how art is made, and who gets to make it, and what art by which people is automatically considered serious and good for you, while the rest is dismissed as frivolous and possibly dangerous.

Unfortunately, opinion-shaping discussions about public taste usually come wrapped up in classist packaging as well as ancient presumptions about what fiction is supposed to "do" for us in the first place. The writer Caleb Crain took to the pages of *The New Yorker* in 2007 and again in 2018 to fret about the decline of reading in the United States; all forms of reading (smart and stupid, fiction and nonfiction alike) have declined in popularity over the last two decades.[2] TV has eroded most of reading's market share, but movies and video games are also to blame. Crain concedes that watching a prestige TV show like *The Sopranos* might be almost as good as reading a literary novel about gangsters: "Both viewer and reader are entertaining themselves while learning something about the Mafia in the bargain."[3] As we've seen with much older arguments on the subject, taking pleasure in literature is permissible if it's presented in tandem with education; an individual work, genre, or medium becomes acceptably "serious" and healthy when it can be passed off as something that's good for you. In fact, as the cultural critic Phil Christman has pointed out, the perfectly accessible *Sopranos* is now "brandished" in the cultural sphere "as if were a difficult text."[4] Now that *The Sopranos* has been elevated to serious business, it's smart and off-limits, even though it's a work of almost universally popular art and even though gangster stories and crime stories were once maligned genres themselves.

This isn't just a quirk of fate for one TV show: this is the loose historical pattern by which new genres or mediums move from frivolity to seriousness, danger to safety, bad for you to good for you. A new form, especially a popular one, is often first regarded as empty entertainment for the lazy, frivolous, childish, multicultural, and often feminized masses (or, as we see with gangster films and video games, the violent male masses). Then there are one or two critically acclaimed hits, nearly always (like *The Sopranos*) by and about white men. After that there's a process of bifurcation: new mediums and genres are split into the serious, generally masculine, largely white, and culturally prestigious against everything else. This is part of how we get prestige TV and regular TV; auteur films and commercial movies; graphic novels and normal comic books; literary novels and commercial genre fiction, etc. We tend to think that these categories are simple—good versus bad art, real artists versus hacks—but anything and anyone formerly consigned to the "bad" category can be raised to the "good category" at any moment if they receive the right kind of critical approval.

I call this the "gentleman's club effect." Whatever art is let into the gentleman's club is good for you, an appropriate and educational use of your leisure time; whatever's not allowed will be called lazy garbage for lazy people, right up until the moment it isn't. The rules change all the time: they've changed for TV, comic books, and video games in my lifetime. Certain well-written genre novels are fine now too; in fact, they're so fine that a book editor might decide, against the actual sales numbers and readers' expressed taste, that they're too intelligent and difficult for the masses to handle. The first rule of the gentleman's club is that you can't let too many people into the gentleman's club.

Not Guilty

I've so far elided the question of whether reading or watching "bad" stories could actually be bad for us, whether they can tranquilize us into stupidity. The gentleman's club effect might tend to skew perceptions of "high" art in racist, misogynist, and classist directions, but that doesn't mean that "low" art is magically good for us. As I've said before, I don't think the "good for us" / "bad for us" binary is particularly helpful when thinking about fiction. It's certainly not empirically provable: any attempted studies on the subject will be necessarily skewed by class and other identity barriers, let alone the difficulty of defining "good" versus "bad" fiction or "healthy" versus "unhealthy." Often when defining bad stories, we use the term "guilty pleasure"—something we know is poorly made or at least flawed, but which we love anyway and genuinely enjoy. I love *Star Trek: Deep Space Nine*, *Buffy the Vampire Slayer*, and *The X-Files*: I will be the first to admit these shows have some garbage episodes, just absolute failures on a conceptual and aesthetic level. They're guilty pleasures—or they were in the 1990s, before they were culturally ennobled as the sacred ancestors of prestige TV.[5] (In 2023, a Gen Z coworker told me that she studied *Buffy the Vampire Slayer* in film school; I was delighted to hear it, once I'd picked my ancient body off the floor.)

Most of the time, if you just wait long enough, what was once considered a popular and addictive but embarrassing bit of pop culture will be universally reimagined as a great work of art, maybe even worthy of academic study. "'Taste,'" as C. S. Lewis once wrote, "is mainly a chronological phenomenon."[6] What you like, and what critics take seriously, changes with the seasons. The culture writer who worries you're watching too much TV and not reading enough books will give way to the one who worries you're watching too many guilty-pleasure reality shows and not enough serious prestige dramas. The "guilty" part of a guilty pleasure, as Phil Christman has wisely noted, really comes from an imagined critic, a "snobby, dominant enemy" who lives in our heads and thinks we shouldn't like what we like: "We are Americans; our national myth is *Footloose*," Christman says. "None of us can enjoy our pleasures till we think someone wants us not to have them."[7] Guilt is yet another manifestation of "other people" anxiety: we fear that other people might find our tastes wanting or elitist, and they might judge us accordingly.

Besides "guilty pleasures," there's another kind of bad art—the kind that isn't even pleasurable and which you won't even psychically defend to yourself, let alone to an imaginary jury of your peers. Sometimes you're just in a dark mood for something awful. In moods like this I tend to watch mindless police procedurals, or bad sitcoms, or extra-bullshit reality shows with unlikely premises and manufactured drama. After a while, TV like this is just enervating—I feel dead, like I do after too much social media scrolling.[8] But even then, a show that I find legitimately stupid and soul-destroying (like *The Bachelor* and *The Bachelorette*—sorry, America) might be for someone else a guilty pleasure, something they really enjoy whether they feel comfortable admitting it or not. They might even take it quite seriously and derive real intellectual meaning from it. Are these people stupid? Are they self-justifying? Has bad art degraded their brain, their soul, their critical thinking, and their political capacity?

Often enough in these situations, *I'm* the idiot who likes the art that someone else believes to be incredibly stupid, or I'm left cold by a famous genius. I have an abiding love for Sarah J. Maas's frequently banned *Court* novels despite her dreadful prose; I'm indifferent to David Foster Wallace despite his good prose, or at least what many critics believe to be his good prose. At the same time, I generally dislike YA and prefer classic novels (unlike most critics, I've tried both, extensively).[9] Taste is surprising: it makes us less legible to one another, not more so. Taste leads to fun arguments with friends in bars and to horrible fights with strangers online who believe that your taste defines who you are and have already slotted you like an advertiser into a demographic Type of Guy. "If you like *this* book or movie, you must be *that* sort of person" is how a marketing algorithm thinks, and it's a very cheap and sad way to interpret our fellow human beings. It's definitely become a popular and ubiquitous way for us to judge each other on social media, itself an algorithmic form, where good taste is so easily slotted into "right taste": healthy and morally justified and appropriate taste, which makes it even easier for advertisers to target us.

But then again, taste is never just a simple matter of taste. It may or may not be intellectually damaging to like one show over another, one genre over another, one medium over another—but taste, in a capitalist society, can be considered a form of power. What art gets funded, or doesn't get funded, is often linked to consumer purchasing power (or at least conveniently blamed on consumer purchasing power). It's always presumed to be a zero-sum game, played by the buying public: if too many people watch superhero movies and not enough auteur films, then there will too much financing for superhero movies and not enough for auteur films; if too many people read trashy genre fiction rather than serious literature, then supposedly there won't be enough intelligent American readers to make the next

N. K. Jemisin or Octavia Butler or Ursula K. Le Guin financially viable. Like everything to do with the dangers of taste, this is partly true, and partly classist and overstated. The downward pressure on different forms of fiction to be less intelligent and contain less variety—a real problem, which is really occurring—is a result of capitalist realism, powered by the corporate conglomerates that now control or exert undue influence over how fiction is made. Both snobs and corporate ownership are united in the belief that *other people* are stupid, and can't handle nice things.

Against this kind of total corporate dominance, consumer buying patterns have little effect. Amazon effectively controls the distribution of both literature and consumer goods; you can personally shop elsewhere, but without a concerted boycott, your lack of dimes won't make a difference to Jeff Bezos's pocket. Large-scale public tastes may shift away from superhero movies (there's evidence that they're already doing so), but Marvel and DC will keep churning out these films as long as there's reasonable profit to be made, and as long as other types of movies can't promise better quarterly returns.[10]

The complicated interconnection of all these factors—taste, snobbery, money, anxiety, access, corporate power, prestige—may or may not lead to a populace that has been made dangerously stupid from exposure to stupid art, but I think it does lead to a kind of social coarsening, where we are unnecessarily cruel to each other and arrive at dismissive judgments about the inner worth of other people over silly stuff like taste in movies. Probably there's a larger public appetite for "good" art than is generally imagined, but the double punch of lack of material access and perceived snobbery successfully gatekeeps and destroys most people's interest in trying it. And the downward pressure on wages makes it harder for good stories to be written—or for artists to survive while making them—in the first place. Cultural production is definitionally "bad for you" (narrow, imaginatively limiting) if only a tiny number of privileged people can afford to do it in the first place.

As we saw in the previous chapter, the image of the poor bohemian writer was only recently swept away by the respectable bourgeois institutionally captured writer; these days, the writer is apparently so bourgeois and respectable that she doesn't need to earn a living. "Never before," Parul Sehgal wrote for *The New Yorker* in 2021, "have so many people made so little from their writing."[11] She was referring specifically to novelists, especially the genre writers who self-publish on Amazon, but she might as well have included TV writers, comics writers, and a host of others. The golden age of prestige television recently came to a crashing halt in the 2023 Writers Guild of America (WGA) strike: aspiring screenwriters from a remarkable variety of backgrounds who had moved to L.A. to participate in the TV boomtown found that they weren't able to make ends meet between gigs. "Must be a coincidence," screenwriter and novelist Kashana Cauley tweeted acidly on the day the strike started, "that every time a few women or people of color enter an industry it suddenly becomes deeply unfashionable to pay people."[12]

It's not a coincidence at all of course, and there's a complex history behind why this is happening right now, why all forms of writing are being devalued—even threatened with outsourcing to the large language models misleadingly labeled as "AI"—just as the gentleman's club of serious art is theoretically more available to every kind of human being than ever before.[13] It's no accident that we seem to have reached a point at which, simultaneously, all forms and genres of fiction have become socially acceptable to enjoy, but it's harder than ever to make a living creating them. To understand this history, however, we have to really look at the poptimist/anti-poptimist debate, which began outside fiction in a different, closely connected art form: music.

Pop Rocks

The battles between "high" art and "low" art, and the associated problems of money and access, have been going on for centuries, but the contemporary terms of the debate owe themselves largely to music critic Kelafa Sanneh. His 2004 *New York Times* essay "The Rap Against Rockism" is often credited with originating the terms "rockism" and "poptimism" (though he doesn't actually use "poptimism" at any point, and the usage of both words in music circles precedes his article by decades).[14] His essay, however, is basically the O.G. and most thoughtful version of poptimism: that is, the idea that popular, "low," commercialized art forms might have artistic value even if most critics, operating from a narrow vision of what "great" art looks like, tend to sneer at them.[15] Poptimism has been such a successful movement in music that critical essays treating Beyoncé or Taylor Swift as serious artists are perfectly normal these days; if anything, there are far fewer rockist or "anti-poptimist" essays decrying the ubiquity and dominance of pop music.[16] It's easy to forget, just as with the relatively recent acceptance of genre fiction, how *new* this all is: the shift has taken place in a twenty-year blink.

But back in 2004, it was necessary for Sanneh to defend pop music against "the rockists": a type of guy that he says first appeared in the music scene in the 1980s. A "rockist" is a guy who loves rock music, but mostly loves it against imagined threats. He constantly bemoans the fact that music used to be better than it is now, more independent, more original, more invested in individualistic genius; the rockist sneers at pop and disco, which he interprets as contamination, trashy virality, poisoning his perfect music scene. It would be easy, especially now, to imagine that Sanneh was overstating the case—as we've already seen, any discussion of high and low art, snobbishness and anxiety, requires a type of guy to get mad at, a person who is imagined to be oppressing you: in this case, the snob who doesn't want you to enjoy your pleasures. Every poptimist needs an anti-poptimist to rail against. But what makes it even more complicated is that sometimes the snob absolutely does (or did) exist, and holds real power. Rockists weren't just annoying guys you ran into at shows (I have run into annoying rockists at shows), but as Sanneh explains, they were ubiquitous among music critics at the time. They had the power to shape cultural appraisal and access: they determined what kind of music was taken seriously and what was denigrated as stupid songs for stupid listeners.

This is where Sanneh's "poptimist" argument rises above normal irritation with annoying fanboys into something quite serious. "Rockism isn't unrelated to older, more familiar prejudices," Sanneh writes, "that's part of why it's so powerful, and so worth arguing about. The pop star, the disco diva, the lip-syncher, the 'awesomely bad' hit maker: could it really be a coincidence that rockist complaints often pit straight white men against the rest of the world? Like the anti-disco backlash of twenty-five years ago, the current rockist consensus seems to reflect not just an idea of how music should be made but also an idea about who should be making it."[17] The guardianship of "good" taste, performed in the name of protecting the public from itself, has often been a matter of dictating which creators get a place in the gentleman's club. Critiques of genres are never as simple as saying "this kind of art is high and noble and sincere, this kind is low and commercial and manufactured," because not every artist will be graced with the automatic perception of their work as high and noble and sincere, even if it is.[18] Criticism isn't a magically neutral art; criticism shapes public perception of what kind of art is good and deserves to last, and critics are human beings with ingrained biases just like everyone else.

Music is hardly the only artistic field to have been historically dominated by white and/or male tastemakers; as late as 2011, fully

84 percent of the reviewers in *The New York Review of Books* were men, covering a nearly identical percentage of books by men.[19] Those numbers have improved somewhat in recent years, according to the nonprofit feminist literary organization VIDA, but still fall short of gender equality (VIDA has not consistently tracked race among critics).[20] Male film reviewers also outnumber female ones—a 2022 study puts the ratio at two to one.[21] But fewer and fewer of these critics are rockists; most embrace popular culture. You may still run into rockists in the wild, or "lit bros," or arthouse film snobs. They will tell you that since poptimism is now more or less dominant in criticism, they are the ones who are oppressed. The anti-poptimists have their own half-real, half-imagined bêtes noires: the insane and too-online member of the Beyhive or a Swiftie, the insane and too-online YA novel reader who refuses to attempt "hard" texts, the childish Harry Potter fangirl or Disney adult. That these half-real, half-exaggerated images of real people are gendered and raced in very specific ways—often still imaginatively pitting straight white men against the world—is once again not coincidental: it still reflects ideas about who does and should make art, and lingering anger over who has the right to decide what's good and what isn't.

The status anxiety—or fear of loss of prestige—that leads snobs to gatekeep their territory is often mirrored, on the other side, by anti-snobs with their own inverted form of status anxiety. Jonathan Franzen once shared a letter from an anti-fan, a woman who had read *The Corrections* and imagined, in a sort of furious fanfic, that Franzen's ideal readers must be "the elite of New York, the elite who are beautiful, thin, anorexic, neurotic, sophisticated, don't smoke, have abortions tri-yearly, are antiseptic, live in lofts or penthouses, this superior species of humanity who read *Harper's* and *The New Yorker*."[22] Here the enemy is high-class but also a woman: a woman who thinks she's better than you, which is intolerable. For a sufficiently insecure person, a weird and difficult novel (or song, or TV show, or movie) isn't just a piece of art they couldn't personally get into but a direct insult to their sense of self and belonging. Somewhere, other people *know* that this insecure person tried and failed, and they are laughing.[23]

Franzen brings up the letter from his anti-fan in the context of a 2002 *New Yorker* essay in which he describes two different ways of looking at literature: the "Contract" model and the "Status" model, terms by which he intends to reconcile appreciation of "low" and "high" art as fundamentally different but still possessing their own forms of validity. In the "Contract" model (low fiction, genre fiction, etc.) the reader presumes they're entering into a contract with the writer to have a good time and have their expectations met. The "Status" model, on the other hand, is about reading something formally risky and difficult: rising to the challenge of a critically acclaimed work that is supposedly too rarefied for mere "enjoyment." The immediate problem with this division is that the "Status" model also relies on an implicit contract between writer and reader: when you open a difficult literary novel, you expect it to match the critical hype. But it's entirely possible that, if you make a serious and good-faith attempt to address this kind of book on its merits, the cloud of Status around it will dissolve, for you, into so much hot air. "Status" is not objectively bestowed by critics, who, again, are not a neutral, objective, or equal body; there is no objectivity in taste, simply more or less intelligent expression of why you like or dislike something, an idea which may seem threatening or even dangerous if you're the sort of person who has based your identity on a sense of cultural superiority or on sensitivity to imaginary elitists who are sitting in judgment. The only truly "bad taste" may be the failure to develop taste of your own.

Franzen puts his own work and preferences closer to the "Contract" model, though in so doing he reveals what this particular discussion of snobbery/anti-snobbery is really about, and why aesthetic taste is such a high-stakes matter in the United States in particular. "Like many other Contract-minded Americans," he says, "I understand that the Contract sometimes calls for work. I know the pleasures of a book aren't always easy. I expect to work; I want to work. It's also in my Protestant nature, however, to expect some reward for this work."[24] Once again, the cultural demand for literature to justify itself by providing some kind of moral or intellectual reward isn't a universal law but just a matter of unexamined history and narrow regionalism: the United States is culturally Protestant, so art in this country remains a guilty indulgence, one which is difficult to justify without pain. (This is also why the *Footloose* censors must be imagined over every shoulder, even if they're not actually there.) It's fine, in Franzen's view, for books to be entertaining—in fact he says he prefers them that way—but they're best when they're also hard work, when they're serious, when they have a clear cost in energy and labor and a feeling of a reward at the end. From this point of view, any book that's *not* hard work, which is just an indulgence, is a dangerously lazy treat.

This is a very unappealing way to look at literature: it makes "good" books feel like buzzkills. Sanneh, writing at nearly the same historical moment as Franzen, noticed the same overseriousness in the "rockist" attitude to music: rockism's most "pernicious" quality is that it views rock musicians as somehow "hardworking" (compared to hip-hop musicians who are "violent" and "too flashy"). This is racially motivated of course, but Sanneh points out that it also manages "to make rock 'n' roll seem boring."[25] If listening to rock music—or reading literature, or watching an arthouse film—is treated as a form of hard work, as labor that frees you from the sin of pleasure, then these works have essentially been tamed into bourgeois irrelevance. If art isn't at least a *little* dangerous, a little bad for you—a little rock 'n' roll—then it isn't any fun. It loses any edge it may have had, any stakes, any potential to transgress. It's no wonder that many people, non-Protestants and Protestants alike, now associate anything that smacks of "difficulty" and hard work with pretension, with snobbishness, and with middlebrow class striving. When something has been gated off into the serious and the difficult, it loses its most vital quality: it stops being *cool*. It loses the power to meaningfully change us or anything else.

Snobbery can lead to a kind of death; it can kill high art, deprive it of air and the ability to evolve. Much of high modernist art was sustained by the CIA and the same kinds of private foundations mentioned in the previous chapter: their mission was not just to counter communism on ideological grounds but to educate the masses through exposure to "good" art that would make them "good" citizens (such as abstract expressionism and serial music, which you may remember as the types of art that Umberto Eco claimed would be good for you).[26] Once the money dried up, all that remained were ossified cultural institutions and the memory of art as an oppressive educational tool, both of which have made it harder and harder for people in the United States to access any kind of difficult art or desire to do so.[27] "While there have always been class and educational hierarchies in the art world," critic Jessa Crispin wrote for *The Baffler* in 2022, "never before have we had such strong barriers not only in the creation of but also the enjoyment of the so-called 'high' arts of modernist literature, opera, and visual art. Not only are tickets to the theater increasingly expensive, not only are arts education programs disappearing from public and rural schools, but there is a pervasive idea that art is for the privately educated while the rest of us get Netflix and YA novels."[28] This doesn't necessarily mean that Netflix and YA novels are evils in and of themselves, but if poptimist culture is all you can access—materially and culturally—then you are being denied something you have a right to, that you might have enjoyed, if only someone had allowed you to enjoy it rather than lecturing you on how terribly serious and difficult and unpleasant it all is.

Many people, as my friend Adrian Rennix has noted, would probably enjoy difficult literature if they tried it, including the famously challenging *Ulysses*.[29] James Joyce's masterpiece has long been hidden by a cloud of Status, considered the sort of platonic ideal of the inaccessible literary novel, but it's really *fun* and—as previously mentioned—was banned on and off for decades because of its sex scenes (and what could be more rock 'n' roll than that!). When people feel comfortable trying novels that were formerly locked behind the doors of the gentleman's club, a degree of healthy danger, even political danger, returns to literature: it suggests that "high" literature isn't out of the public's reach, in fact that nothing is out of their reach, and the common heritage of humanity belongs to everybody.

When you can pull back from the idea of literature, or movies, or TV, or music as labor, and see it rather as joy, then there's far less anxiety about pleasure, whether your own or others'. (Some joys are naturally painful, like playing sports; imagining pain and joy in opposition to each other is a telltale sign not only of Protestantism but also of dorks.) "The problem with rockism is that it seems increasingly far removed from the way most people actually listen to music," Sanneh points out. "Are you really pondering the phony distinction between 'great art' and a 'guilty pleasure' when you're humming along to the radio?"[30] Of course not: you're just having a good time, until today's guilty pleasures become tomorrow's critically reimagined "serious" art. The wounds of high art are largely self-inflicted, and on purpose. If you really wanted people to engage with risky and challenging novels, movies, or television, you'd tell them how *great* it all is, how much you loved it, and what it meant to you. Unless, of course, you wanted your likes to stay a special art for special people—if you wanted to keep it all for yourself. In that case, you might lament the death of art, only so you can preside over its corpse.

Two-Hour Ads for Toys

There is, however, another way that art can die, a problem which Sanneh glosses over much too quickly. Whether art is the province of special people or the larger public, it still has to be financed by somebody, and increasingly, that financing has come from large corporate powers. Exploitative labels and music-streaming companies have swallowed up artists, as corporate movie studios have done to filmmakers, and publishing houses (and Amazon) have done to writers. The rise of poptimism over the last two decades is inextricable from the corporate consolidation of art forms and from the new critical perception that popularity, which often boils down to marketing and resources, is all that matters. It's much harder to be an independent artist in any genre, medium, or field. Some kind of corporate backing or distribution channel is more than common or helpful; it's simply required.

Even major stars lack true artistic freedom. Taylor Swift, whose tours have a Mansa Musa–like ability to enrich local economies, has struggled to claw back the rights to her music from an unscrupulous producer.[31] This isn't a new phenomenon: music labels have long exploited their stars, particularly women and people of color, and Swift is hardly the only artist who doesn't own full rights to her music. But poptimism's uncritical celebration of pop stardom too often glosses over the problems inherent to corporate art and corporate ownership. At its best, poptimism lets formerly maligned and dismissed artists and art forms have a fair chance to be meaningful; at its worst, it leads to a worship of popularity for its own sake and a contentment with the corporate status quo even as the vast majority of art workers are brutally exploited, their independent ideas quashed, and their labor funneled only into the most popular and easily sellable forms of art. Poptimism has done the necessary work of dethroning some cultural gatekeepers, but it's also contributed to the flattening of what's possible for everyone who remains. Cheerleading for popular art helps defeat the kind of cultural snobbery that can damage what it's ostensibly trying to protect, but it elides the issue of who really gets to create art and how that affects all of us.

If Sanneh's *New York Times* essay kicked off the cultural poptimism conversation, then the definitive anti-poptimist riposte would be Martin Scorsese's 2019 op-ed about Marvel movies, also published *in The New York Times* (whether poptimist or anti-poptimist, the authoritative and influential opinions on the subject are usually printed in the same small gentleman's club of publications). Scorsese had recently come under fire for an interview in which he said that Marvel movies aren't "cinema" but something "closer to theme parks"; his op-ed is meant to reiterate and expand on what he meant. Marvel movies—and superhero movies more generally— are, in his view, lacking in technical artistry, real characterization, surprise, and risk. They're effectively the "Contract" model in its worst form: you show up and get exactly what you expected to pay for. "The [Marvel Cinematic Universe] pictures are made to satisfy a specific set of demands," Scorsese says, "and they are designed as variations on a finite number of themes." Because of their lack of creativity and stifled ability to experiment, they aren't an "art form," in his opinion, but something qualitatively different. They're not risky, and not interesting; they're corporatized, artless, and safe.[32]

I like pieces of Scorsese's argument, but not the whole of it. For one, I think it's useless to divide creative work into "art" and "not art." These are temporal and subjective definitions—much of what we now consider "art" endured a period of being considered "not art." There's also no quicker way to annoy and harden the people who love the supposedly wrong stuff than to say that the things they love don't count. As a criticism, it goes beyond even saying someone's taste is "bad" to saying that it's totally mistaken and inappropriate. And even if you believe a claim like this to be true— that the people who like Marvel and other superhero movies (i.e., most people on the planet) love something absolutely stupid and wrong for them—you'll never convince them by saying so. The response to "what you love is not art" will always be "fuck you."

In some ways, the critique of Marvel movies as "not cinema" is just a rehash of much older criticism of comic books themselves, which were also considered "not art" or at least not "fine" art or high literature.[33] It's also a rehash of the old "novel versus romance" distinction, valorizing individual originality above serialized reworkings. Superhero films in the MCU (Marvel Cinematic Universe) and DCEU (DC Extended Universe) borrow from the logic of comic book universes: individual films aren't discrete entities any more than an individual issue of a comic book is a discrete work. Instead, the characters interact across movies just as they do across books, hopping into different timelines and special events and reboots, held together by variations on a finite number of themes and the corporate oversight that makes a hugely interconnecting and evolving history like this possible to coordinate and control.[34] Superhero films and TV shows aren't really doing anything that the comics hadn't already done before: they're just doing it in a new medium.

And, like the comics before them, these films are commercialized and tied into the marketing of consumer products. Each movie is, as a Marvel coworker once admitted to me, "a two-hour ad for toys." This "toyetic" quality is simply an acknowledged part of the business model: each film exists to sell consumer products and runs promotional tie-ins with other large corporations, in addition to operating as advertisements for the other films (you gotta collect them all). This is where Scorsese's argument has unequivocal merit: beyond the unwisely antagonistic framing of art/not art lies an indictment of a method of creating movies in which salesmanship comes first and technical competence comes last, if at all. An MCU/DCEU film isn't meant to be a *film*, in the normal sense of the term—even if some people do enjoy it and find aesthetic value in it; rather, it's mainly meant to sell itself, and the tie-in toys, and the next movie.

But even this highly necessary anti-corporate part of Scorsese's argument is still predicated on certain assumptions about the gentleman's club, which are also closely connected to what kind of person gets to make art, and under what circumstances. When Scorsese was coming of age as a young filmmaker in the late 1960s and 1970s, movies were not yet universally agreed upon as "real" art, or at least not as a serious form; in his op-ed he comments that he and his fellow New Hollywood directors previously had to defend "cinema as an equal to literature or music or dance."[35] Again, this almost always happens to popular young art forms: they are always labeled "not art" or a lesser sort at least. It's one of the eternal stages of the gentleman's club effect: the new genre or medium is considered silly garbage at first, until it produces enough serious works by brilliant individuals who are labeled as such by the right critics. This is another key assuption: we generally understand a serious work of art to be something that can only be made by a creative genius, an always-lauded artist who understands and elevates his chosen form out of the muck of popularity. Scorsese doesn't think corporate filmmaking allows for this kind of personal genius: while he acknowledges that some of the corporate action flicks of the last twenty years might be "well made by teams of talented individuals," he says that "they lack something essential to cinema: the unifying vision of an individual artist." Cinema becomes *real*, and an art, when—and only when—it's created by a lonely genius.

Filmmaking, of course, is a collective art, involving dozens or hundreds of people. What Scorsese is really referring to is a specific vision of a film as something made by an auteur: a single artist-director-writer with nearly absolute control over the production. "Auteur theory" has been the subject of ferocious debate in recent years; bringing it up may be the critical equivalent of tossing a bomb in a theater. "Auteur" is sometimes used simply to mean "artist": a director who tries to take a thoughtful, creative, and noncommercial approach to filmmaking. But some women film critics have labeled "auteur theory" a misogynist trick to diminish the contributions of women, who have historically been shunted into the roles of editors and low-level producers, their contributions ignored or viewed as less serious than that of the (nearly always male) director.[36] Leslye Headland, filmmaker and cocreator of the TV show *Russian Doll*, has called auteurism a "myth," saying that "women have always been major collaborators with men, yet we're often stuck with this story of a guy who came up with everything on his own, never ran it by anybody and didn't respect anybody's opinion."[37]

Some women directors and directors of color embrace the title of auteur, but most famous "auteurs" are white men.[38] The term has never been applied evenly, because access to it has never been even. In his essay, Scorsese mentions twelve filmmakers, including himself: nine are white men, two are white women (Claire Denis and Kathryn Bigelow), and one is a Black man (Spike Lee). I don't mean this as a gotcha; Scorsese is simply giving a representative sample of established, respected directors, who have mostly been—and continue to be—white men. As of 2022, the numbers have improved a little, but not significantly: out of every ten directors of theatrical films, only one or two are women or people of color or both.[39] The barriers are structural, both in a social and a material sense: movies are expensive to make. And films, even independent auteur-directed serious works of art, are still expected to bring in box office returns and streaming view counts. Scorsese's own *Killers of the Flower Moon* (2023) was released by Apple TV to help boost the corporation's streaming service, while *The Irishman* (2019) debuted exclusively on Netflix; this is simply what the business is like for everyone.

The problem with superhero films, as critic Sam Adler-Bell suggests in *Dissent*, isn't that they invented "crassly subordinating the creative instinct to the necessities of commerce" but really that they do so "shamelessly, without the obligatory pretense of past eras of Hollywood."[40] The movie business has never been a place where individual creative geniuses just got to make whatever they liked; box office failures could tank careers, especially those of non-white, non-male directors. Elaine May never directed a film again after the failure of *Ishtar* (1987), which had poor returns and was called one of the worst movies ever made.[41] In recent years, however, *Ishtar* has been critically reevaluated: Richard Brody of *The New Yorker* calls it a "thoroughgoing, beginning-to-end masterwork."[42] C. S. Lewis is right once again: taste is mostly a matter of chronology. Yesterday's unacceptable failure is tomorrow's cult classic; a critically regarded film with significant ticket sales can virtually disappear after a decade.

The movie business may always have been a business, and always about money, but it can still be *too much* about money; resources may have been unevenly distributed among artists in the past, but that doesn't mean giant corporations distribute them any better. Quentin Tarantino, when asked if he would ever direct a Marvel movie (celebrated directors and actors are regularly asked about Marvel movies, in hopes of generating public outrage and therefore clicks), dismissed it as working as "a hired hand" for the corporation. "I'm not looking for a job," Tarantino said.[43] Auteurs were never quite "independent" artists in any sense, but they also weren't corporate employees. Whether Marvel movies qualify as "cinema" or not, the work of directing them does amount to being a temporary employee: to helping a multiconglomerate synergize and hit its goals across all divisions. Money always forecloses on what's possible to make, but too much money—and the expectation of extraordinary returns and commercial tie-ins—can foreclose on it further.

Pauline Kael, the great and highly idiosyncratic film critic, appears to have predicted the current state of filmmaking back in 1981, when she panned *Raiders of the Lost Ark*.[44] It's breathtaking to read the review now—*Raiders* being one of those films that's been elevated from a guilty pleasure to a classic—and there are moments where Kael's criticism seems out of date. She doesn't like George Lucas's attempts to hybridize cinema with a "low" pulpy romantic form (in this case, TV adventure serials). She finds the now-beloved characterization shallow, as Scorsese does of Marvel movies; she finds Steven Spielberg's direction merely technically competent—Spielberg's extremely recent critical reevaluation from mere pulp technician to genius auteur is yet another example of the chronology of taste.[45] She even dismisses John Williams's score as "klunky" (a line I dare you to read without singing the iconic *Indiana Jones* theme out loud). But Kael's primary criticism—that the movie is basically a marketing exercise, that it exists to sell toys—is still dead-on. "George Lucas," she concludes, "is in the toy business." Lucas had already made *Star Wars* and had evinced a proprietary control over the many, many toys generated as tie-ins; *Indiana Jones*, Kael correctly sussed out, was just going to be another of Lucas's franchises, turning out toy after toy and sequel after sequel, regardless of their quality. Mel Brooks caught on to this tendency too; in his *Star Wars* parody *Spaceballs* (1987), he plays a Yoda-like figure who sells movie merchandise within the film itself, solemnly promoting a fake sequel titled *Spaceballs 2: The Search for More Money.*

The movie business has steadily gotten worse since the 1980s: we're stuck in the sequel, the search for more money. The era of neoliberal deregulation just so happened to coincide with the era of blockbuster action films, which critics claimed at the time would rot brains and now look back on nostalgically as examples of "real" cinema. There are ordinary chronological factors at work here: bad art is often forgotten, and the good stuff remembered, so that the past always seems like a more fruitful artistic time than it really was. But it's also true that big, profit-generating serial films—prequels, sequels, and remakes—have become what most movies are like and, increasingly, the only thing they can be like. "And if you're going to tell me that it's simply a matter of supply and demand and giving the people what they want, I'm going to disagree," Scorsese writes. "It's a chicken-and-egg issue. If people are given only one kind of thing and endlessly sold only one kind of thing, of course they're going to want more of that one kind of thing."[46]

It's impossible to run any kind of controlled study on what audiences would opt for in a vacuum, if every film received equal levels of support, marketing, and availability, but there's at least one interesting data point we can examine. In late 2021, as the pandemic was theoretically winding down, film distributors tried to encourage viewers to return to theaters through several big- and small-budget releases. There were a few auteur films available, along with a host of sequels and prequels and remakes. But audiences overwhelmingly chose one movie: *Spider-Man: No Way Home.*[47] They didn't just go see it, but they packed theaters: the movie made $1.4 billion in the first two weeks.[48] The enormous crowds may even have led to

COVID spikes, making *No Way Home* a literally dangerous movie that may have sickened and even killed people. And yet, people went: it was the only movie they were willing, en masse, to risk their health to see.[49] You can blame this on marketing, or you can invent all sorts of sociological and chronological explanations (audiences felt pent up after the lockdowns and other restrictions and wanted contractually guaranteed entertainment). But maybe, also, people just like (certain) superheroes; they want to see pictures of Spider-Man, and they have since his inception in 1962.[50]

Ultimately, though, Scorsese is right that the dominance of corporate superhero films represents something dangerous for movies, as the dominance of corporate control over every art form represents something dangerous for art more generally. This isn't just regular old capitalism, which was bad enough, but an exceptional and unusual form of deregulated greed. And it's a kind of capitalism that propagandizes itself less through the medium of the fictional stories themselves (though you can, if you like, analyze superhero movies as tortured metaphors for the desire for limitless power and control) but much more directly through the systems of financial power that build themselves around those stories. As the actor Stellan Skarsgård (one of our finest Skarsgårds) said in an interview, the problem with movies these days is "not the fault of Marvel" but "the fault of an idea about how the economical [*sic*] systems of the world should work. It's all fiction. But it's the fiction that we had for the last couple of decades," and it, he says, "has led to this."[51]

The Dark Satanic Content Mill

The opposite of the individual is not necessarily the corporation: these are not the only two categories of things that exist. It's possible to believe in the importance of individuals (plural) getting a chance to make art without endorsing either corporate art or the myth of the solo genius auteur. The stunning victory of the WGA and SAG-AFTRA in the 2023 strike may have won back some of the creative autonomy that's been otherwise lost in the corporate consolidation of Hollywood, and it may help continue to open the gentleman's club of respectable art to everyone. But even so, these efforts can feel like something of a losing battle against corporate consolidation: whether art appeals to "good" or "bad" taste, it's still going to be made in the same profit-seeking industries and by the same profit-seeking corporate powers.

Increasingly, there's less interest in whether art is even "good" or "bad" at all; and not just as difficult-to-prove objective and eternal categories, but as matters of subjective and personal critical opinion. The new word we see for all art is "content," which actually functions a bit like the "not art" label, though leveraged in a very different direction and for different reasons. Rather than naming some genres "art" and some genres "not art" for the sake of taste and snobbery, every kind of media these days is just "content"—interchangeable stuff for us to consume. Mark McGurl, in his somewhat bizarre follow-up to *The Program Era*—titled *Everything and Less: The Novel in the Age of Amazon*—argues that the rampant commodification of novels in particular will be healthy for fiction in the long run. If fiction has long been considered dangerous because it's an idle pursuit that can only be sometimes pegged to Protestant notions of use-value, then turning it into a commodity grants it an innate usefulness. If a book has a price tag, that means it has an immediately identifiable value; whether it's "good" or "bad," it *does* something for you, the consumer. You can order a novel at Amazon along with toothpaste and paper towels and a butt warmer for your car; it's just the same as any other item.[52]

But of course, this also makes fiction as interchangeable and disposable as toothpaste and paper towels, and as meaningless.

This is how every form of fiction stops being an art form and becomes a consumable *thing*, no different than a factory-produced wall painting or a streaming Prime TV show—though of course the TV writers went on strike until they were treated more like artists and less like interchangeable producers of commodities whose work could be outsourced to machines.

If fiction is only a commodity, then a writer is a mere content producer, or as McGurl puts it, a "servant" and a "service provider" while the reader is a "consumer."[53] If a writer is a service worker—a corporate employee/contractor—it naturally follows that a work of fiction is a service and is judged on whether it fulfills that service accordingly. Once again, it's the worst form of Franzen's "Contract" model: consumerism over any and all aesthetic experience. There's a subtle but key difference between being socially permitted to have your own opinion about whether something was good—whether it met your version of the implicit contract—and the decision that you are "owed" customer satisfaction in a literal, actionable sense. If you read a book or saw a movie and you didn't like it, you're allowed to say so: but it's not a mattress, and you don't get your money back. But on the other hand, if a novel or film or TV show isn't art, only more stuff you bought, then the writer *does* owe you, as does the corporation who sold you that product, from whom you can demand everything you want.

Many of the ugliest contemporary debates about fiction are really debates about corporate responsibility and about what large corporate products—such as franchise TV shows and movies—really "owe" to their viewers. If Amazon and other corporations are one-stop shops for all contemporary forms of storytelling, they have increasingly become one-stop shops for our politics as well. This is another way that we skip past the importance of fiction as fiction and concentrate on its use-value as a commodity: we judge it on whether it displays the political values we consider important, satisfying us as moral consumers. We've largely accepted the role that corporations play in shaping our politics, and we tend to only argue about whether the content satisfies our expectations or not. In this way, we've tacitly accepted McGurl's queasiest claim in *Everything and Less*: the corporation really is "the super-author of our time."[54]

CHAPTER SIX

The Enemy of My Enemy Is—

The release of a corporate pop culture property is now a regular political event; you could set your watch to it, like Old Faithful. The usual pattern goes like this: first, a media corporation announces the latest remake, reboot, or other permutation of some unit of intellectual property in its possession—a live-action Disney movie, a new *Star Wars* show or film, a new *Star Trek* series, a prequel to *Lord of the Rings*, etc. The new story usually has some improved amount of racial diversity and gender parity, at least in comparison with older iterations, a fact that sends conservative and far-right fans into a screaming meltdown long before the show or movie even airs. Professional far-right attention artists make bigoted and often deliberately stupid comments designed to win headlines and social media impressions (such as professional troll Matt Walsh's claim that it's scientifically impossible for mermaids to be Black, or amateur troll Benny Johnson declaring the multi-racial dwarves in the 2024 *Snow White* to be a sign of "a Nation in Decline").[1] The far right often engages in serious harassment of actors of color, going so far as to dox or send death threats against anyone associated with a movie or TV show they've decided in advance they don't like.[2] This sort of nonsense infuriates liberal-minded people, who vow to see and support the media object in question. All this attention, negative and positive, results in free publicity cycles for the corporations that create our pop culture, whether their (almost exclusively) wealthy white male ownership is remotely interested in diversity or not.

This cycle can be deeply frustrating, especially if you agree that diversity on-screen is a social good (on-screen diversity being basically the first baby step of a social good). It's also frustrating because a lot of these shows and movies end up being *bad*—and I don't mean bad as a matter of personal taste, but bad as a matter of a corporate conglomerate burping out superficially diverse content rather than intentionally fostering the creation of serious art. If audiences end up liking them, that's essentially an extra as far as the companies are concerned: their only intent is to make money through ticket sales and streaming subscriptions, and to sell toys by one means or another. And yet criticizing these cynical corporate products is often miscast as agreeing with the far right, which hates them As with most modes of binary thinking, this creates superficial and destructive patterns: pretending that the conflict over pop culture is a simple battle between the right versus the woke corporatists allows the right to dictate the shape of reality, recasting diversity as a sincere corporate concern. It also ignores how the owners of pop intellectual properties often throw actors of color to the fascist wolves, and in 2023 tried very hard—before the WGA and SAG-AFTRA pushed back—to replace as many writers and actors as they could with AI. They don't give a damn about the people who make these movies and TV shows, let alone the stories themselves, many of which already feel produced by algorithm.

But at the same time, this is also a real war, in the sense that the threat of pop culture is taken very seriously and that the far right is energetically devoted to forcing culture to conform to their image. This effort may not always win them elections, but it does win them attention, and there's some anecdotal evidence that these sorts of moral panics can be an effective tool for far-right radicalization.[3] We may be dealing with a fake and foolish binary, but when it comes to fascists attacking the very existence of marginalized people on-screen, most progressives end up at "critical support for comrade Disney" for valid reasons. Twenty-first-century pop culture bears a resemblance to presidential politics in this respect: we seem to always face a choice between frothing fascists and corporate mediocrity. That being said, we might continue to work and hope for a better third option, but when one side of a culture war wants to sweep all the marginalized people out of its fantasy realms (in imaginative anticipation of doing so in physical realms), the only real option is to oppose them.

And yet corporate control remains an ugly, untrustworthy thing—it changes with the wind, and the wind can always blow in another direction. The Walt Disney Company has its own ugly fascist or fascist-adjacent history; it also has a much more recent history of mistreating and underpaying its workers, especially workers of color.[4] It would be cool if the far-right fantasy about an ultra-woke Disney was actually true, but mainly the company just profits from the appearance of being progressive while maximizing the profits of its exploitation. We can see clear evidence of this in Disney's reaction to the racist harassment of actors Kelly Marie Tran and John Boyega: the company reduced their roles in the final installment of the trilogy, pandering to the worst and noisiest fans.[5] The far right's claim that shows and films that "go woke go broke" isn't true in an empirical sense—the actual box office and streaming record is mixed, as would be expected of any random sampling of media properties—but it's also a convenient excuse for media corporations themselves, who can use conveniently poor numbers as an excuse to not pursue diverse casting in the future.[6] Progressive fans, being generally aware of this corporate unreliability, have often responded by insisting that it's a political duty to watch (and praise) what are frequently just glorified toy commercials.

In the end, this whole fight is about toys. That makes it sound childish—which I think it both is, and isn't. The accusation that only *other people* are childish, only *other people* want to see new versions of the things they loved when they were young, always has convenient carve-outs for personal taste, and it ignores the immortality of certain stories while making a modern and insincere demand for novelty above all other considerations. (Novelty is good; many good things are still not novel.) Even the idea that toys and imagination belong to children alone is modern and insincere; the fact is that just about all of us care about toys, dress-up, and imagination, long after we're supposed to stop. (Search your life and you'll find it: fashion is an awful lot like dress-up, makeup is character creation, playing sports is a form of adventurous nonbeing.) Thanks to western modernity, adults have few acceptable outlets for imaginative play—Halloween for most, cosplay for the brave, drag for the best of us—but these few outlets can hardly contain the common desire to not be oneself, to be *other people* in a different world. (Or, for the right, the *fear* of not being oneself, plus the fear of other people and different worlds, a set of anxieties that are inextricable from desire.) It's no coincidence that most of the pop culture properties in question are some variant of science fiction and fantasy, with their wide-open strata of conceptual possibilities. Grown adults are fighting over remakes of their favorite childhood stories not necessarily because *they* are childish people—though of course, sometimes they are—but because the territory of the imagination remains serious business into adulthood.

And *who* gets to populate the imagination is the most serious business of all for a reason. The far right finds depictions of marginalized people in fictional stories to be dangerous, and corporations find them dangerously useful as a profit mechanism; both of these turns of events are, for stories and for people, potentially quite dangerous in their way. To unpack what's really happening here, and understand what the actual stakes may be, we need to start with the precipitating factor. I've referenced it several times in this book but it's time now to address it in full: the most important contemporary fight over fiction was started by grown and very childish men who demanded that everybody else play the same game, their way.

Hands Off My Stuff!!!

Gamergate should really have been a passing fad, a toxic belch in the internet's indifferent ocean. And yet it's the origin story for a lot of the far right, and a precursor for a dynamic that has shaped every pop culture panic of the past decade and probably more to come. The first hint of trouble came in the form of a series of misogynist complaints on gaming forums and social media about the supposed incursion of women and women's interests in video games. Casual misogyny and the gaming community have long been friends, but Gamergate separated itself from the muck of ordinary nerd bigotry and social media misbehavior through its tactics: the movement weaponized internet harassment and abuse on a scale that hadn't been seen before.[7] Game designers and journalists were doxed and harassed, subjected to rape threats and death threats to the point where several people had to flee their homes. The gamers soon graduated from harassing a small number of women to abusing anyone who seemed to them like an "SJW" (social justice warrior), meaning anyone who supported a more complete representation of race, gender, and sexuality in video games, both in terms of the content of the games and who was playing them. Gamergate was so toxic that advertisers started avoiding game review sites targeted by the gamers; it was effectively the harassment campaign version of a consumer boycott.[8]

In the 2020s, a spot of doxing and abuse may sound like the regular cost of being online; after all, people have been harassed on Twitter just for posting photos of homemade chili and threatened with public execution or worse for daring to criticize Taylor Swift or BTS.[9] But back in the hoary days of 2014 these were relatively new extremes of internet behavior. Some media critics dismissed Gamergate as a passing fad, but others, like Kyle Wagner of *Deadspin*, correctly identified it as the start of something new and ugly. His article, titled "The Future of the Culture Wars Is Here, and It's Gamergate," reads now like a prophecy.[10] In the mid-2020s, Gamergate is everywhere: essentially any doxing and harassment campaign by the right carries its distinct musty signature. The ecosystem of YouTube videos *DESTROYING* the latest "woke" pop culture franchise, the harassment campaigns against actors of color who dare to appear in them, the coordinated "review bombing" of these shows and movies in advance—all of these tactics effectively originated with or were perfected by Gamergate.[11] Every successive wave of the new right has adopted these strategies, even when pursuing targets outside of pop culture; there's seemingly a "new right" every year, and they are always very mad about diversity in video games and everywhere else.

But Gamergate was always more than just a set of tactics, a way of organizing disaffected young men into right-wing political activity. It also opened an entirely new front in identity politics itself. Most of Gamergate's partisans were men—largely white, cis, and heterosexual men—and they usually insisted that their objections to women gamers or multicultural characters in games had nothing to do with identity. It was their opponents, they often claimed, who "saw" race and gender everywhere, and weaponized it, such as people like game designer Zoe Quinn, whom the Gamergaters claimed had violated journalistic ethics by sleeping with a games reviewer (she didn't), or critics like Anita Sarkeesian who ruined the immersive quality of video games by pointing out that bikini armor doesn't provide adequate protection for women warriors (it doesn't). The real issue, the Gamergaters said, was media coverage, or "ethics in video game journalism," a matter closely related to the public entrance of women into gaming. As journalistic coverage of games took a single faltering step away from the interests of the classic white, male, heterosexual gamer, many gamers reacted furiously. They were no longer being marketed to exclusively; they were no longer the only imaginable consumers.

This was part of a legitimately huge cultural shift. Until quite recently, most big pop culture entertainment—especially of the sort so easily gobbled up by megacorporations and turned into IP franchises—was designed with a white, male, heterosexual audience in mind. If other people engaged with these things and enjoyed them, that was fine, but non–white men weren't catered to as audiences through representation or marketing or anything else. The original *Star Wars* films have only one Black male character and one white woman (who is absurdly sexualized at one point). This is typical of many big pop culture products prior to the late 2000s or so. When games or films or TV shows are made or remade with more characters of color and more women—especially women who are portrayed not as sex objects but as real people—this is greater than a mere aesthetic change: it's a signal to the previous consumers of this kind of media that they're no longer the only desirable demographic. "Gamergate is right about this much," Wagner wrote in 2014. "When developers make games targeting or even acknowledging other sorts of people, and when video game fans say they want more such games, this actually does represent an assault on the prerogatives of the young, middle-class white men who mean something very specific when they call themselves gamers."[12] When the white male customer is no longer prioritized above everyone else, that means his money is just as good as anyone else's—no more meaningful, and no less.

This sudden loss of consumptive monopoly was perceived by the Gamergaters as an existential threat, a decentering and destabilizing moment. Suddenly, these guys were just a set of consumers adrift in a sea of other consumers, no longer catered to, no longer the center of the universe. Being a middle-class white man used to *mean* something in this country: it meant you could buy more stuff than other people. Buying stuff—being *able* to buy stuff, being targeted as a consumer of stuff—was an expression of power and importance, and often the only real expression of power and importance that this sort of person might have in his daily life, which would otherwise be taken up with the daily humiliations of modernity (bosses, commutes, bills, existential dread). And even though the average middle-class white man can still usually buy more stuff than other people, not quite everything is marketed to him anymore. Not every toy and film and advertisement says to him, "Hey, you! You're great! Buy this!" To be forgotten as a consumer—or in this case, very slightly deprioritized—made for a genuine loss of status and identity for these men, especially in the United States, where buying power so often *is* who you are, and often the only real freedom you possess.

It's possible that the right-wing backlash started with video games before leaping to all other forms of popular fiction because games are an expensive consumer product—effectively, the most expensive form of popular storytelling we have. A new video game usually costs two or three times as much as a movie ticket or a novel, and the systems required to play them cost hundreds of dollars each. Only some "high" culture products (theater tickets, opera tickets) regularly cost more than video games. It's true that the content of games happened to be diversifying in 2014, but so was every other form of media; women and other nontraditional "gamer" types may have been becoming more visible as well, but people who are not cis straight men have always played games. (I played *Zelda* and *Final Fantasy* as a kid; I'm sure I'll play *Zelda* and *Final Fantasy* forever.) Nothing particularly different was happening in games in 2014, nothing especially dangerous to the average white male fan's sense of identity and control—except that no pop culture fan is more of a consumer than a gamer, and with great expense comes great entitlement. If you're accustomed to buying things that remind you of yourself, you may become very annoyed when even a small number of those things aren't about you anymore.

Gamers and other pop culture fans spend their money on more than just entertainment: they also spend heavily on toys and the other products of fandom. As an identity category of its own, fandom has long been perceived as something mockable, even psychically damaging; people can become so devoted to their particular fandom that they supposedly lose connection with reality. There's a creative end of fandom (fan fiction, fan art, cosplay) and a consumptive, possessive, dominating end (collecting Funko Pops, memorizing superheroes' first appearances and correcting other people about them, etc.).[13] The creative end may have its risks: a person could theoretically become so invested in cosplay that they become, like Don Quixote, inextricable from their character (though like Don Quixote, how could you look around at this world and blame them?). The consumptive end, however, is definitely perilous. At a certain point, consumptive fandom becomes purely greedy and self-centered; as Roger Ebert noted back in 2009: "A lot of fans are basically fans of fandom itself. It's all about them. They have mastered the 'Star Wars' or 'Star Trek' universes or whatever, but their objects of veneration are useful mainly as a backdrop to their own devotion."[14] This kind of fan doesn't really care about *Star Wars* or *Star Trek*, not as they actually exist. They are, however, hugely invested in how these worlds can be leveraged to bolster their sense of identity, their ability to buy the stuff that makes them feel like themselves.[15]

And this is why, though the new versions of *Star Wars* and *Star Trek* and other IP properties may be violently nostalgic, conservative white male fans remain offended by them. In fact, the more conservative and nostalgic a fan may be (and conservatism is nothing if not a nostalgic movement) the more likely it is that they'll claim the new pop culture event "murdered their childhoods." Rather than returning them to the past, the new thing demonstrates only, hatefully, that they have aged. It feels different, it looks different, and it's marketed at different people—the same complaints that Gamergaters had about the new wave of games and games journalism in 2014, and the same complaint that these successive right-wing panics have had and will continue to have about each new thing.

That this accusation of unacceptable difference is even leveraged against *Star Trek*—which has always had a diverse cast and progressive politics at least relative to other TV shows of its respective eras—illustrates that this complaint has never really been about fidelity to the original stories. Rod Lampard of the Australian *Spectator* was one of many right-wing critics to come out against the newer *Trek* shows (called "NuTrek" by fans); he claimed that the original series—which was about a crew of diverse professionals engaged in scientific space exploration—"maintained the concept of family, faith, and freedom" and was "a far cry from the 'Woke' alienation of healthy traditions, and the 'burn it all down' social justice warriorism of deconstructionism."[16] This is a very silly bowl of word salad, and it could have been written about any show, movie, book, or game that the right dislikes, ever since Gamergate started railing about social justice warriors in 2014. Whatever the new thing is, it's always gone woke; it always symbolizes the movement of history and changing social mores, the death of a childhood that has always been murdered by time.

As Adam Serwer notes for *The Atlantic*, to pretend that universes like *Star Trek's* have "suddenly gone 'woke' is to ignore almost everything about them."[17] To borrow one of Serwer's more famous phrases, the ignorance is the point: to a certain kind of fan, these stories have always been meaningless objects to collect.[18] For these fans, the politics and the diversity of *Star Trek* failed to impact their imaginative space and their construction of reality, just as it failed for *Star Trek: The Original Series* fan Stephen Miller. They saw what they wanted to see, and they decided it meant what they wanted it to mean. There used to be a certain power for fanboys in being able to interpret nerd culture—their supposedly exclusive property—exactly as shallowly as they liked, without being subject to the opinions of women or professional critics or anyone else who might offer a different interpretation. It was a place where they could be architects of their own reality, heroes of their self-insert dreams.

The right-wing fan base may no longer be able to claim *Trek* and the other intellectual properties as their sole territory, but these stories remain useful to them as a different kind of meaningless object: a rallying point for their grievances. Persecution creates group cohesion; pretending to be menaced by Hollywood (i.e., not being marketed to by Hollywood) helps build the kind of group identity that can be translated into advocacy and action. Serwer's piece—titled "Fear of a Black Hobbit"—was written in response to the racist panic over *The Rings of Power*, Amazon's prequel to *The Lord of the Rings*, which cast several Black actors as hobbits and elves and other fantasy beings. Brandon Morse of *RedState*, a prominent right-wing website, made the usual noisy complaints that the new product looked different from the old product, and that this was clearly a woke political act designed to hurt white people. He was also sure it couldn't possibly be good. "If you focus on introducing modern political sentiments, such as the leftist obsession with identity issues that only go skin deep," Morse said in an interview with CNN, "then you're no longer focusing on building a good story.'"[19]

Morse made his comments without—as is typical—actually having seen *The Rings of Power*; he could easily have made the same comments about one of the new *Star Trek* shows or *The Little Mermaid* or anything else. The far-right reaction to these pop culture events is lazily algorithmic: it could be performed by a bot. But at the same time these shows and movies are often not even trying to be good, a fact that, given the actual agendas and practices of the corporations that make them, is fairly easy to predict.

The Ratio of Suspicion

With all due caveats about the subjectivity of taste, I will say that, subjectively, *The Rings of Power* is the worst TV show I've ever seen, and I don't mean to brag, but I have watched a *lot* of bad TV. I'm grading on a curve, since *The Rings of Power* is also the most expensive TV show ever made and supposedly draws from J. R. R. Tolkien's source material.[20] If it were a derivative 1990s Sci-Fi Channel original fantasy series, it might be excusable as a cute but ill-advised failure. But it's made by Amazon Studios in the 2020s with an outrageous budget, and the result—of the first season, anyway, since only the first season has aired at the time of this writing—is a loveless disaster. The CGI is incompetent, the camerawork shockingly amateurish, and the production values inconsistent at best (some of the costumes are quite pretty, but the titular rings themselves look like the prizes from a carnival machine). The show's diversity, so hated by the right, is its sole positive element: Ismael Cruz Córdova, who received death threats for his role as the only dark-skinned elf on the show, is also the only one to capture that all-important and elusive elvish quality. It's a sign of his strength as an actor that he manages to do so without a single good line.

There are plenty of viewers who don't really pay attention to visual narratives, or even dialogue—they don't "watch" as much as "read" a story, and so they don't really care if a show or a movie *looks* or *sounds* bad.[21] This is why critics of Marvel movies tear their hair out over sloppy visuals and irritating dialogue, while many viewers only see the story—the characters that they love, doing things that mostly make sense. But in the case of *The Rings of Power* (and also many of the later Marvel movies, which have greater diversity coupled with underinvestment on the production level), the story is also bad and the characterization often incoherent. There are a few charming moments here and there, but also *major* editing mistakes, including clumsy action sequences and outright continuity errors, which apparently nobody involved in the creation of such empty content products cared enough to catch.

The worst element of *The Rings of Power*, however, has to be the embarrassingly shallow gestures toward contemporary political concerns. The arc of the show is meant to cover the movements of various groups of people before the events of *The Lord of the Rings*. In one scene, a mob of angry humans expresses fear that elves will take their jobs and take over their country. The moment is clearly meant to reference the fascist "great replacement theory," but this racist anxiety conveniently vanishes from the show as soon as the plot requires those particular humans to act as the good guys. This frivolous and passing evocation of a real-world fascist ideology that has real consequences for real people might be offensive, if it weren't so stupid—the whole show is remarkably stupid, made by a pair of white male showrunners with literally zero prior experience, a hiring move which is proof of real contempt for its audience, not to mention the marginalized creators who would never be able to swing such a gig.[22]

The Rings of Power is so terrible that, for me, it even unseated the former title holder of the worst show I've ever seen—*Star Trek: Picard*, the first two seasons of which also gesture shallowly at progressive politics and which also happens to be part of the suite of "NuTrek" shows despised by the far right. Again, this is literally a case of the stopped clock being right twice a day: the far right would have hated these shows before they debuted even if they were brilliant. (The only contemporary IP content this crowd has ever really liked was *The Rise of Skywalker,* and only because it seemed to stick it to the right's perceived enemies by mothballing actors of color and undoing much of the clunky but earnestly progressive second film.)

But I hate these shows too. I hate a lot of this new IP stuff, honestly. It's not a problem of genre; I love this genre. I am exactly the target audience. (I can tell because of all the Strong Female Characters I am clearly supposed to find relatable, even though they mostly just yell, make stupid decisions, and hit things.) This is just *bad* art, the kind of bad art that's so bad it isn't even fun anymore; the kind of bad art that makes me feel dead. I watch these shows and feel despair.

Shows and movies like these aren't just an aesthetic disappointment. They're also a serious political problem: they let the Gamergaters and the Brandon Morses of the world walk backward into being right. In the case of *The Rings of Power* and *Picard*, audiences seem to largely agree with my opinion: neither show has made much impact on the cultural conversation besides the right-wing backlash, and if you're not a huge nerd for the original versions of these stories in the first place, you may not even be aware that they exist.[23] TV shows, unlike films, have no visible box office returns, and streaming companies tend to keep their stats to themselves.[24] Still, Amazon admitted that only 37 percent of people who started *The Rings of Power* in the United States actually finished, and an otherwise enthusiastic *Polygon* article about the NuTrek shows made a joke of the fact that *Picard* seemed to have no particular audience even among Trekkies.[25] Audience scores on sites like *Rotten Tomatoes* are likewise unreliable, thanks to the far-right practice of negative review-bombing, but the audience score for the first season of *The Rings of Power* squats at a lowly 38 percent, while the first two seasons of *Star Trek: Picard* likewise never left the 30 percent range.[26] (The third and final season of *Picard* brought in a different showrunner and was widely agreed to be much better, which led to an increase in the overall ratings; this seems improbable if the negative scores were *only* review-bombing due to the casting, which didn't significantly change in terms of diversity.)

Critical ratings for these particular shows, however, are much higher: 80–85 percent of critics, per Rotten Tomatoes' own mysterious algorithm, have declared these shows to be good and worth watching. I've started calling this 50 percent gap "the Ratio of Suspicion": whenever critics appear to like pop culture *that* much more than the actual public, it suggests that something strange is going on. It could be simply a matter of racist review-bombing (but then the Ratio of Suspicion would always show up for these types of shows and movies, and it doesn't). Or it could be that the masses have failed to appreciate something genuinely groundbreaking and original (but then these shows are notably not original; in fact, nostalgic extended universe properties are designed to be as unoriginal as possible). What I think is much more likely than either of these possibilities is that critics are judging these shows by the purported "value" they provide, by their position in the cultural conversation as diverse big-budget media properties, rather than by whether they're entertaining or aesthetically interesting.[27] It's possible that, as the Gamergaters said, there's an issue of ethics in TV journalism . . . Oh no . . .

But of course, there really are ethical issues in play here. If all that matters to critics is that these corporate shows and movies are superficially diverse (in front of the camera, rarely behind it) and that they make brief and obvious stabs at progressive political topics, then there's no reason to interrogate whether they're actually "good" or even something that most people like, not to mention the actual politics of the companies that made them. Progressive critics (and most critics are indeed progressive) have no reason to evaluate IP products according to their own informed, interesting subjectivity; they're not viewing these shows as works of art but as hollowed-out baseball bats for both sides in the culture war to hit each other with. On top of that, criticism is as underpaid and unstable as any other media profession, and no sensible critic wants to alienate future employers or lose access to sources. Wagner remarks in his Gamergate essay on the fact that the angry gamers wasted their critique of "ethics in video game journalism" in misogynist and racist fury. Of course game reviewers are chummy with the game companies; of course there's grade inflation.[28] This is how criticism often works: there's very little incentive to be honest, and reviewers can—and have—acted as stenographers of power just like many other bad journalists.[29]

And this is exactly why media-tech companies devalue criticism; this is exactly why they think critics are replaceable by AI. A machine is always going to be a much more reliable stenographer for corporate power than a human being. When progressive critics pretend that a piece of corporate media with a sprinkling of minority representation is good and enjoyable art, every time, regardless of its actual quality, they're simply acting out the right-wing playbook in reverse; they're giving automatic condescending compliments instead of automatic reactionary contempt. It's algorithmic thinking all around; a machine could replace both sides. Like many algorithms, this discourse is also racist by design: it suggests that popular art featuring marginalized characters can't ever be complex and serious art but only ever good medicine, the kind that tastes bad going down. And it lets the corporate powers that make this shallow content get away with a PR sheen of progressive identity politics while they grind poor and marginalized workers underfoot.

The Zombie Cinematic Universe

The term "woke-washing" has been used by garment industry activist Aja Barber and others to refer to a corporation's weaponization of diversity and progressive politics to cover up real crimes.[30] Many companies rely on woke-washing, but nobody does it quite like Amazon—or has more to cover up. The company is notorious for mistreating its warehouse employees, who are disproportionately women and people of color.[31] Injuries at Amazon facilities are so common that in 2023, the company was under simultaneous investigation by OSHA, the Department of Justice, and the U.S. Senate.[32] A number of employees in different divisions have sued the company, claiming racial and gender discrimination.[33] Chris Smalls, the union organizer, has alleged that Amazon fired him for racist reasons and because he was advocating for the largely non-white warehouse staff.[34] Jennifer Bates, another Black union organizer, claims she was fired for similar reasons and immediately after recovering from an on-the-job injury.[35] In June 2022, just a few months before the debut of *The Rings of Power*, a leaked internal report from Amazon revealed that the company was worried it might run out of people to hire in its warehouses; thanks to injuries and low pay, they've been burning through their disproportionately minority labor pool faster than it can replace itself.[36]

The superficial diversity of *The Rings of Power* doesn't just help woke-wash Amazon's reputation; the company's TV and filmmaking arm is inseparable from the rest of its business. The streaming service effectively exists, as Bloomberg reported in 2023, to drive new customers to sign up for Amazon Prime—and therefore to order more toothpaste and butt warmers, further burdening an already overburdened workforce.[37] The convenient use of TV shows as advertisements for Prime is why Amazon chose to spend so much on *The Rings of Power* (Jeff Bezos was reportedly hoping for a *Game of Thrones*–style cultural hit) and also why they were able to afford such a wild expenditure in the first place.[38] Amazon makes so much elsewhere, from monopolizing markets and exploiting labor, that it had the resources to outbid all other media companies for rights to the source material. These rights are limited in scope, and I was told by a source that Amazon allegedly described its remit in an early internal email as not including "The Simulacron." They must have meant *The Silmarillion*, but substituted a different generic sci-fi/fantasy kind of word, probably because they didn't really know or care what they'd bought, just that it was valuable intellectual property that could be leveraged into even more value for the company. Amazon is above all else a retailer, and increasingly for knock-off products; if *The Rings of Power* feels like it was produced by a third party with an inexplicable vowel-less name, that's just the company brand.[39]

Amazon is hardly the only company to churn out content for woke-washing and profit-seeking purposes; pretty much all the major media companies engage in these practices, including Paramount, which owns *Star Trek*. There are five or so NuTrek shows at any given time, created as part of an effort, according to Paramount executives, to have "year-round *Star Trek*" that will ideally drive customers to sign up for Paramount+.[40] The point of this isn't actually to give a devoted and toy-buying fan base what it wants—a surfeit of the thing it already loves—but to make sure that fans don't unsubscribe and resubscribe between shows. But here again the corporate bet may not be panning out: the NuTrek shows range in quality, and have their partisans, but it's too much content even for serious Trekkies (including me) and doesn't appear to have resulted in the same level of mad and acquisitive devotion as previous *Trek* shows.[41] Paramount even appears to be tabling or delaying some of its planned *Trek* offerings, pivoting to support of *Yellowstone*, its unexpected neo-Western hit, and launching somewhere between four to eight spin-offs.[42] This feels like too much *Yellowstone*, or too much anything, but this is the current business model: find something that the public seems to like, beat it to death for profit, and move on.

If these shows are just interchangeable units of content meant to sell subscriptions, then there are no incentives for them to be written well, or even to be written by talented human beings. It's no wonder that the streaming companies tried to replace writers and actors with AI; the dialogue for *The Rings of Power* already sounds as if it were generated by an AI that ate and spat out the *Lord of the Rings* movies, while *Picard* sounds like chopped-up, Twitterized therapy-speak.[43] I wasn't joking when I said that the *Rings of Power* showrunners had zero experience—literally zero; they didn't even have prior writing credits.[44] *Picard* seems to have had about twenty writers and still relied on ideas filched from other science fiction universes (key plot points from *Battlestar Galactica* and the video game series *Mass Effect* were stolen outright).[45] These seem like lazy and strange choices for companies that are trying to build MCU-style franchises, unless the audience is regarded with absolute cynicism if it's regarded at all; these properties are just assets in a portfolio and everyone's lying about their numbers anyway.[46] It's also a clever choice if the badness is somewhat deliberate—that is, if corporations are choosing to make bad shows on purpose to feed the right-wing take machine. The right-wing racist who signs up for Amazon or Paramount+ just so he can scan for clips to insert into his garbled YouTube DESTRUCTION takedown is still a guy who is spending money; if obvious clips of bad writing and bad acting aren't easy for him to find, he might choose to skip these shows entirely.

Rather than hiring genuinely talented people to build out already popular universes, media companies seem to be invested in zombie universes with both zombie fan bases and zombie haters, cynically orbiting around a zombie progressive politics that remains the most disturbing part of the whole business. This is a genuinely dangerous use of fiction: not as the right imagines it, where the existence of actors of color means that white viewers are being unfairly dethroned or that audiences are being indoctrinated into progressive ideology, but because the companies who mass-produce these things are only pretending to care about actors of color and real-world political problems in the first place. The right calls this "virtue signaling"—an update of the way that "political correctness" or "wokeness" is sometimes used to mean that a person is only pretending to express progressive political virtues. But the frustrating truth is that virtue signaling is sometimes real: when media corporations and their hired showrunners wield characters and plot points in the service of contemporary political statement making, it often feels clunky and *wrong*. "When art gets made to check a box for positive representation, you feel it," Elaine Castillo comments in *How to Read Now*. "You feel its intellectual limits, its political lassitude, its flat affect where a complex emotional life is supposed to be."[47]

This is the kind of flat affect that James Baldwin talks about in "Everybody's Protest Novel," where characters are used as instruments for good politics but not represented in all their humanity. This type of characterization may serve a political purpose, but not an artistic one, and certainly not a human one. It also bows to the bigots who already believe that marginalized people can't and shouldn't exist as fully realized characters.

Still, many progressive critics seem perfectly fine with this type of flat characterization, and not even the contestable flatness of humanity-abrogating villains but that of undeveloped side characters stamped into temporary avatars for moral lessons. *Star Trek* has always been willing to use allegory and metaphor to address contemporary political issues, but they're painfully direct about it in *Picard*, where a Latino character gets transported back to the year 2024 just to be kidnapped by ICE. The character never gets any real development, and the storyline is soon abandoned when it becomes inconvenient, but it does momentarily signal "ICE is bad" at a progressive viewer who is supposed to nod, knowingly, and agree that ICE is bad.

Conservative viewers are far less threatened by this kind of weak progressive signaling than they may imagine. The anticipated *Picard* viewer is probably still white enough to please *RedState*, or at least isn't the kind of person who feels personally threatened by ICE. If you had real concerns about being arrested by the immigration police, then watching a careless fictional treatment of such an important issue might be upsetting, or at least annoying; you might have a similar reaction to the one I had with *The Rings of Power* and its short-lived, trivializing reference to fascist white replacement theory. *The Rings of Power* also makes a few attempts to address the previous usage of Tolkien's work as fuel for fascism: it briefly tries to complicate the image of orcs as monstrous invaders, only to conclude that they are indeed monstrous invaders who can't live normally with other people. These shows feel written only for a distracted viewer; it's hard to imagine how anyone could enjoy their undeveloped themes and dropped plotlines if they were really paying attention.

In fact, there's a kind of stutter-stop quality to this sort of storytelling, almost as if these shows aren't ever meant to be taken in as complete narratives but just as GIFs and tweetable moments.

It's the cinematographic equivalent of "reading" a book via a few tweets and screenshots and forming an opinion about it: piecing bits and bobs into a narrative you can either praise or condemn. Many contemporary streaming shows are literally designed to function as "second screen" content, the other screen being your phone.[48] This is why so much IP content has successfully descended into incoherence—as well as why there's an apparent need for so many "ending explained" videos, and also why the right-wing takedowns are so easy to compile. You're not really meant to watch these kinds of shows or movies with your full attention, but to half watch and react on social media. The right-wing racist looks for easy aesthetic missteps to exploit, while the progressive viewer is meant to pick up the scattered references to contemporary politics and think, "Wow, what good politics! How good I am for watching it, how justified I am in my consumer choices!" But neither of these anticipated viewers is really watching and isn't really thinking about what they saw, and in the meantime the company quietly collects their subscription dollars.

When the act of consuming fiction becomes a kind of politics—when viewing and promoting something that the far right dislikes is reimagined as a political act in itself—then there's something very nasty at work, something that's bad for both art and politics. "Just as the reduction of art to political propaganda leads to bad art," says the critic Adam Kotsko, "the aestheticization of politics leads to bad, irresponsible politics."[49] It's easy for progressive viewers to convince themselves that they've done something meaningful about ICE when they only watched a story that mentioned ICE for a minute; it's easy for them to believe they're personally anti-racist because they publicly support the kind of art that racists hate (art that often seems lazily designed to encourage and satisfy that hate). And this is especially bad when the art is bad, and the politics are trivialized, because then the entire exercise is flat and insincere, reducing both fiction and politics to you, the viewer-consumer, posting about how brave and anti-establishment you are for watching TV on your couch.

The Rebellion Has Been Televised

When IP shows and movies are actually well made, and trying to be good, racist fanboys often retreat: great art makes poor fuel for their outrage engines. The best of the IP shows so far is probably *Andor*, a *Star Wars* show beloved by many on the left for its depiction of revolutionary politics. Diego Luna is luminous as the title character, a complicated and rough and not always likable person who grows from selfish mercenary into selfless revolutionary. The show eschews the usual *Star Wars* convention of magical heroes and villains in favor of a gritty, more realistic story of ordinary people struggling against imperial domination; it also depicts the crushing, almost boring daily maintenance of imperial control. The show is quite political, but thoughtfully so: it treats its diverse characters like real human beings, and its audience like grown-ups who are paying attention.

For all its lovely qualities, *Andor* is still aesthetically imperfect, with pacing issues that feel like an ambitious attempt to break out of the structural expectations of the IP streaming show that haven't quite yet been realized. I agree, nonetheless, with politics writer and critic Jamelle Bouie, who called the first season of *Andor* "the best *Star Wars* anything in quite a while." Bouie took special note of the show's interesting (though "not *that* sophisticated") political approach, especially given that it's a Disney product. "Considering the source, a risk-averse and creatively stagnant multinational conglomerate," he says, "*Andor* is the closest thing you can imagine to a triumph."[50]

I do wonder, however: Who exactly is it a triumph for? It's a triumph for *Star Wars* fans, certainly, who finally get something interesting to watch. (As with other streaming shows, it's unclear how many people have watched *Andor*; we do know that it doesn't suffer from the Ratio of Suspicion, with an 80–90 percent rating from both critics and audiences.) The show is good for Disney, to be sure: probably good for its subscription numbers and good for its continued reputation-laundering. It's also good for the U.S. military-industrial complex, which loves its *Star Wars* imagery and now gets more of it to play with. Activist Leah Bannon has written for *Jacobin* about the U.S. military's love of *Star Wars*–related stuff: a Department of Defense cyberteam, she says, "name[s] every team, project, office, conference room, contract, and software application after a Star Wars reference" and their office is "reportedly littered with Star Wars collectibles." To quote Marge Simpson, these people are clearly nerds—and nerds who are apparently unaware of the deeper meaning of the story they love so much. The *Star Wars*–loving cyberdefense unit is employed by an American government that somewhat resembles the evil empire depicted in *Andor*, which, as Bannon writes in *Jacobin*, "extracts resources, displaces Indigenous populations, turns prisoners into slave labor, and partners with corporations for profit."[51] And yet this fiction fails, apparently, to have any effect. It remains—for this team and for many other people living inside this empire—just inert, collectable stuff.

The kinds of fans who find political meaning in *Andor* and *Star Wars* more broadly will keep finding it; the ones who can't, won't. There's probably no level of political sophistication that will ever stop this stuff from being mere *stuff* both to the nerds that would collect it to define themselves and to the companies that own it in the first place. It's possible, as writer Adam Fleming Petty says, that *Andor*'s message—"the ordinary heroism of ordinary people is what brings down empires"—might resonate and might be useful in some future revolutionary context.[52] It's how all these small messages work in the aggregate, as always, that defines fiction's potential power and its danger; it's why marginalized representation matters so much to the marginalized. The depiction of many kinds of people as complex and interesting human beings isn't necessarily important in any particular story, but at scale. But when all these stories are made by very big companies, when they can devour even diversity and revolution and make either good or bad TV out of it, then the most obvious political ends these stories can serve will always be corporate ones. Better art will only ever mean better PR.

But it's also no small thing for a TV show to try to be good. TV should try to be good; all art should try to be good. *Andor* may end up being politically useful, or not; its only job, really, is to try to be good. And this is why it's so bothersome when these extended IP adaptations are almost always so deliberately bad, when they can only be praised on the grounds of their weak and temporally relevant political gestures. The original versions of these stories have remained popular because they were well made and interesting, and we know they were well made and interesting because they have enduring power. The new versions really ought to be better, and if they were, they probably would be popular with just about everyone except the kinds of conservatives who squawk at all change.

And on top of that, it would be nice to have new stories too; the importance of novelty may be slightly overstated in certain contexts but it's no mean thing either. In their desperate attempt to imitate the MCU, media companies have been trying to leverage all intellectual property, of any kind, into some kind of extended franchise universe; the Mattel corporation has been attempting to do this with all the toys they can drag out of their closet.[53] Greta Gerwig's *Barbie* film made a lot of direct (if annoyingly underdeveloped) statements about feminism and patriarchy and commercialism;

it had a running gag about Mattel being run exclusively by men. I have a certain special irritation for *Barbie*, which however cute and fun was clearly a discourse movie, designed to provoke certain public conversations as if by algorithm. The takes are predictable, and might have been written by AI: the far right hated *Barbie* and called it gender ideology, while progressive critics noted the film's cynicism and incomplete representation but defended it as important for women. (The women for whom *Barbie* is important presumably played with Barbies as children; I didn't, having generally preferred boy toys, and I still resent the implication that I need to care about something just because it's marketed at me).[54] Certainly the Mattel corporation is happy to co-opt feminism, stoke debates about representation, mock even its own misogyny, and sell more toys and more movies based on those toys, until the formula stops working entirely, if it ever does.

One of the most interesting things about *Andor*—and maybe one of its points of real failure—is that it didn't necessarily have to be related to *Star Wars* at all. It's set in the *Star Wars* universe but so divorced from the magical elements and the old established characters that it could easily have taken place in a new and unique science fictional galaxy, with a different imperial bureaucracy and a different aesthetic. *Andor* is a *Star Wars* story partly because *Star Wars* is one of the science fiction stories that TV and film writers are allowed to tell. In one episode, an imperial commandant brags about how easy it is to control the simpleminded people under his rule. All you have to do, he says, is "put a number of options on the table, and they're so wrapped up in choosing they fail to notice you've given them nothing they thought they wanted at the start . . . They've basically choked down everything we've thrown at them the last twelve years." This is a remarkable allusion to capitalist control and the illusion it provides of options on the table, provided by the handful of media corporations that control the handful of IP that's allowed to be used. And yet this speech is still made in the context of a Disney+ show; *Andor*'s rebellion can only ever go so far.

But again, if fiction's primary use is just to fight the culture war, then the structural limitations of art under capitalism are irrelevant, and the critics giving high marks to good and bad art alike haven't done anything wrong. If it doesn't matter who makes it and how, just that these shows and movies exist—and that they annoy the right people and spark the right algorithmic discourse—then all of it is perfectly good and good for us, the same mediocre level of healthy progressive culture. If something depicts "good politics" in our terms, then we can be proud that we didn't waste our time with it; we can consider ourselves freed from the sin of political complacency, even as political conditions in the United States and elsewhere mostly continue to devolve. But if fiction matters for its own sake, then our consumption of it is both less burdened and more complicit—less burdened because we aren't always anxiously searching for political use-value, and more complicit because it suddenly matters very much how it's made, and who made it, and why, and what isn't getting made at all.

The Next Generation

In the same way that "cancellation" as a term of public shame or loss of status is mostly dangerous to poor and marginalized people, the narrowing of options and the outright cancellation of TV shows is most dangerous for marginalized creators or anyone with a risky, non-mainstream vision. HBO has canceled shows like the Latinx family comedy *The Gordita Chronicles*; Netflix has canceled shows like *Warrior Nun* which featured lesbian characters.[55] Even presumably safe IP projects have had little protection against the corporate hangman: *Batgirl*, directed by Adil El Arbi and Bilall

Fallah and starring Latina actress Leslie Grace, was canceled by HBO before it could be released. The film, which was already complete, cost $90 million to make, which the company wrote off as a loss.[56] The James Gunn–directed *Coyote vs. Acme*, as shameless a toy-grab as one could imagine, was also shot, finished, canceled, and written off for $30 million.[57]

Often, when these shows or movies are canceled, they're not just ended but destroyed. HBO/Warner Bros. and Disney have a particularly nasty habit of not just canceling shows but deleting them from their libraries.[58] Since its merger with Discovery, HBO/Warner Bros. has removed over eighty titles, and because streaming has replaced physical media, these shows and movies are effectively wiped off the face of the earth.[59] Even the creators don't always have access to physical copies: Aaron Burdette, a writer and producer of the canceled animated show *Close Enough*, tweeted, "Cool, love to work on something for literal years and then have it totally vanish, it's extremely good that TV writing has become building sandcastles at high tide."[60] Some of the deleted TV shows seem to have been popular with large audiences, while others were offbeat and niche; the clear message of these cuts in either direction is that "peak TV" is over, and corporate owners will only seek out the kinds of shows that guarantee huge returns (or the zombie illusion of huge returns or acceptable losses that look good on a balance sheet).

The far right isn't the only force interested in deciding what gets to be preserved and what doesn't; what will become part of our cultural history and the art that future generations will look back on with nostalgia. It's in media companies' financial best interest to keep narrative fiction as narrow and easily replicable as possible, which means endless iterations of intellectual property that already exists, and discouragement or outright destruction of the genuinely new and different (or the profitably destructible). The major capitalist myth of the postwar era is that capitalism rewards innovation:

simply show up and be talented, and media companies will help you produce your dream. But creative people often *do* show up and *are* talented, a fact which means absolutely nothing whatsoever to a corporate balance sheet and this quarter's needs.

It's hard to know exactly what we're missing in our lives when new storytelling is destroyed or never gets to exist in the first place; as is usual with censorship, it's hard to track the meaning of an absence. How do you understand a profound aesthetic experience you didn't get to have, or the formless feeling of not seeing yourself represented? According to GLAAD's 2022–23 *Where We Are on TV* report, that year's bout of cancellations removed around 23 percent of all LGBTQ+ characters on television.[61] Young queer kids in particular are impoverished by this loss, just as they are by queer books being removed from libraries. This is one area in which media companies and the far right end up causing the same kinds of fascistic havoc with fiction, even if they claim to have different politics. Amazon canceled its series *A League of Their Own*, an IP reboot beloved by both fans and critics that *Pink News* declared to be "one of the greatest queer shows of all time."[62] Reportedly, the cancellation decision was based on focus group feedback and testing, though Amazon's testing practices are known to have a bias in favor of TV shows starring straight white men and against everything else.[63] In the end, whether the motive is bigotry or bigoted data, the outcome is the same: more of the same art made by the same well-connected white men, and less by everyone else. The damage this causes to both creators and audiences is incalculable.

Most TV shows and movies, regardless of their content, are never going to be hugely successful pop culture events; they aren't going to be useful assets in a corporate portfolio, whether as profit or as losses that can be written off. And that's fine; no work of fiction needs to be huge and enduring to matter. But the big stuff is always going to get the most attention, and it's no surprise that people look to the big pop culture properties to save us; they're likely to be viewed by the largest number of people, and so they appear to be the medium through which the culture can be fixed. In fact, they're often seen as the *only* way it can be fixed, because the big media companies that own everything don't appear to be going anywhere (except maybe to keep eating each other and getting bigger). The right will never have any real interest in regulating these companies, just in policing their content and making the existing culture even narrower than it already is. Trying to battle the right with diverse corporate art is understandable but misguided; it gives the companies far too much credit.

Diversity in pop culture is at this point a baseline requirement, not a get-out-of-jail-free card, and the tendency to cast people of color mainly in knock-off versions of preexisting, white-dominated properties rather than original work is disrespectful and a disservice. Activist Leen Dweik put it simply in a tweet: "classics can be retold in whatever way like idc but i think this era of colorblind casting is actually harming bipoc storytellers. why are we taking traditionally white stories and throwing in poc instead of just . . . making new media based on bipoc stories?"[64] It's a good question, and the answer is that media companies have decided to believe that BIPOC stories wouldn't be profitable enough or reliable enough— and also they just don't want to. They have proved themselves entirely insincere in their commitments: they only care about *looking* as though they're interested in diverse media to trick critics and audiences into believing it, and to reaping the discursive rewards of their shoddy craftsmanship.

Far-right backlash has confused this era of corporate power, making it seem more progressive than it is; and it's allowed consumption of media to be mistaken for political action, which too often gets in the way of real political action. When one of the major pop culture properties has a diverse cast, that's good, but it isn't everything; if it contains an allegorical or metaphorical or openly political progressive statement, that may be interesting, but it's not actionable. The accumulated weight of symbols in stories we know to be unreal and untrue creates an unidentifiable amount of pressure in the real world, but they can't act for us, and we shouldn't expect a corporation happily creating art about itself to meaningfully alter corporate power.

But there's another kind of storytelling—much of it on television—which I've largely neglected so far. Stories set in the "real" world and about real institutions (government, police, national security) are often given less pop cultural weight, even if they're technically quite popular in raw statistical terms. They also tend to get less critical coverage and provoke much less right-wing outrage, though they may have an even greater impact when it comes to representation and identity, since it's even easier to "see" yourself in an actor playing a person with a real job than a fantasy hero. And a lot of this stuff is even more dangerously narrow and algorithmic than the flagship corporate properties that get so much more attention and sell so many toys; these kinds of stories often blur the lines between reality and fantasy, bleeding into both worlds.

CHAPTER SEVEN

The Dramatic Condition

There was a time in my life when I watched every episode of *CSI* in existence. I can't really tell you why I was so invested— *CSI* is just a normal crime procedural like a hundred others, featuring a bloody murder solved every week by a rotating cast of very attractive people. I got attached to this particular set of attractive people, I guess, and the predictable rhythms of each episode: the murder, a morbid pun about the murder leading into the credits, the forensic investigation, the frustration over insufficient evidence, the dramatic twist!!!, more evidence found, and the bad guy arrested. The characters began to feel familiar and trustworthy, like friends. Of course I didn't think for a moment they were *real* people, or *real* friends, and I never thought that their work was remotely like actual police work. I always knew I was watching procedural TV: formulaic, satisfying, and safely unreal.

One of the primary anxieties over fiction that we've encountered so far is the fear that other people will mistake a story for reality, and that this mistake will lead them into unhealthy or disreputable situations. Or, if the story in question is an obvious fantasy, they'll be so distracted by the joys of escapism that they won't think about who is making these stories and why, and how their goodwill might be manipulated in the process. But that's always a fear about *other people*, and I was sure, while I was watching *CSI*, that I wasn't like *other people*: I wasn't deluded into believing a fictional TV show accurately represented anything like reality, and I especially wasn't deluded about the realism of the police procedural itself. *CSI* falls into the category of TV shows that can be fairly labeled "copaganda": media that presents the police as far more effective, dedicated, and useful than they are in reality. Often enough, this kind of media is financed and assisted by the police themselves.[1] But real crime and real police work don't follow tidy and predictable episodic patterns; real forensic techs don't just happen to be gorgeous, disinterested scientists dedicated to discovering the truth at all costs. I knew all of this going in—I was sure that I was wise to the tricks of copaganda, and immune to all of it.

But at the same time, I harbored a tacit belief that forensic science itself—even if the show exaggerated or misrepresented its techniques for dramatic effect—was at least a real, established form of science. At worst, I assumed, what I was seeing in *CSI* was "like true" in the way that thrift stores mark some clothes as "like new": close enough, at least for everyday life. So I was very surprised, some years later, to run across articles explaining that forensic science— as celebrated on *CSI* and also in real-life courtrooms—has been widely criticized for inaccuracies and outmoded techniques. Certain practices do have real evidentiary basis, like DNA, but other areas such as bloodstain pattern analysis and microscopic hair comparison (both favorites of television) are now mostly considered to be junk science.[2] In the case of microscopic hair analysis, the FBI admitted in 2015 that an "elite" FBI forensic team had misrepresented evidence in real-life court, claiming that certain hairs clearly matched when there was no real evidentiary basis to suggest they did. Essentially, they came to the kinds of conclusions that a fictional forensic scientist would reach in the last five minutes of an episode, supposedly identifying the bad guy beyond a shadow of a reasonable doubt. And this real, elite FBI team did this not just once in a while, or regularly, but *in almost every criminal trial for two decades.*[3]

These errors and exaggerations of real-life evidence resulted in hundreds of flawed convictions, including those of prisoners on death row. At least fourteen people died by execution or in prison before the FBI admitted that their junk hair analysis had condemned them to death.[4] And in the meantime, *CSI* was playing on millions of TVs across the country and the world, followed by its many spin-offs and imitators, including *NCIS*, a show which has run for over twenty seasons and remains one of the most popular TV dramas ever made.[5]

Media and legal scholars alike have worried that "the *CSI* effect" can manipulate jurors' perception of how forensic evidence should be evaluated, since people who watch TV shows also serve on juries. The *CSI* effect, however, has never been empirically proven to be true, in part because it's impossible to prove exactly how people come to believe what they believe and what specific factors may influence their unconscious world-building.[6] This isn't a case where fiction is telling a lie and real-world courtroom experience or news media is telling the truth, but a case where both reality and fiction are giving the same lie. It's hard for most of us to grasp the difference between fiction and reality when both appear to agree, and both are wrong.

Historically, most anxiety over fiction has been pointed toward the popular taste for the obviously unreal, like romantic fantasies or science fiction (with, as we've seen, special anxiety about who gets to participate in those genres and what messages are propagated). But I've so far largely neglected the kind of popular media that's supposed to be set in the real world, aka the given world.

Beyond terms like "the *CSI* effect" or "copaganda," it's rare to hear this type of fiction treated as especially dangerous. I've left discussion of this sort of thing nearly to the end, however, because I think "like-true" fiction has some unique qualities that make it different from clearly established fiction, and almost represents a separate problem entirely. Any story that purports to be about the "real world," and especially the kind that depicts real institutions such as the legal system, hospitals, and government bodies, can end up selling "truths" that are actually fictions, especially when they comport with popular nonfiction narratives. As C. S. Lewis put it in 1961: "Adults are not deceived by science fiction; they can be deceived by the stories in the women's magazines."[7]

And when something deceives us by purporting to be genuinely "real"—based on true events that happened to actual people, or could have happened to actual people, we tend to give them more weight: we think of them as truth in a fiction jacket. This problem bleeds over into related half-fictions like true crime and government conspiracy theories, which dip in and out of reality, applying the techniques of fiction to real life. What connects all these types of fiction and half fiction is that they're often treated *like* reality, and touted for their "like-true" qualities, and sometimes fervently believed in as if they were true, as if reality looked like that.

The most useful term for this effect is "dramatic conditioning," a phrase that was coined by maritime safety expert Mario Vittone. In a 2010 blog post that has since gone viral and is still regularly reprinted by *Slate* at the start of beach season, Vittone explained that there's a huge difference between the way drowning is portrayed in pop culture, especially on TV, and what it looks like in reality.[8] On-screen, drowning people usually splash around and yell for help, but in real life, that rarely happens; thanks to something called "the Instinctive Drowning Response," people who are drowning physically can't raise their arms or call for help.

Children have drowned, often within a few rescuable feet, because their parents had an inaccurate picture in their heads—thanks to movies and TV—of what a dangerous situation is supposed to look like.

The police have long relied on the deliberate inaccuracy of dramatic conditioning; the shows they fund are often constructed around a false sense of actual reality.[9] *Dragnet* effectively inaugurated the cop-show genre, first as a radio show, and then as a 1951 TV drama with direct financial support and advice from the LAPD. The show purported to be about police work as it really happened, and opened with a declaration of absolute realism: "Ladies and gentlemen, the story you are about to see is true."[10] It wasn't remotely true of course—if anything, the sober, principled *Dragnet* cops were an ironic inversion of the famously corrupt LAPD of the era—but the construction of "truth" helped burnish the LAPD's image. The fact of *Dragnet* being deliberate and constructed propaganda doesn't mean that viewers literally believed the show was "true" in the sense of being "real," like a documentary; after the opening line, *Dragnet* is obviously a TV drama with actors. But the suggestion of being true or "like true" always lends the fictional an extra seriousness and importance: it requires less overt suspension of disbelief and is therefore more immediately believable.

The later, trashier *Law and Order* shows followed *Dragnet*'s lead, sometimes basing episodes on ripped-from-the-headlines cases and filming in the grittiest parts of real cities. *Law and Order: SVU*, one of the most popular and longest-running TV dramas of all time, begins every episode by describing the titular NYPD unit's mission and concluding: "These are their stories." This framing is deliberate: these *are* their stories, in the present tense. Like *Dragnet*, we know it's a drama, but it's framed as if we're watching live unscripted reality.

Mainstream American TV is silly with procedurals and stories "about" reality—not to mention reality TV—and cop shows are especially dominant. Of the ten most popular new and returning broadcast shows in the 2022–23 season, half were about the police, and four of the other five were medical, firefighting, and legal dramas (the rebooted *Quantum Leap* was the lone sci-fi exception).[11] In terms of their portrayal of actual lived reality, cop shows are really not much different from science fiction: most police procedurals take place in a world where dangerous criminals are everywhere and only a well-armed and respected cadre of officers and prosecutors can stop them. This consistent representation of cops as heroic and successful is belied by statistical reality, where the police commit one in every twenty gun homicides in the United States and murder Black people at disproportionate and disturbing rates.[12] These killings are happening at the same time that, according to the FBI's own data, the police clearance rate for the murders they are supposed to be investigating has hit historic lows: not even half of the murders committed in the United States are solved.[13] Sex crimes are notoriously underinvestigated, as are thefts, and crimes of any sort against Black women are far less likely to receive real police attention.[14] But if you didn't already know this, you won't get it from fiction: nothing on broadcast TV—where the cops solve a murder or catch a vicious rapist every hour of every week—will tell you otherwise. And that's the result of deliberate actions taken by the police to finance and advise shows that will make them look more powerful, more impressive, and more effective to the public at large. These official consultants know quite well what policing is really like: they are spinning fantasies of heroism on purpose. The police and other institutions try to fool us for a reason. Dramatic conditioning has a clear return on investment.

But at the same time, dramatic conditioning doesn't deceive everybody to the same degree. A well-designed 2015 study of the effects of entertainment on public perceptions of law enforcement found that Black people are less likely than white people to think that cop shows are true or "like true." According to the same study, Black people are also less likely to believe that police use justified force against recalcitrant suspects or that law enforcement officials are effective at catching criminals in real life. But of course, Black people are more likely than white people to have had direct experience with the police, and especially with the violent and unhelpful end of policing.[15] Direct knowledge and professional expertise can be effective inoculants against misleading stories about reality: nobody who's ever been at the wrong end of faulty forensic evidence or works for organizations like the Innocence Project could be fooled, as I was, by *CSI*. When you know from personal or professional experience that something portrayed as "real" or "real-like" on TV isn't real at all, that forensic hair analysis is bunk or that doctors in a real hospital absolutely wouldn't host a prom? with their patients??? (this happened on an episode of *Grey's Anatomy*), then you can't be fooled by a fictional depiction of it. Expertise of one sort or another will always be an effective shield against dramatic conditioning. A lifeguard knows what drowning looks like, and what it doesn't. A medieval historian isn't likely to watch an inaccurate medieval bloodfest movie and conclude, "Wow, I guess that's what the Middle Ages were really like."

But nobody is a subject expert in everything, and we all invariably fill in the blanks in our understanding of reality with what we encounter in fiction, and especially what we see on TV (since seeing a moving image of something on screen often makes us feel like we "saw" it in real life). Still, fiction *is* fiction: accurately representing reality isn't in the job description. It's generally considered the business of journalism and nonfiction to represent reality, especially when it comes to important public institutions like government and the police. The largely sensationalism-driven news media has often engaged in its own forms of copaganda, dutifully repeating police statements as facts and failing to emphasize the inconsistencies inherent in a lot of police "science," including forensics.[16] Journalistic ethics really should bar such pathetic deference to power, as TV production ethics should bar the use of police assistance on cop shows, but until such behavior is disincentivized by professional or legal codes, the police are going to keep getting away with it.[17]

A lot of writing about cop shows tends to imply, if not outright state, that fiction about "real" things has a moral and political responsibility to accurately represent reality, especially when it comes to oft-misrepresented and mythologized institutions such as law and government, since mythologizing them can cause real harm to real people. As always, I'm skeptical of censorship as something that can be applied wisely or for good purposes, but when it comes to this kind of supposedly realistic fiction, I do tend to pause. Drowning is hardly the only situation in which dramatic conditioning can be dangerous; white people going around calmly believing that real-life cops are just like the crime-solving action heroes they see on TV can easily take these factually wrong beliefs into the voting booth and the jury pool. And the police themselves are seduced by their own media portrayal: in a 2019 survey, over a quarter of officers said they were attracted to law enforcement because of how cool it looked on TV.[18] The gap between the fictional presentation of crime and its actual reality easily results in a knee-jerk public respect for police as the thin blue line between civilization and barbarity, and the police's knee-jerk respect for themselves coupled with rage at any hint of disrespect. Journalistic portrayals of real-life cops have tended to mirror the techniques of fiction, grafting police officers with magical qualities only possible in stories, and real situations with the conventions of fantasy. The bullet strikes, of its own will.[19]

But again, not *everyone* is consistently fooled; not everybody believes every piece of copaganda on sight, and, as we see with fascist art, there's a lot of willing belief in play. The combination of dramatic conditioning and willing belief can be found in the reaction to plenty of other stories that fall under the umbrella of "realistic" fiction: for example *The West Wing*, a show that represents politicians mainly as fast-talking selfless public servants, resulted in many viewers choosing to believe that the show was true, or "like true," or even though it wasn't true it *should* be true. An entire generation of Democratic political operatives thought they could make *The West Wing* really happen, only to be desperately disappointed by the reality of governing. No amount of Aaron Sorkin snark and quotes from Marcus Aurelius could sway political opponents in real life, just like no amount of cop shows starring ever-braver officers and ever-more-diabolical murderers can actually result in higher clearance rates for real-life crimes. Reality is something qualitatively different from fiction, and fiction is only dangerous when we don't respect that difference—when we forget that it serves a fundamentally different purpose and appeals to different needs.

As crime clearance rates go down, the number of crime shows seems to go up: the copaganda increases in fervor and in laziness. I can't keep up with it, or tell one show from another. Ads promote each show with the same debauched primitiveness, the same childish desperation. A recent ad for the popular *FBI* show included the line "there's nothing more important than putting the bad guys away" while an ad for *NCIS: Hawai'i* confidently declared, "Case closed, bad guys in jail." Another ad for an *FBI* spin-off showed a very handsome officer saying to a beautiful woman, "Someone's got to get the bad guys, sweetheart."[20] These actors could be kids playing cops and robbers for all the seriousness and complexity of their supposedly realistic shows. But nonetheless, these shows still enter many people's consciousness as a picture of what reality is *like*, or should be like, or close enough anyway.

As always, the question isn't "Why are *other people* foolish?" or "Why are *other people* fooled?" We are all foolish depending on the circumstances, and we are all fooled from time to time by stories that pretend to be real but aren't. But I'm curious why so many of us stick around for police procedurals and other deceptively "real" fictions, even though we know they're treacherous, even though we know they're poor guides to reality. Plenty of people are aware of copaganda, whether because they've experienced police brutality or only read about it, and yet a huge number of people in the United States and around the world still watch police procedurals. Many of us are aware that it may be risky to cross reality and fiction, and yet we still enjoy media that crosses reality and fiction. This kind of storytelling—whether it's deliberate propaganda encouraged by the government or just fun fiction with a breezy relationship with the facts—can create, in the aggregate, an unconscious image of reality that isn't actually true. Yet many of us still enjoy this picture, even while knowing there's a possibility that it could actually be bad for us.

To fully understand how and why these various forms of "realistic" "like true" fictions can be risky, I want to examine, in some detail, what makes them compelling to us in the first place. We may have gaps in our knowledge of reality, but I don't think we turn to police procedurals or true crime or bureaucratic soaps like *The West Wing* because we're trying to fill intellectual gaps. We're trying to fill emotional gaps, and there's a particular fulfillment that we only get from narrativizing reality, from the satisfaction of familiar procedure and familiar if incorrect facts, from reducing public institutions and individuals into something we can easily grasp. This, I think, holds the key to why this kind of story takes up so much space in most of our lives, and why we sometimes choose to let it stand in for reality.

The Consolations of Copaganda

Dragnet may have been the first modern cop show, but copaganda really originates from the half-realistic, half-romantic world of detective stories. The modern form of the detective story is another repetitive romantic hybrid, in this case blending the bloody genre of nineteenth-century "sensation" novels with a certain clinical and "realistic" detachment. The popularity of sensation novels, especially among women, caused another literary moral panic in nineteenth-century Britain; the new detective novel, set in solid reality and relying on logical reasoning, was supposed to satisfy the public taste for violent literature in a safer, less emotional way. According to historian Kate Summerscale's lovely book *The Suspicions of Mr. Whicher*, detective novels also served to resolve the previously dangerous and unsavory image of the police detective into a man that the public could trust.[21] The great fictional detective was (and still is) nearly always a man—a self-assured, rational genius who can tell the ashes of a Hetlock cigar from those of a Shayfield at a single glance.[22] Sherlock Holmes was really an early *CSI* guy, and every bit as bullshit. But the bullshit is part of the appeal: or specifically the confidence we have in the bullshit, and the confidence that Holmes has in himself. A detective can't tell the difference between two different kinds of cigar ashes just by looking at them, any more than a real forensic tech can tell the difference between two hairs under a microscope. But it's comforting to think that someone could, that somebody out there knows what they're doing: that the truth itself is knowable.

The Holmes-inflected detective story tradition soon spread from the United Kingdom to the United States and everywhere else, influencing the TV procedurals that borrow their tropes from—and are often based directly on—these novels. A 2022 report in *The Conversation* suggests that crime novels may be "the most global of literary genres," and many countries produce tons of their own crime TV dramas and movies in addition to importing British and American ones.[23] It's tempting to find a sweeping historical or sociological explanation for this popularity: an effect of Anglo-American imperialism, maybe, though detective novels weren't a significant part of the CIA's cultural playbook, and the tradition of investigation stories doesn't derive solely from western sources. Another possible culprit could be global social instability: detective stories (and police procedurals) provide a sense of logical stability and security in uncertain times. But Scandinavian countries, which generally rank highest in indices of social stability and happiness, are absolutely wild for detective stories, and have been for decades. Iceland, a country obsessed with murder mysteries, probably has more crime novelists per capita than actual crimes.[24]

If the detective story and the police procedural work on a global and personal level, it may be simply because we all face fear and uncertainty from time to time: we're all subject to mortality, loss, and the inexplicable cruelties of the universe. A fictional detective solves a case with a satisfying click of absolute certainty we rarely get from everyday life. Summerscale concludes *The Suspicions of Mr. Whicher* by suggesting that "the purpose of detective investigations, real and fictional," is "to transform sensation, horror, and grief, into a puzzle, and then to solve the puzzle, to make it go away."[25] This is true for real *and* fictional cases; even in the rare instance where a real-life murder is properly investigated, the act of putting "bad guy in jail" rarely provides closure. It's impossible to answer for all the social forces and individual aberrations that lead to terrible crimes like murder, not to mention how we can be so vulnerable to one another in the first place. And so the figure of the heroic detective cop—in fiction and reality—stands in for someone who can solve the puzzle of reality, someone who can make us feel safe.

When asked in June 2020 about the discrepancy between the

heroic cops on *SVU* and the reality of policing, Warren Leight—
SVU's then current showrunner—said that the show is a fantasy
and viewers understand that. "I think the audience is sophisticated
enough," he said in a podcast interview, "to know this is not the
reality of day-to-day life in the world of sexual assault." The most
sophisticated audience members, he added, are sexual assault survi-
vors themselves, many of whom have contacted *SVU* star Mariska
Hargitay over the years, expressing the wish that their rapes had
been investigated in the same way that Hargitay doggedly pursues
each case on the show.[26] Whether less informed and less sophisticated viewers are fooled by dramatic conditioning into believing
that sexual assault cases really are something that most police take
seriously, and investigate thoroughly, the show's fundamental attraction is its unreality, not its "these are their stories" projection of
factual truth. Viewers love *SVU for* its falseness (and also Ice-T's
line delivery, which is flawless). The appeal lies precisely in the fact
that we *know* we're watching something that isn't real: a fantasy
world where justice actually exists and authority figures care when
bad things happen to us.

Nonetheless, the fantasies of justice these stories provide weigh
heavily on our actual reality, especially since there are few alternatives.[27] Leight has claimed that he and other showrunners have
tried pitching Innocence Project–type dramas, where scrappy defense attorneys try to free the wrongfully convicted. I'm sure this
would make for great and unusual television—one that could still
console the viewer with the fantasy of justice and the episodic satisfaction of the mystery resolved—and yet, per Leight, producers
always refuse. It's hard to say whether this is because producers
are unwilling to take risks on a tried-and-true formula, or whether
they're just ideologically opposed to a crime procedural that would
decenter the police. (The somewhat paradoxical capitalist aversion
to potentially unprofitable risk-taking and conservative ideology

are natural allies.) An Innocence Project show, Leight added, especially wouldn't work in the Dick Wolf–produced *Law and Order* universe: it's not "part," he said, "of Dick's brand."

Other showrunners have tried to create TV outside the hero cop narrative exemplified by Dick and his brand. *The Wire* is often touted as a satisfactory alternative to the false realism of the typical procedural: David Simon's prestige drama centers both police and criminals, framing each season around a different set of systemic problems that plague the city of Baltimore. Sitting through all five uneven seasons of *The Wire* is often touted as a sort of personal political achievement, a sign of liberal bona fides. (The well-meaning white progressive who excitedly asks, "Have you seen *The Wire???*" has been a cliché for years).[28] Investigative journalist Taya Graham, a longtime Baltimorean who covers police brutality and the criminal justice system, has a different opinion of the show. "It genuinely hurts my heart," she told me, "to see smart, politically engaged people view *The Wire* as a realistic and compassionate view of Baltimore city."[29] Baltimore, unlike New York or L.A., has little fictional representation, especially on TV; *The Wire's* unvarnished aesthetic and its emphasis on systems over individuals suggests a gritty realism, and matches the common contemporary presumption that gritty realism naturally possesses the proper level of vraisemblance. But the show isn't "real" in any meaningful sense, even if dramatic conditioning might delude non-Baltimoreans into thinking so: it's just a work of fiction, and one that made Simon rich and famous. Graham points out that many women in *The Wire*, especially Black women, are poorly written stereotypes, and many plot points (such as the Baltimore police department being partially defunded by a kindly mayor) not only didn't happen but simply couldn't have happened under Baltimore's real-life leadership. "[Simon] appropriated our histories and struggles and wrote a fictive universe," Graham said. "He found a way to monetize the poverty and despair of the people of my city and gave nothing back to us."[30]

The Wire, for all its fine aesthetic qualities and complicated (male) characters, is just a TV show; for all its efforts to be "like true," it's really just another fantasy. And that's absolutely fine—all fiction, no matter how much it resembles gritty reality (or our accepted image of true reality as gritty) is always going to be fantasy to some degree. The problem is solely the extent to which these stories are framed *not* as fantasies but as reality, and how that framing contributes to a false view of what real-life police work is like through its falseness. In June 2020, after the murder of George Floyd, cultural critic Alyssa Rosenberg called for a shutdown of all police movies and TV shows regardless of their orientation. "There are always gaps between reality and fiction," she wrote in *The Washington Post*, "but given what policing in America has too often become, Hollywood's version of it looks less like fantasy and more like complicity."[31] The semi–reality show *Cops* actually did get temporarily canceled in the summer of 2020 but soon returned.[32] The police sitcom *Brooklyn Nine-Nine* decided to run for one final season, with rewritten storylines that attempted (bravely but poorly) to address the issues raised by Black Lives Matter. I've always liked *Brooklyn Nine-Nine*, which I consider cute and unrealistic enough to count as an obvious fantasy, though journalist Steven Thrasher has argued that the show's very cuteness and zany, loveable cops make it especially good propaganda and maybe, he argues, "an even more effective form of social control than *Dragnet*."[33] Whether it was successful propaganda or not, *Brooklyn Nine-Nine* may have ended up being an ethical cop show in the end—by recognizing its own complicity in perpetuating dangerous myths about the police, and ceasing to exist.

I asked Graham what she personally thought an ethical cop show might look like, and she countered with a better question:

Who exactly would an ethical cop show be *for*? "Would police officers," she asked, "actually watch it?"[34] The public might be misled at times by fantasy, but the police are even more so; it's the police, after all, who declare that Black suspects like Michael Brown are actually demons, and it's the police whose guns can apparently fire magical self-willed bullets.[35] The police create their own hype through TV consults and press conferences, but they're the ones who choose to believe, or pretend to believe, their own hype, presumably in the hopes of willing it into reality. But this again takes us back to the matter of fascist art, and what happens when people actively choose to believe in fantasy. In situations like this, it's not about being misled through images by simple ignorance, as we see with dramatic conditioning, but about making a deliberate decision to live *inside* the dramatic condition itself: to pretend that life, real life, is a story, and that it follows narrative conventions.

Murder She Ate

If we turn to stories ("true" or otherwise) to compensate for the uncontrollability of the real world, then that's a coping mechanism; if we turn the real world into a story, then we're engaging in something much darker. This is where not knowing the difference—or not caring about the difference—between reality and fiction can become genuinely dangerous. True crime is occasionally held up as a healthy and favorable alternative to cop shows, especially since true crime stories often portray the police as the bunglers that they usually are.[36] But the audience for true crime is also notorious for a certain ghoulish attitude toward their beloved subject matter, engaging in creepy behaviors such as joking about murder victims on podcasts, or stalking real-life victims and suspects.[37] We're on tricky ground here, because an estimated 70 percent of true crime consumers are women, and women readers have so often been accused of failing to grasp the difference between fiction and reality.[38] And yet a decent number of true crime fans really *don't* seem to grasp the difference between fiction and reality, and are genuinely fucking ghoulish about it. Summerscale's description of the moral panic over women readers of sensation novels and true crime stories 150 years ago ("It was as if the domestic angel of Victorian fantasy momentarily gave way to a bloodthirsty ghoul") is echoed by contemporary headlines about the mostly female "true crime ghouls" who post AI renderings of real murdered children on TikTok.[39]

A certain number of true crime fans (of every gender) have become notorious for creating conspiracy theories about old cases and picking apart fresh murders, usually from behind the comfort of their computer screens. Once in a while, these internet detectives have helped solve real crimes, but mostly they've just hounded innocent people.[40] When four college students were brutally murdered in Moscow, Idaho, in 2022, some true crime fans investigated with enthusiasm, as if the case were a new episode of their favorite mystery show and they'd all been deputized as Sherlock Holmes. Facebook groups speculated together about whodunit; TikTokers and YouTubers turned every bloody update into engagement. The news media, in turn, played up to this audience of detective ghouls. As journalist McKay Coppins wrote in a long exposé of "murder fandom" and the Moscow killings, "Perhaps more disturbing than the vulturous reporters or the vortex of TikTok speculation was the way the media and the sleuths seemed to encourage and sustain each other—their priorities converging in a vicious ouroboros."[41] The real deaths of four college students were algorithmically beneficial for both the news media and clout-chasing true crime fans: they fed off each other.

Of course, not every person who enjoys true crime is a ghoul who can't tell the difference between fiction and reality, and not all attempts to investigate unsolved horrors are ghoulish. The HBO documentary *I'll Be Gone in the Dark* details journalist Michelle

McNamara's careful efforts to identify the Golden State Killer, who had stalked and raped women in the California area for decades and had never been caught by the police. The documentary suggests that McNamara's fascination with these crimes was partly related to a past trauma; she couldn't solve or undo what had happened to her, but she felt that if she could solve *these* crimes, she could exert control and bring closure to the Golden State Killer's victims. (McNamara ended up dying during her obsessive pursuit of the killer; her research helped identify him, some years later, as a local ex-cop.)[42] Probably this displaced desire for control and closure is closely tied to why many women are drawn to true crime: women are statistically more likely to be victims of trauma and abuse.[43] True crime also tends to overemphasize violent crimes against women, especially young and photogenic white women who were attacked by strangers—this overemphasis has been anecdotally linked (though not proved) to lead to an increase in paranoia and fear of outsiders.[44] Misleading narratives like these can end up being much more dangerous than pure fiction, especially because it's all presented as "true": true crime has half-fictional, storylike qualities but feels more plausible even than a procedural, and the feeling of delicious vulnerability coupled with fear of the other can be justified as a sensible reaction to a harsh and terrifying reality.

But none of that quite explains the ghoulishness: the choice to become involved in cases just like a fictional detective would be, which is once again hardly limited to women fans alone. If the unmet emotional needs that lie behind true crime fandom are the same as those that lie behind the love for detective stories—the quest for solved puzzles and tidy explanations, for order, safety, and control in a scary world—then why are some true crime fans so bloodthirsty about it? Why do they take investigative work outside of its received form—the book, the documentary, the podcast—and into stalking real people in real life?

What's so disturbing about murder fans (and they really are murder *fans*) is how the worst thing that can happen to somebody else can be turned into fresh juicy content for themselves.[45] And it really does become *content*, in the same way that so much fiction has been degraded into mere consumable stuff. Murder fans don't just treat murder victims and suspects as characters in a detective story, lined up in the drawing room to be accused, but as living toys to be moved or crushed or discarded. Most of us have a degree of feeling for imaginary characters; the real trick of fiction writing is to make us care about people who don't exist. But a murder fan sits in the role of the detective without any emotional connection to the other characters in the story, with no stakes and no danger other than the stakes of being proved correct and admirable and brilliant, and the danger of being embarrassed in front of fellow sleuths. And, since this a fandom and fandoms can be turned into cash, the various TikTokers and YouTubers and journalists who play to this audience function as a content-production machine, no different in form than the worst excesses of consumptive geek fandom, except for the obvious distastefulness of turning real tragedy and real people into the entertainment product of the week.

Much of internet cruelty, in any context, is the result of crushing real people into units of entertainment: not simply blurring the lines between reality and fiction but reducing both into consumable content, into Happy Meal toys for daily enjoyment.[46] This process is mediated by the simple fact that all our online engagement is found inside the same small metal boxes, and we tend to reduce everyone and everything we see to the same size. But I think it's also once again about legal judgment: our desire to solve for the guilt or innocence of our fellow human beings, to know their unknowable inner lives and judge them as we're trained to know and judge a fictional character. But whereas in American literary fiction we might still expect a three-dimensional protagonist to embody our judgment and our values, the blending of people in real life with fictional techniques tends to render them more flatly and without the potential for change. Someone is as bad, forever, as their worst social media post, which is supposedly a clue to their true and unchanging inner being. Their most casual statement is evidence in a whodunit, and we always know who's guilty.

This tendency to treat real people as characters, or worse than characters, is considerably older than postwar literary fiction or the internet: Summerscale describes it happening in the nineteenth century. *The Suspicions of Mr. Whicher* is centered on the real and publicly sensationalized 1860 murder of a young boy; the police were unable to get a conviction, but some years after the murder, the boy's older sister confessed to the crime. This launched a new wave of headlines and murder-fan consumption—did the sister really do it, and did she confess because she was really contrite, or was she only pretending to feel guilty? One Protestant minister put out a pamphlet describing the woman as a vicious and unrepentant killer: "Very cruel, very close, and very callous. And much as she was, she probably is . . . She is simply a very wicked young woman."[47] This kind of conviction about what people are actually and permanently *like*, based on what we may have read about them and a certain demotic Protestant certainty about the absoluteness of human guilt and innocence, is a form of fictionalizing people, a way of turning real human beings into consumable narratives and moral object lessons.

The practice of reducing fictional characters in fictional stories to a mere lesson in values may be annoying and critically suspect, but it's outright disturbing to do it to real people in real life. We never really know who did what, or why: we never achieve objective, unmistakable access into people's inner lives. I tend to like true crime best when it deliberately doesn't try to offer novelistic, omniscient third-person insights into real people, when it concludes that perfect knowability is for detective stories only. I especially like investigations into grifters and scammers, because there's absolutely no way to know why a real-life human being might have pretended to have cancer when they didn't, or attempted, say, to pull off a fancy music festival with no logistical support and no planning.[48] You invariably want to know, in this sort of story, what the grifter thought they were doing: whether they believed their own lies, and how deeply. But the only person who can provide insight is the grifter themselves, a known and prolific liar whose self-narrative can never be trusted. We turn to fiction to gain the types of knowledge that are impossible in real life, and sometimes, in the process, we misuse fiction by filtering reality through an unreal lens.

It could be argued that, as with copaganda, the solution here would be to create a kind of ethical true crime: narratives that embrace ambiguity, don't giggle over death, and avoid the cheap fictionalization of beginnings, middles, and ends while making it clearer to potentially stupid audience members what the differences are between reality and speculation. *The Suspicions of Mr. Whicher* and thoughtful documentaries like *I'll Be Gone in the Dark* would probably make for good examples of ethical true crime, or about as close as we can get. But probably all audience members, including me, are at least a little ghoulish about death, deceit, and distress: it's the blood that's interesting, the unsolvable puzzle of why people hurt each other, why reality can be like this. The itch to solve it, to have answers, isn't something that can be waved away by simply being more ethical about it, by being clearer about the differences between fiction and reality. The problem, as usual, isn't really with fiction at all but with reality: that it's broken and unsolvable, and it makes us itch to complete it. And for that, we sometimes entertain obvious fictions about reality, in hopes that they can someday be turned into truth.

The President's Neck Is Missing

Police procedurals rely on dramatic conditioning to rewrite reality; true crime can deceive by painting reality with the techniques of fiction, but there's also the somewhat rarer and extremely influential pop cultural blending of reality and fiction that can best be described as the aspirational lie. This is the category in which we find a show like *The West Wing*, a story that was so popular with a certain type of young enthusiastic Democratic operative that it both did and didn't permanently alter American politics. Many Democratic staffers in the twenty-first century have been "Sorkinized" by the show: they fell in love with the image of themselves as heroes who could save a damaged world through liberal bureaucracy.[49] But they also struggled to pass laws against stiff Republican opposition; they struggled to accept that turning reality into an Aaron Sorkin show, or any kind of show, is impossible.

What makes *The West Wing* weird—besides its popularity with a very specific set of upper-middle-class liberals and its dated gender and racial politics—is that its fans usually knew perfectly well that it was fiction, but tried to make it real anyway. The Obama administration was infamously crowded with bright young things who loved *The West Wing* and wanted the Obama administration to resemble what they saw on television. As an unnamed White House staffer told *Vanity Fair* in 2012, "Yes, the show was sexier, faster-paced, and more idealistic than Washington really is, but what's wrong with that? We should aspire to do big and ambitious and idealistic things in this country—even if it takes longer than one hour, or one season."[50] In theory, there's nothing wrong with fiction being aspirational: one of the things that fiction can provide is a space to imagine what doesn't exist in reality. But in the case of *The West Wing*, aspiration and inspiration went further into something like delusion, a desire to patch the problems of American political reality through the re-creation of a TV show. This desire has never been limited to staffers and politicos: a 2019 report in *The New York Times* explores how the show underwent a renaissance during the Trump years, providing many viewers with a wistful view of a reality that never existed, but was hard not to fall for.[51]

Sorkin's heroes walk fast, they talk fast, they are impossibly witty. They give speeches backgrounded with soaring music; their words have weight and meaning. Stupid opponents (leftists, women) are stunned into silence; intelligent opponents (Republicans, military men) acknowledge the importance of these words with a grudging *goddamned respect*. It's still something of an enjoyable show, I think, despite its cringey and dated moments: the dialogue is sharp, and the episodic structure carefully paced and rounded. Problems are raised and solved with a satisfying neatness through discussion and compromise, not to mention statements of soaring principles about freedom and goodness.

One of the common truisms of the 2020s is that we live in a fractured reality, where different groups of people can't agree what's real and what's really happening. *The West Wing*, for all that it's fiction, also represents one of those fractures, a glimpse into a particular imaginative construction of the United States as a flawed but ultimately noble place. *The West Wing*'s reality isn't attempting to be true, or even "like true," operating more like a belief somewhat around the level of a religious faith: that the world could be like this, and that well-meaning idealistic people can get us there. As a number of leftist critics have pointed out, there was always a hard limit to *The West Wing*'s idealism and utopianism. Writer Luke Savage commented that "after two terms in the White House, [President] Bartlet's gang of hyper-educated, hyper-competent politicos do not seem to have any transformational policy achievements whatsoever. Even in their most unconstrained and idealized political fantasies, liberals manage to accomplish nothing."[52] There was no real governing in the show, only the image of power and good governance upheld by all those soaring words and music. It was a portrayal of reality if reality were an aesthetic only; reality if it weren't real. In the end, the show says much more about the unreality of a certain perspective than about the world as it actually exists.

Still, *The West Wing* made gestures toward realism: it embedded itself firmly in the real world and in the expected constructions of realistic fiction. Characters were flawed, well rounded, aspirational; they taught and received lessons about virtue. The reaction to the show ended up being much like a real-life *Don Quixote*, as *West Wing* fans treated the supposed realism of the show like actual reality and went into politics expecting rational, hard-minded but decent opponents, a respected opposition written in an appropriately nuanced, lit-fic sort of way. But the reality of the Republican Party, undergoing a far-right radicalization throughout the Obama years and beyond, was anything but that, and Democratic attempts at compromise and bipartisanship were mostly met with hatred and loathing. Trump Republicans don't resemble the tough but fair foes of *The West Wing* in the slightest. Their motives have proved to be more elemental, maybe even medieval: power and cruelty.

America Is Canceled

The far right, looking at the world through the fractured lens of an entirely different reality, doesn't generally see nuance and the power of American decency; it sees a violent struggle for power. The QAnon conspiracy theory, which has captured a frighteningly large percentage of the Republican imagination, views the U.S. government as the setting for a titanic fantasy battle between good and evil.[53] The story has never really made any sense—Trump has somehow always been battling "the deep state," even when he was commander in chief of it—but that doesn't really matter. QAnon is not a good fiction; its primary writer, the anonymous poster known only as Q, seems to have permanently disappeared.[54] The movement has always been on the cusp of something happening: Hillary Clinton's imminent arrest, the resurrection of JFK, the fall of the deep state.[55] In a way it's the opposite of episodic television, with every plot point held at the peak edge of tension at all times—like *Lost*, really, and just as likely to have a disappointing ending for its fans. But as with any popular fiction, it's serving a purpose for now, giving reality a shape for those who desperately want to see it. Conspiracy theories are always a form of fiction in one way or another, a narrative about reality that makes more sense than formless chaos.

When reality feels formless, scary, and dangerous, it's not surprising that many people try to impose patterns, locating the dramatic condition in reality. Few of us manage to understand our lives without any sense of narrative, especially without a narrative for our larger political reality. Since COVID, at least, it's been common to joke online about how "this season of America has really jumped the shark."[56] It does feel implausible, especially lately, that so many political events could happen without the presence of some kind of overarching narrative, whether it's the soft utopianism of Aaron Sorkin or the terrifying apocalypticism promised by QAnon. Mike Rothschild, a journalist who has written a book about QAnon, commented that "2024 could be the series finale for America as we've known it. It's all too easy to imagine a scenario where state legislatures are given the green light by SCOTUS to throw out results they don't like, nobody having any idea who won the election, and civil war kicking off."[57] Regardless of what actually takes place, the framing of this is interesting: the future understood through the structure of a TV show, the primary way we've been dramatically conditioned to understand reality. *The series finale of America*. Even that has a feeling of safety and comfort about it: after all, when one show is canceled, there's always another to watch.

The Fascination of What's Difficult

As usual, we don't really have a problem with the fictional; we have a problem with the real. Reality is unsatisfying and scary; fiction about reality fixes those problems. It's much easier for us to navigate reality if we can reduce it to simple, digestible patterns: if our public institutions and our fellow human beings can be flattened into immediately legible images of good and bad. I don't think this can be easily resolved, even through responsible journalism, even through the recitation of statistics and lived experiences, even by questioning yourself as you engage with a story that bills itself as true, or "like true." Nonetheless, I think it's always useful to ask yourself whether you're falling for a convenient narrative that feels true but may not be so. Does something like this—forensic hair analysis, identifying a killer through a single Facebook post, making a big dramatic speech that convinces the other side, inventing a giant secret conspiracy that explains the entire world—make sense in real life? And if not, what does it mean that you still want to believe in a certain picture of given reality?

No matter how careful you are, it's still likely that you'll be deceived at some point. Governments facilitate propaganda; individuals tell fake stories online. I've been taken in by more than one bullshit fabulation, and I'm guessing I will be again. As our shared reality likely continues to fracture, there will probably be more perceived versions of reality, more difficulty in figuring out what's invented and what's real, and what any of that means. In the end, I think we mainly seek reaffirmation of what we already believe: we're attracted to stories that fit our preexisting narratives, whatever they may be. I was raised in a logical, liberal, scientifically oriented environment, a "trust science" kind of community, so of course I liked the forensics show. Despite having been misled by it, and by the public perception of forensics more generally, I still think it's probably a good idea to rely on scientific evidence in a generalized, trust-but-verify-as-best-you-can way. Distrusting everything only leads people toward conspiracies or toward another kind of absolute belief: yes, this one narrative of reality may be false, but a different one is completely true.

Conspiracy theories normally remain on the fringe, contributing relatively little to the creation of popular fiction (they're usually too busy insisting on themselves as *true*-true to spawn much in the way of novels and TV shows).[58] But there are some exceptions. *Sound of Freedom*, an action flick supposedly based on the life of anti-child-trafficking advocate Tim Ballard, was billed upon arrival as "the QAnon movie."[59] The movie, like Ballard's highly fictionalized life story, portrays Ballard as a white savior rescuing kidnapped children sold into sex slavery by villainous brown people.[60] This film doesn't even remotely depict what real child trafficking is like, and it exaggerates Ballard's real-life attempted heroics along the lines of any action movie. And yet it opens, as real-ish stories like this so often do, with "based on a true story." As film critic Miles Klee has pointed out, the expected audience for *Sound of Freedom* wouldn't have a problem with this obvious bit of dishonesty: the movie's "hackneyed white savior narrative" and the "wildly immature assumption that abused and traumatized children go right back to normal once the bad guys are in handcuffs" are, in Klee's view, "the whole appeal."[61] The expected audience wants the story of the white-hero-vigilante-unofficial-cop fed back to them. They're choosing to believe in this version of the dramatic condition: they're seeking it out on purpose, and making a particular choice to believe its pretended truth.

Interestingly enough, for all that *Sound of Freedom* is a very politically motivated movie, it doesn't contain a direct call to political action. Or, more specifically, it concludes only by asking viewers to donate money so that other people can see it (a request that itself appears to have been a scam, worthy of its own true crime podcast).[62]

Despite the fact that the film was clearly made to push a particular narrative about child trafficking, it's mainly interested in making money off that narrative and that engagement. This is generally true of copaganda, as well as other half-real, half-fictional forms: they may be constructed on purpose to push particular narratives, but they also exist to get you to pay attention to them, meaning, they exist to make money. These stories might be created, to some degree, to affect reality—all fiction does affect reality in one way or another—but they also exist to replicate themselves. For any work of art to exist in this current iteration of capitalist realism, it has to be expected, first and foremost, to appeal to an existing consumer demographic; for any narrative to be promoted it must be intended to make a buck.

I think that's important to keep in mind as we turn to the final question about fiction, which is what is to be done about it, and how much can we expect of art and entertainment to fix our problems with reality, especially under our current economic and political system. Some of our problems may in fact be unsolvable; reality has always been disappointingly unscripted. But it's still the case that our current set of political problems is a very frightening one, and the level of fear and uncertainty about the future is much more extreme than usual, especially as—thanks to rising fascism and climate change—we face the shivering breakdown of the real. It's easy to suggest that if people just consumed better and more accurate narratives about reality, they'd be more equipped to handle it. But it's less easy to determine what those healthy fictional narratives are, and what problems we can realistically expect them to solve for us.

CHAPTER EIGHT

How to Blow Up Reality

W hen the climate change allegory *Don't Look Up* debuted on Netflix in December 2021, it was imperative—per its filmmakers—for audiences not only to watch it, but to love it. Director Adam McKay insisted on social media that unhappy critics of his film must have lacked "even a small ember of anxiety about climate change" and were like "a robot viewing a love story."[1] It's normal for any artist to feel defensive about their work, and especially normal for artists to imagine their critics as unfeeling hunks of metal, but in the case of *Don't Look Up*, the creators made especially serious demands. Since climate change is an underrepresented element in fiction, both in visual media and in novels, any movie that addresses such an important subject couldn't be a target of aesthetic concerns, for example whether the run time is too long or whether a film about a meteor striking the earth really works as an effective allegory for a slow-moving man-made ecological crisis. Instead, the movie—or so its makers insisted—had to be judged solely on the level of its political importance, meaning its immediate relevance and its potential to impact reality. And since climate change is arguably the most important issue of our time, one that interpenetrates and exacerbates all preexisting social and political concerns, the free exercise of personal taste in a situation like this could be literally deadly: refusing to watch a climate movie, or honestly disliking it, might kill us all.[2]

I didn't enjoy *Don't Look Up*. My objections were political as well as aesthetic, the political being so often inextricable from the aesthetic. The movie casts the central barrier to tackling climate change as a fundamental problem of *awareness*. Human beings (Americans specifically—in the film basically all human beings are Americans, with the rest of the world existing largely offscreen) are too distracted by media and gadgetry and depraved public institutions to simply *look up* and realize there's a problem. Greedy billionaires and corrupt public officials are also to blame, but they're at least aware that the oncoming meteor (i.e., symbolic climate crisis) is quite real: the core issue, as the title of the film suggests, is the broader public's refusal to *look up* and view the crisis in the face. And therefore the solution to climate change is exactly the one meta-suggested by the film, and by so much recent overtly ideological art regardless of political orientation: watch this movie to raise awareness, since awareness is all we need.

But *is* awareness all we need? And if "raising awareness" is the only noble and appropriate role for fictional stories in such terrible times, then is any other goal—such as aesthetic ambition—just a signal of outdated privilege, of a cozy and conceited art for art's sake? No work of art is apolitical, as I've said before, but the kind of fiction that's designed to raise awareness—that instructs people to look up—doesn't just *have* a political point of view. This kind of art is supposed to also *do* politics: it's supposed to lead directly to political action. And there's a kind of implicit math involved there, a logical progression between the awareness and the act. It's much like the formula used in the Underpants Gnomes episode of *South*

Park; the gnomes' plan is: "collect underpants + ? = profit!" while the formula for fiction seems to be "raise awareness + ? = problem solved!"[3]

I'm sure that fiction is always going to have some role in "raising awareness" just like any other form of media, and certainly the construction of reality in fiction has at least some effect on how we regard reality in real life. But it's still not clear to me what's supposed to happen at the "?" stage of this imagined gnomic formula, how reading or watching political art is meant to translate into action. And it's likewise unclear to me how much responsibility fiction has to make the "?" part happen. Many people did watch *Don't Look Up*: for all its mixed reviews from critics, the film was relatively well liked by audiences (78 percent on Rotten Tomatoes) and per Netflix's own numbers it was one of the company's most popular original films.[4] Neither source is completely reliable, but let's take it at face value that many people around the world did watch *Don't Look Up* and enjoyed it. It doesn't matter: climate change still remains an inescapable reality. The comet has already struck the earth.

A 2023 study found that the planet is "well outside of the safe operating space for humanity," having broken six of the nine boundaries necessary for sustained human life.[5] The year 2023, in which I wrote most of this manuscript, was the hottest year on record, and 2024 will almost certainly be worse.[6] On the morning I originally drafted this paragraph, an unthinkable amount of rain in Derna, Libya, overwhelmed the local infrastructure; the resulting flood swept whole neighborhoods out to sea, killing thousands of people.[7] By the time this book will be published, the Derna floods will likely have been forgotten outside North Africa, superseded by a hundred more recent climate tragedies: forest fires, murderous heat, blizzards in places that don't get blizzards, rain in desert nations that never see rain like this. Are we really, at this point, not *aware?* And is a film like *Don't Look Up* to blame for *only* attempting to raise awareness, for not solving climate change on its own, for not being dangerous enough to change reality?[8] Political fiction may no longer possess the occasional power it once had in the centuries before the age of mass media; raising awareness for the sake of changing reality may no longer be a service that fiction can provide. Lack of awareness is not a twenty-first-century problem. We are drowning in it.

The final problem to tackle when assessing whether fiction is dangerous requires us to first examine our deepest assumptions about what art is, and does, and what our own responsibilities are toward it and toward real-world problems. In fact, fiction is dangerous in part because we tend to outsource our political problems to it, and to hold fictional representations accountable for not fixing our reality as it presently stands. The 2022 independent climate film *How to Blow Up a Pipeline* has not, as of the time of this writing, directly inspired anyone to blow up an oil pipeline. I did think it was a pretty good movie, however, and that its relative goodness matters—not because better aesthetics necessarily make for better propaganda that might convince climate skeptics and deniers (given the constant weird weather at this point, the deniers are willfully dishonest rather than ignorant or misinformed) but because an honest and brave artistic attempt to represent reality is a meaningful end in itself. In the case of *How to Blow Up a Pipeline*, the filmmakers seem interested in the specific reality of various types of flawed and interesting idealists who might end up drawn to climate terrorism. Imagining complicated realities is what fiction does, whether through real-world settings or refracted through unreal, romantic forms. And whether it does that imagining well—convincingly, beautifully, honestly—may be all we can really ask of it.

To that end, we can also ask why there's so little climate fiction of any kind in any medium: not because we need it at this point to raise awareness of what we can see out our windows or on the news, and what only ideological stubbornness could lead us to deny, but because it's a lacuna in the representation of reality. You can count the films about climate change, including the two I already mentioned, without taking off your shoes. On TV, the absence is even more violent: we have all those supposedly "like-true" cop shows and not a single dedicated climate thriller.[9] (This kind of show, much like an Innocence Project series, seems easy to imagine along the lines of conventional genre formulas. Picture a climate procedural about brave first responders, traveling from place to place, handsomely rescuing people from floods and fires—a "monster of the week" show, in effect, but for monstrous weather, strung along by a couple larger story arcs and some will-they-won't-they sexual tension. You can have that one for free, CBS.) For the most part, big-media film and TV companies have been disinterested in climate change; we might get an environmental allegory in films like *Don't Look Up*, or in big-budget action franchises like the Aquamans and the Avatars, but allegory is often the form you rely on when it's politically risky to be direct about what you mean (e.g., Rod Serling's attempted Emmett Till allegory and his later *Twilight Zone*).[10] Since climate change is a real, omnipresent, and inescapable problem, there's no need to hide it behind a meteor, mer-people, aliens, or anything like that. We could just address it directly—but we usually don't.

The enforced "climate silence" in fictional storytelling has been noted, with frustration, by activists and journalists.[11] The usual excuse provided is that climate change is a buzzkill: stories that depict apocalyptic devastation just bum people out and make them feel hopeless. But I don't think that's the entire issue. When we're forced to acknowledge the reality of climate change in fictional storytelling, we're also forced to address larger problems with the way that our reality has been constructed, both on the page and off it. Specifically, we're forced to grapple with the fact that centuries of capitalism and imperialism have brought us to this terrible point, and that these forces have also inflected storytelling, especially the idea of the "real."

In his short, excellent nonfiction work *The Great Derangement*, novelist Amitav Ghosh studies the strange failure of fiction—and literary fiction in particular—to reckon with the living reality of climate change. It's true that there's an increasingly robust prose genre of what's usually called climate fiction, or cli-fi, but, as Ghosh points out, cli-fi remains adjacent to science fiction. This categorization is fine from a marketing point of view—science fiction is no longer disreputable, and climate novels are often taken seriously as works of art—but it's not fine in the sense that there's no ontological reason for climate fiction to be separate from literary realism, which is supposedly the record of *this* real world, where every summer is the hottest on record and fire tornadoes roam the woods.[12] The absence of climate events—catastrophic hurricanes, floods, fires—from most realist novels of the past two decades is a kind of soft denialism, an *over there*, with events always happening somewhere else to someone else in the near future, not here and not now. Climate change may be new, physically present, and tremendously modern—yet it doesn't belong in the pages of the realist novel as we understand it.

The problem, as Ghosh sees it, is that the parameters of reality demanded by the western novel—parameters that have been adopted worldwide, including in India, where he grew up—have always been deliberately, excessively narrow. At the birth of the western novel, the literary imagination was reconstructed around the idea of bourgeois stability and the lack of improbable events. Therefore, the depiction of natural disasters like sudden storms and floods can feel, as Ghosh says, like "a contrivance of last resort": an improbable romantic coincidence, lacking in that all-important vraisemblance.[13] The appearance of a natural disaster in a story—and in reality—suggests that the world itself is *alive* and has some degree of agency: that the natural world, as Ghosh writes with awe, "is [itself] a protagonist."[14] Improbable events, a wild and living earth—these have long been the properties of fantasy and magical realism, not literary realism where a windmill is only ever just a windmill. If fiction is the story of *other people*, then the most extreme—and extraordinary—form of otherness must be the non-human itself.

The rise and respectability of climate fiction, even as it remains a separate genre, is itself part and parcel of the victory of the nerds; it *had* to start becoming respectable to depict the improbable, as the improbable increasingly occurs all around us. We have all sort of new mini-genres now, such as the "speculative epic," which critic and novelist Lincoln Michel has described as the kind of world- and time-spanning novel that crosses different centuries and story-lines.[15] Most of these novels are considered literary or literary adjacent, such as Emily St. John Mandel's *Sea of Tranquility* and Hanya Yanagihara's *To Paradise*. But famed science fiction writer Kim Stanley Robinson's novel *The Ministry for the Future* is also included: set in 2025 and onward, the book follows a plethora of characters as they successfully battle climate change through a number of political and scientific strategies. Whether or not the novel is successful as a novel (the climate journalist David Roberts called *The Ministry for the Future* "a bunch of position papers & blog posts & white papers, lightly fictionalized, and I mean lightly"), it was widely hailed as one of the most important books of the year and, according to *Vox's* Ezra Klein, required reading for "policymakers and citizens" alike.[16]

Here, as with climate films, climate novels and speculative epics are largely marketed on the grounds of their usefulness, which may be another clue as to why they remain marginal or, at least, usually categorized as something other than unmarked literary fiction. The criterion of "usefulness" places particular demands on both individual works of fiction and their audiences: engaging with these stories is supposed to be politically important, aesthetically unpleasant, wearying moral work. These novels' flaws or virtues as works of art are less important than their potential power to change our minds for the better, to save the world that we've destroyed. In Michel's survey of the speculative epic, he does praise the aesthetic qualities of several novels, but concludes his summary with the usual touting of the use-value of these books to "help us process and understand the issues we face. And if we're lucky, they can help inspire a better future." It's interesting—and illuminating—that Michel chose to phrase this as a matter of luck and not certainty. The demand for more climate fiction is generally portrayed as a matter of inputs and outputs: if sufficient inputs of right-minded literature, then sufficient outputs of right-minded action. But the truth is that we only *might*, if we're lucky, get that right-minded action, with the implication that we'd better hope we do, since nothing else can save us.

When it comes to climate fiction and other political art, consumption itself can be a form of distraction and denialism, especially when we insist that if only *other people* consumed the right art, everything would be improved. We already know that there's no type of political entertainment that capitalism can't absorb, no level of critique or dissent it can't co-opt. (The 2023 film *Dumb Money* advertised itself as "a riotous middle finger to the capitalist swine of Wall Street"; this film about the stock market was made by a division of Sony and distributed by Sony.)[17] Even if and when fictional stories do reference climate change, there's no reason to presume that the mere act of watching, by itself, will make much difference, and too much watching may even be detrimental to the cause. "It's like we're all entertaining each other while the world burns, right?"

says Aubrey Plaza's character in season two of *White Lotus*, itself hip streaming entertainment.[18] We don't actually require climate novels or references to the burning world in our prestige TV shows to fix our sense of political possibility; our problem is that we can't, or we won't, take action to change our present reality as dramatically as we should.

The Big Bad Feedback Loop of Power and Death

I think the core problem with fiction, the real heart of the matter that I've found after examining it from so many different angles, isn't actually that fiction contains the power to potentially mobilize people for good or evil. Fiction certainly *can* have that power, from time to time, but the deeper problem is simply power itself: who's got it, and who doesn't. You could write the most popular and critically acclaimed climate novel in the world, it could sell millions of copies and win every imaginable literary award . . . and Exxon-Mobil would still be there to sponsor your prize. A story can't threaten the kind of power that's aware of climate change and still chooses to willfully exacerbate it—that is, the kind of power that most corporate and government actors still have, and use.

Even to be able to sit and write a climate novel in the first place implies a kind of distance from the worst climate effects: you must necessarily have time and leisure to instruct and amuse other people. And being able to sit and read a climate novel—having the luxury to process climate anxiety in general—is also proof of time and leisure, the *over there* quality of the problem.[19] Ghosh speculates in *The Great Derangement* about what future generations will think when they read novels or see art in museums from this period of human history—it's bold of him to hope we might still have libraries and museums.[20] The apocalyptic world of a four-degree Celsius rise is unlikely to have either writers, readers, directors,

or audiences, obviating the question of whether fiction is dangerous altogether. Maybe future generations won't wonder why we
didn't use art to address climate change: maybe they'll only wonder why we believed art could—and should—be our salvation in
the first place.

In the end what fiction does, and what it's capable of doing, is
something quite different from political action. Only human beings can take political action: only human beings can dismantle the
existent fossil fuel infrastructure and build the new structures of
energy and mitigation that will be necessary to cope with tempera-
tures that will keep rising even if we cut all emissions tomorrow.
It's true that climate fiction, including—and maybe especially—
policy paper regurgitations like *The Ministry for the Future* can help
us think through these problems. It certainly makes sense why climate journalists such as Mary Annaïse Heglar claim that what the
climate movement "desperately needs is more artists."[21] But at the
same time, I think we need to be very clear that imagining different
futures isn't the same as creating them; watching *How to Blow Up
a Pipeline* will not, by itself, blow up a pipeline. Watching a movie
isn't the same as committing an act, and the situation calls for action, not for being entertained as the world burns.[22]

But there's a risk here too: if fiction—and art more broadly—
isn't sufficiently conducive to the goal of saving the world, doesn't
that render it useless? And isn't it especially useless now, given the
scope of the threat posed by the climate apocalypse? I've been opposed throughout this book to the consideration of art as "useful"
because I don't think that's a meaningful way to evaluate fiction
and what it means to us; uselessness too only makes sense as a category if we've accepted the framework of "use" in the first place.
But if fiction isn't useless *or* useful, then it's reasonable to ask what
it's supposed to be and whether it matters, especially under these
pressing circumstances.

I think fiction and all forms of art matter quite a bit, even as we struggle to understand what mattering might look like outside of the use-value framework. This is another lacuna, as wide and shocking as the absence of climate fiction itself. By judging fiction solely as "useful"—judging it by that ability to teach this or that lesson, by its ability to show us how to behave, and deciding that it's useless if it fails to do so—we've misplaced the cause and the effect, or, more specifically, misunderstood a feedback loop as a simple matter of cause and effect. (Appropriately, much of climate science relies on the cycling of feedback loops rather than cause and effect with its directional arrows.) The limitations of our fiction are the result of larger social failures of imagination, which lead to greater limitations in our fiction, which in turn lead to greater social failures of imagination. Or to put it more directly, we aren't stuck in a capitalism-induced climate hellscape because our fictional stories have failed to adequately describe it; we don't have fictional stories that adequately describe our capitalism-induced climate hellscape because we only got to this point through an inability to grapple with the consequences of this system, which in turn makes it harder to imagine a way out of it. Fiction may represent and inform a changing reality: it can contribute to the disruption of that feedback loop. But it can't change reality on its own, by itself.

I think it's important to examine these feedback loops directly: it's important to ask why it's so hard to see outside the doctrine of use-value, why, again, it's so much easier to imagine the end of the world than to imagine the end of capitalism. It isn't just the CIA's old dead hand on the scale of fiction, or the total capitalist control of nearly every medium and form of production. It's also because the two, capitalism and apocalypse, increasingly appear to be twinned together. Death lies at the root of a system that believes the natural world is dead and voiceless, and that it can be abused without consequence forever.

The world is in fact alive, despite imperialist-capitalist attempts to render it a dead and exploitable thing; we are alive, and much more complex than algorithmic input-output machines. Stories too are alive, and complex beyond imagining. This is exactly why we imagine them, to say what we can't, and to be who we aren't.

Useful, Useless, Helpful, Helpless

If we don't rely on fiction to save the world, then we have to rely on ourselves, and that's much more complicated and difficult than demanding good results from fictional stories. Quinta Brunson, the showrunner of the lighthearted school comedy *Abbott Elementary*, tweeted in May 2022 that it was "wild how many people have asked for a school shooting episode of the show I write. [P]eople are that deeply removed from demanding more from the politicians they've elected and are instead demanding 'entertainment.'"[23] School shootings have become such a commonplace horror in the United States now that, like climate disasters, it's easy to lose track of which events happened where if they didn't happen to you or your family. And as with climate change, the solutions are both simple (ban what's killing us) and nearly impossible to implement in political terms.

The final-straw demand Brunson received from a viewer was to "formulate an angle [on *Abbott Elementary*] that would get our government to understand why laws need to pass."[24] It's up to a TV show, this viewer seemed to believe, to do the useful work of raising awareness to (and for) politicians, as if the problem with senators opposed to assault weapon bans was a lack of properly formulated angles rather than gun lobby influence. And the viewer didn't frame this as a request to Brunson, but as an order in the imperative mode: "formulate." In fact, the whole sentence sounds almost exactly like a command typed into an AI prompt, insisting that an artist respond not as an artist but as a machine, churning out optimally useful episodes instead of merely entertaining ones. But at the time, as Brunson noted, the viewer was still demanding entertainment—only the sort that could be directed at stubborn and paid-off politicians in hopes of persuading them.

Many people do feel so alienated from their elected officials, so politically helpless, that forcing their leaders to action through art may indeed seem like one of the only available options. This is exacerbated by the fact that politicians often play helpless, even creating a deliberate characterization of themselves as the makers of dramatic gestures rather than political action. Democratic politicians in the United States have been particularly adept at creating situations in which they simply can't act, except symbolically and artistically. When *Roe v. Wade* was overturned by the Supreme Court in June 2022, Speaker of the House Nancy Pelosi—who had been aware for several months that the ruling was imminent—chose to respond by reciting a political poem about being sad for one's country.[25] Other congressional Democrats gathered on the steps of the Capitol to sing "God Bless America."[26] These weren't just useless gestures; they were an ironic inversion of Plato's ancient concern that poetry would inflame the people and incept them with dangerously anti-authoritarian ideas. This was the use of poetry as complacency, similar to—though not quite the same as—Plato's other idea that the only proper use of art would be to instill noble and sobering values in the public. Poetry, as it turns out, is just as powerful when wielded as an excuse; art can be held up as a screen to hide the nothingness of political inactivity. But many liberals have become so accustomed to protest art as a supposed site of power—and the demand for protest art as a tool to sway politicians—that Democratic politicians themselves have started to co-opt the form, performing acts of protest art to an unclear audience (God, maybe, or Republicans, or themselves).

Phil Klay, a writer and an Iraq War veteran, has expressed concern that political poetry—and political art in general—can end up being useless and enervating in this exact way. "The mismatch," he wrote for *The Point*, "between the urgency of the cause and the form of the response always leaves me with the sinking suspicion that such literature is less 'political' than parasitic on politics, drawing more emotional power from the underlying cause than it adds to that cause's support."[27] For this parasitic relationship to occur, the literature in question has to be elevated to a status of usefulness: a poem or a story has to be understood not as art but as an especially direct and compelling form of speech. This is what happens after poetry and fiction and other arts become gentrified and respectable, after they've been ossified into the gentleman's club of "Well, I say!" When words are just things you *say*—when their use-value as seeming political acts replaces actual political acts—then they become quite useful to power and no longer dangerous to it. The misuse of art *as* politics tends to collapse art and politics into one mutually inert glob.

It's a paradox, but when art becomes useful, it also becomes useless at the same time: usefulness/uselessness isn't as much a continuum as a single point. And this dead singularity of use-value diminishes fiction into a form of dramatic communication, and writers into mere dramatic communicators of ideas. Film scholar Racquel Gates commented on this in a July 2020 essay about the lists of "anti-racist" movies and TV shows; these lists tend to pop up online after a terrible event like a police murder of a Black person, offering up helpful numbers of Black films and TV shows, as if these shows and movies primarily exist, in Gates's words, "to be an educational primer on race in America." These lists usually purport to celebrate Black art, but they don't treat these stories *as* art, just as potentially useful lessons for non-Black viewers. In fact, Gates points out that these lists tend to overemphasize the didactic qualities these stories may or may not have, and fully ignore the kinds of movies and TV shows that are simply about complicated people living their lives. What happens, she asks, "to movies [that] may not have been deemed 'important' because they cared more to focus on the lovely intricacies of Black life rather than delivering Black pain for white consumption?"[28] Treating Black movies, and Black art in general, as valuable only for its political usage is an expression of total disinterest in these works as art and in their creators as artists. The usefulness/uselessness framework terminates in a machinelike attitude toward art, and toward human artists as valuable only insofar as they function as a conduit for this usefulness—which means they are fundamentally unimportant, unindividuated, and interchangeable.

I don't think many people have noticed this yet, but the reduction of art to its supposed political value alone—to the useful/ useless/helpful/helpless framework shorn of any judgment of actual aesthetic qualities—is a strong argument in favor of AI authorship. If *only* entertainment can save us, if protest art is the *only* meaningful way to battle damaging Supreme Court decisions, and if art by marginalized people is *only* valuable in hopes that it will combat bigotry, then we just need lots and lots of fiction, tons of books and movies and TV, churned out very fast and maybe sensitivity-checked by real underpaid human beings before being marketed to the right people. Our politicians just need the *right poems* about racism and climate change, which they can presumably read aloud on the House floor to themselves. An AI could be trained on overtly political art, on long lists of anti-racist movies. It could even steal from the very best, so that it might educate the very worst.

But if art matters for its own sake, if it's not useless or useful but simply itself, then artists matter too; in fact, they might matter much more than any effects that may or may not result from their artistic output. The various concerns about the dangers of fiction have largely fixated on whether fiction is dangerous *to readers*. Writers and other kinds of storytellers tend to enter the conversation largely in relation to these vulnerable readers and audiences: whether they're damaging the public or representing them sufficiently. Even the question of diversity in creative industries has often been constructed around how various segments of the public respond (positively or negatively) to stories created by or featuring marginalized people. But if we center writers, artists, actors, directors, and other art workers in the discussion, then I think the story changes. Dropping the usefulness/uselessness framework restores us to the living purpose of fiction, which is for it to exist: for people to tell stories because they want to tell them. And it also puts artists in the same uncomfortable seat as everybody else; it's our job to save ourselves, and not to use art as a substitute for doing politics.

Like Deodorant

There's a quote that fiction writers love for all the wrong reasons. It comes from Ursula K. Le Guin's barn-burner speech at the 2014 National Book Awards, and you may have seen it lovingly screenshotted and passed around by writers online. "We live in capitalism," the quote begins. "Its power seems inescapable—but then, so did the divine right of kings. Any human power can be resisted and changed by human beings. Resistance and change often begin in art. Very often in our art, the art of words."[29] When taken out of context—as it usually is—this fabulous quartet of sentences has been interpreted as a paean to the power of art and its ability to shape political realities. But Le Guin only says that such power *begins* in art, not that it ends there—and the main thrust of her speech is about something else entirely.

In fact, her declaration of war against capitalist realism begins and ends as a critique of the publishing industry. "Books aren't just commodities," Le Guin says before those four famous lines. "The profit motive is often in conflict with the aims of art." Elsewhere she talks about the "ignorance and greed" she saw in profit-seeking publishing houses, in Amazon's attempt to drive out its competitors, and in the overall industry effort to trim the art of writing into mere sales units.[30] Le Guin doesn't just blame publishing in the abstract, or capitalism as a distant force; she specifically calls out writers, editors, and other industry professionals for allowing such bullying to occur. "I see a lot of us," she says, "the producers, who write the books and make the books, accepting this—letting commodity profiteers sell us like deodorant, and tell us what to publish, what to write."[31]

These other lines are much less flattering for writers, and they aren't quoted nearly as often. If resistance and change can begin in the art of words, then it matters very much *how* those words are produced. The most important issue, as we've seen repeatedly in this book, isn't actually whether the words in question are sufficiently revolutionary—whether they can change the world for us, which again, they generally can't on their own—but how they're made and how they're sold. Novelists may talk a big game about shaping the world through art, but they can't have any control over everybody else's reality until they win some control over their own.

In this sense, writers have a political responsibility that goes far beyond some misty dramatics about the power of stories to overthrow capitalism. The real work of overthrowing or at least mitigating the worst of capitalism can be found in a unified workers' resistance—including writers' resistance—to being sold and commodified. This is something that screenwriters (and actors) have so far understood much more clearly than novelists. The 2023 WGA strikers defended themselves first and foremost as workers who deserved fair compensation for their labor and who shouldn't be reduced to merely editing the slop exuded by AI.[32] In terms of its impact on the reality of workers' lives, especially in the broader context of all the other strikes that have been occurring in other industries, the Hollywood strike may end up being more valuable to the cause than one or even a hundred Hollywood movies *about* strikes. As labor journalist Sarah Jones wrote for *Intelligencer* the morning after the WGA announced its victory, "Labor is telling America a story it has long needed to hear."[33] It's *labor*, the unions themselves, that are telling the story—not an individual writer here or there writing a story *about* a story and hoping that it hits.

The power and threat of this kind of direct action was apparent to film studios from the beginning; they even used this book's magic word. At the June 2023 Sun Valley Conference (which has been labeled a "summer camp for billionaires"), Disney CEO Bob Iger said that the WGA strikers had "a level of expectation . . . that is just not realistic" and were "adding to a set of challenges that this business is already facing that is quite frankly very disruptive and"—get ready for it—"dangerous."[34] The strike was indeed very disruptive and dangerous to the film and TV business, which has long relied on outrageous inequality to fuel profits to CEOs like Iger.[35] And the strikers were indeed, in Iger's words, acting in a way that was "just not realistic," in that they were attempting to shift this realism. And they *did* shift it: they won. That's what happens in real life, where anything is "real" if you can make it happen. Capitalist realism is much more fragile than it seems, and easily threatened—not necessarily through the indirect mechanism of stories to inspire us toward better action, but *always* through the direct action of workers refusing to give their labor until their demands are made into reality.

The novelists that Le Guin was addressing at the National Book Awards, however, don't have the same sorts of union protections as the WGA. Novel writing is an individualized kind of labor, much more so than screenwriting, and it's hard for individuals typing away in separate rooms to look up and recognize each other's shared interests. The Authors Guild—the oldest and most extensive writers' organization in the United States—has at least followed the WGA's lead in opposing the attempted AI takeover of writing. The guild's initial tactic has been to go after OpenAI (the creator of ChatGPT) for copyright infringement. Most authors already earn less than a living wage, and if ChatGPT—which has allegedly been programmed on data sets of stolen ebooks—continues to drive down the market price for writing, then wages will degrade even further.[36] Novelist and Authors Guild member George Saunders, who is part of the Authors Guild's class-action lawsuit against OpenAI, made a strong statement in favor of writers as laborers. "Writers should be fairly compensated for their work," he said in the guild's press release. "Fair compensation means that a person's work is valued, plain and simple. This, in turn, tells the culture what to think of that work and the people who do it." But Saunders concludes—as so many writers simply can't help doing—with a defensive statement about the use-value of art and its social impact. "The work of the writer," he says, "the human imagination, struggling with reality, trying to discern virtue and responsibility within it—is essential to a functioning democracy.'"[37]

It really should be enough to say that writers are workers, and all workers deserve both a fair wage and not to be replaced by machines that have been trained on their stolen work. But there's still an unconscious pressure to establish art as useful, especially under capitalism and in the context of a broader western culture in which the art of writing has been regarded, for over two thousand years, as a potential threat. This is why writers like Saunders respond with such automatic defensiveness, why they try to fend off Plato's bullets before he can fire (and the dude didn't even have a gun). Writing *has* to be established as good and useful for a democracy;

otherwise, it could only be bad and useless. If writing is *just writing*, if a story is just a story, if Saunders's own bright and bleak short stories about a dystopian service economy don't shift that dystopian service economy in a happier direction, then their social value is indeterminate. The value might even be negative: the output-value of a fictional story could be less than the input-effort of the writer that went into it. If writing is just art, then it's impossible to justify—and to explain—by the standards of value that we have decided are normal, real, and uncontestable.

The danger—and the power—of defending writing as art, and art itself as art, is that it suggests there's more to human life than mere functionality, more to our relationship with one another and the natural world than the transformation of raw materials (human talent, natural resources) into tangible profits. The propriety demand placed on writers to perform good political labor—to be good for democracy—is echoed by the proprietary demands of publishing houses who only sign writers if they think their outputs can be turned into units of direct monetary value. We've been led by decades of capitalist realism and market conglomeration to think of this as a normal model, but it really isn't—there's no requisite or natural relationship between talent and profit. The free market isn't a god; it doesn't determine good or useful literature based on what can sell. It also isn't a demon; the unprofitable or unpopular isn't, by the transitive property, magically good or useful or aesthetically better than the popular. Profit is a wholly *unrelated metric*, which we have treated as if it has meaning in human life, when it really doesn't.

I say "human" life because profit has a great deal of meaning for machines, as we see with AI. The suit by the Authors Guild focuses on copyright violations alone, but this doesn't account for the big tech companies—including Meta, Google, and Microsoft—that are already seeking to avoid future plagiarism charges by hiring writers across the globe to create original works that are meant to be used as the base material to train new generations of AI.[38] (Taking a job like this ought to be considered disgusting scab work, but I worry that fiction writers have too little solidarity with one another to acknowledge or enforce that, especially across national borders.) These new AIs, trained on original fiction and poetry written in English, Hindi, Japanese, and many other languages, would be perfectly legal in copyright terms and just as well equipped to drive down wages. And they'll even be able to sell AI fiction in the name of being good for democracy, because there's nothing about writing being "useful," "essential"—and above all, profitable—that necessarily requires it to be human.

Saunders did specify that "the *human* imagination" and its struggle with ethics and virtue is an essential part of civic functioning, but the history of art shows us that this isn't true: even in capitalist democracies, the human imagination can be quite easily cut out of any process. Many of our mass-produced commodities—clothing, bedding, dishes—were more like art forms until the industrial revolution, when they became machine-produced crafts. This was the reason for the original Luddite rebellion, committed by workers who (despite popular reputation) were not stuck-in-the-mud anti-technologist grumps but skilled weavers who didn't want their art to be replaced by machines.[39] It's taken a long time for machines to catch up to the work of writing, but they're getting close. Novelist and essayist Vauhini Vara has written with dread and fascination about her own experiments with AI—she used ChatGPT to help write a piece that was later anthologized in *Best American Essays*, but she questions whether AI could or should be allowed to write fiction and whether a preponderance of it could destroy human-created stories altogether.[40]

As of the time of this writing, AI struggles with most fiction and is useless at poetry; I doubt any AI will ever be as good as a really gifted human novelist or poet.[41] But then, no mass-produced dress is ever as good as an evening gown designed and sewn by a haute couture artist either. AI writing doesn't need to be as good as human writing to supersede it; it doesn't have to wrestle with questions of ethics and virtue inside the limitless depths of the human mind. It just needs to be close enough to sell, and to sell enough units to undercut wages so far that the only remaining novelists will be much more like high-fashion designers: relatively rare and rarefied, making products that are mainly intended for the rich.[42]

In this scenario, the non-rich wouldn't be able to afford to be writers, as they basically can't afford to be now, and readers would be inundated by mass-produced fiction on an industrialized scale. The corporatized production line is already too fast and too dangerous, with novelists having to assemble stories at speeds that are unhealthy both for their art and for themselves. Self-published Amazon writers are advised to churn out a new novel every three months or less; the rise of AI has made this crunch easier to bear while also exacerbating the pressure on everyone else.[43] Many traditionally published genre novelists have sped up their own processes, writing almost as fast as algorithmic Amazon garbage; to avoid competing with themselves, they sometimes opt to use one or more pseudonyms. Delilah S. Dawson, a novelist who also writes under the name Lila Bowen, once claimed that she can turn out a new draft of a novel in forty-five days. She also complained, in the same social media thread, that writers have little control over the publishing process and no security: "Authors are already doing everything in our power to succeed. All we can do is keep trying to level up. It's frustrating."[44] "Level up" in this sense doesn't mean "become better at writing, and write successfully to your own taste"—when you work at that speed it's virtually impossible to improve as an artist—but just improve your efficiency, like a machine. But of

course, a machine will always be more efficient than a human being. Too many novelists have already bowed to the conditions by
which they themselves will become replaceable.

The event horizon for AI evangelists isn't actually the one
where writers are supplemented by AI, but where they don't exist at all: a world in which readers and viewers autogenerate their
own novels and movies, calibrated to their exact tastes and prejudices. This is the reader as ultimate consumer and reading as ultimate consumption: art reduced to a vending machine.[45] And the
art is almost guaranteed to be—as AI art and writing already is—
extremely same-y, training itself on a database only of itself: the
same dreary grocery store, the same boring flavors of chip, just in
different combinations. Here we have another paradox: by emphasizing the individual consumer, we end up with more conformity;
by "democratizing" the writing of fiction through a technology that
technically lets everybody do it, we let nobody do it in practical,
professional terms. By insisting that the potential political impact of
fiction is so important that it trumps any aesthetic qualities—that
the artist doesn't matter except as a conduit of ideological priors—
we encourage people to customize their own version of fiction for
themselves and their politics, whatever they happen to be. (Incidentally, Nihar Malaviya, CEO of Penguin Random House, has
managed to stake out a position that is both anti-book-bans and
pro-AI; both book bans and human writers cut into his profits.)[46]

Junk heaps of AI writing already clutter the formerly helpful
parts of the internet; they resemble nothing so much as the worldwide junk heaps of cheaply made clothing that contribute to the
climate crisis.[47] This is the danger of treating writing only as use,
clothing only as use, the entire world only as use. Children's education too has been reduced to the merely useful, the most basic
training for adulthood. It isn't just libraries that have been attacked
across the United States—by book banners, by extractive licensing

agreements, and by government defunding even in blue cities—but also arts programs and humanities departments in high school and colleges.[48] And this is dangerous not because of lofty and unprovable claims about democracy and training smart citizens who can spot misinformation, but because if education is *only* training—if books are only inputs to the output goal of useful worker-adults— then conservatives will always have an argument regarding the content of school libraries. If books only exist to shape young readers, then conservatives have a valid reason to force that shape to conform to their desired profile. But if children are more than mini product units and mini social replicators, if there's more to childhood than training for adulthood, if there's more to being alive than simply maximizing your potential along the lines of the ideological agenda of whoever happens to be in charge at the moment, then books—and the writers who write them—have a fundamental right to exist that can't be subject to political vicissitudes or changes in technology. If we take art seriously as art, and artists seriously as artists, and labor itself as something that deserves respect and compensation, then we start moving toward a view of human existence that's bigger and stranger and more alive than anything the last four centuries have allowed for or could understand.

Roses for Roses' Sake

Let's say I've been correct so far. Let's say that art isn't useful, or at least doesn't need to prove itself useful to exist. We're still left with the question of *What good is it?* and whether it's just a distraction in the context of melting ice caps, rising fascism, mass shootings, mass incarceration, and mass deportations, plus book bans and other threats to the written word. If stories are "just" art, and art can't do politics for us, then what's the point of it right now when political action is desperately necessary? Why read a book at all when organized labor is on the march? Why *write* one, for god's sake, in this environment? aren't we just entertaining each other while the world burns?

Answering this is difficult to express in words, or at least difficult to express in a nonfictional style. There are writers who have tried to express this point in fiction—who have tried to explain art in art, which is a much more sensible way to do it. Take Michelle Tea's 2015 semi-autofictional and experimental queer novel *Black Wave*, which is about a woman named Michelle trying to write an autofictional and experimental queer novel as the world burns and drowns. The prose is recursive, beautiful, ugly, obsessed with granular detail; the protagonist is obsessed with herself and with meta-speculations about capitalism and feminism and queerness all while trying to write her book and figure out who she is. The book doesn't blow up a pipeline; I didn't blow up a pipeline after reading it. So what does *Black Wave* do, then? Something else. What is that *something else*? I can't really say. At one point the protagonist sees herself in a vision, writing: "Michelle writes another book. She stops drinking. She writes another book and then another. She continues writing books, the world gone, long exploded."[49] Michelle writes through the end of the world, and after it, because there's nothing else for her except writing: nothing except the act of creation, which has its own inexplicable meaning.

Sally Rooney gets at this too, I think, in her not-a-Marxist-novel *Beautiful World, Where Are You*. As I mentioned back in chapter 4, there's been frenetic critical effort to figure out whether Rooney is writing Marxist novels, which is really a question of whether her novels are successfully *doing* Marxism—that is, helping to bring about the revolution. As I said, I think her project is totally different, partly because no book can successfully bring about the revolution, and partly because Rooney is exploring a totally different set of questions. *Beautiful World* is something more like *Black Wave*, an experimental novel/anti-novel asking the basic question of why the novel as a form exists and what it means in a dying world. Alice, one of the protagonists of *Beautiful World*, is a successful literary novelist; she keeps expressing how much she hates the world of literary publishing, how sick and suffocating and pointless it all is, especially in the face of catastrophe and instability. But at one point she concludes, "I find my own work morally and politically worthless, and yet it's what I want to do with my life, the only thing I want to do."[50] Whether or not all writers would agree with Alice in full (many do believe in the moral and political value of their work, or have hopes for it at least), the last part of the statement is true, I think, for just about every kind of artist. The act of creation is what you want to do with your life, and the only thing you want to do. That's why you do it no matter what, even though it doesn't pay enough to live, and even though the world you live in may be ending.

Most people are creative in one way or another; many people write fiction, or draw, or sing. Not everyone is a great artist, but at the same time not everyone (and increasingly few people) possess the time and the support to really become great. And anyway being "great" in a critical or a public-approval sense isn't nearly as important for many artists as the creative work itself. Creative people *will* create art, even if it sucks: the need to make art is something like a sickness, a curse, a blessing. Visual art in the United States has been murdered by profitability, by starved public funding and unscrupulous collectors and tax-dodging millionaires—and yet it appears everywhere, tattooed onto every building, posted online even through the flood of AI images. Beyond questions of good, or useful, or helpful, or healthy, creating art is necessary for the artist: an expression of indefatigable being.

Making and experiencing art is really just part of being alive: as ordinary—and as extraordinary—as eating and drinking and

having sex. And fiction is simply—and astoundingly—the most
ordinary art with the lowest bar, since all it requires is the materials
of everyday communication, which are so casual in our mouths, and
so fiery when raised to art. "They're just words," writes the journalist Talia Lavin, "like life is just life, or oxygen is just oxygen."[51]
If words have their own value, if the material of everyday life can
be reimagined and elevated into something never seen before on
this planet, then it really begs the question why anybody ever does
anything else with their time. Art can't be our *only* lives—there's
still plenty of other necessary labor, not to mention political activity that we ought to engage in to help ourselves and other people
(unionizing, organizing, all the hits). But the ultimate end purpose
of this political activity isn't suffering and more suffering; the end
goal is to create better conditions for everyone, full of pleasures
that can't be pegged to value, and to create art that is for itself, and
is an end in itself, and words that are said because they have no
choice but to be said, because the artist wanted to say them.

The great critic Barbara McClay has written about the "politics
creep" in every corner of human life, though really of bourgeois
Anglophone human life, where every act from reading a novel
to lighting a scented candle can be justified—and in fact, self-
consciously needs to be justified in advance—as a bold act of resistance.[52] Pretending that self-care is a brave political act detracts
from actual political acts, and it sucks the life out of life itself: turning every moment into a performance for an audience, for an imagined crowd of other people on social media. This is *other people* not
as fellow complicated human beings, but as fearful object, whose
inner lives are imaginable only insofar as they might be watching
and comparing and judging us for whether we've done enough,
whether we're wasting our time. And books and movies and TV
shows and every other form of fiction will always be, to some extent, a waste of time, as having friends will be a waste of time, as

being in love is a waste of time, as every possible action or thought you may have could be considered a waste of time if every second of your life has to prove its value, and has to get a job.

Reclaiming life from the constant need for necessity, to prove its value to an imaginary jury of other people, makes it easier to take actual political action, i.e., to be actually useful to other people. And removing the pressure from fiction to change the world makes it, paradoxically, much more important. In his essay "On Becoming an American Writer," the novelist Alexander Chee said that he spent much of his education "doubting the importance of my work, doubting the power it had to reach anyone or to do anything of significance." But all the same, he found that literature remained the key element of his life: "Books were still to me as they had been when I found them: the only magic."[53] Books may not be useful, certainly less useful than action, yet they're still magic. And not magic as a corny slogan or a metaphor in a fantasy novel, but as something literal, and strangely ordinary. Chee describes the job of the writer as distilling everything they have ever known and seen and thought, all their experiences and knowledge, into something that "meets and distills from you, the reader, something out of the everything it finds in you. All of this meets along the edge of a sentence like this one, as if the sentence is a fence, with you on one side and me on the other." This is lovely, prose writing at its finest: a fence is a normal, forgettable, man-made object, but Chee studies it, infuses it with magic, and transforms it in the context of other words into an image rarely seen and used. And at the same time, it's still familiar: something we meet. We're transformed by great writing, not *beyond* our own powers and capabilities but *into* them. Writing doesn't fix us or save us or make us better people: it just makes us more of what we already are, and what we want to become.

The world might burn to the ground, and people will still write; I imagine people will probably be telling stories as the last fire winks out. The nature of these stories will change, as they always do. There are going to be panics over these changes, as there have been for centuries, and as there will undoubtedly continue to be until we break out of this feedback loop of incorrect certainty about what human art and human life is supposed to be like, and how we measure its value. But what's amazing about this is that we don't have to sit and wait for stories to take their lucky effect: we don't have to wait for other people to watch the right movie or read the right book and wise up around us. We are all *other people*, and we aren't prisoners of reality, as constructed by fiction or anything else. We can get up any time, and go outside.

ACKNOWLEDGMENTS

Thanks to John for his infinite patience with me while I wrote this book (and always); thanks to Erik Hane for everything; thanks to Emma Whitney, also for everything; thanks to Adrian Rennix, Allegra Silcox, Kate Gauthreaux, Vanessa A. Bee, Cate Root, and Aisling McCrea, who are all simply the best of the best; thanks to Jaya Rajamani, for always being in my corner; thanks to Max Alvarez and the Real News squad, with special thanks to Taya Graham for a really interesting and vital interview; thanks to the Book Cranks, too many to name here but all beloved; thanks to my parents, Paul and Sari; thanks to my siblings and their various kiddos—both human and animal—for lots of love and support; thanks to the Zaldonises, who are very dear to me; thanks to Stephen, Bethany, and Seth, for much-needed vacations during this time; thanks to Evelyn Liu, for vital coffee breaks and cat wrangling; thanks to Helen McEvoy and the crew for lots of patience as I disappeared for a while; thanks to Ilena Osma, who knows why; thanks to Jessica Lam, Kevin Joffre, Anthony Pasquarosa, Ivy Ingber, Hussein Najafee, Bierka Castellanos, and Chris Liu for being yourselves; thanks to Talia Lavin, for commiserating; thanks to Bertrand Cooper, Amanda Hanna-Mcleer, and the other brilliant and inspiring writers who I've had the joy of editing, and who have made me a better writer in the process.

NOTES

INTRODUCTION: MORAL PANICS OLD AND NEW

1. Mike Hixenbaugh, "A Mom's Campaign to Ban Library Books Divided a Texas Town—and Her Own Family," *ProPublica*, August 11, 2022, www.propublica.org/article/texas-book-banning-libraries-lgbtq -hood-county.
2. Ibid.
3. According to an April 2022 report by PEN America, 72 percent of the books banned from July 1, 2021, to March 31, 2022, were fiction. See Jonathan Friedman and Nadine Farid Johnson, *Banned in the USA: Rising School Book Bans Threaten Free Expression and Students' First Amendment Rights* (New York: PEN America, 2022), pen.org /banned-in-the-usa. The 2023 PEN report did not separate banned books by genre, but trends appear to be basically identical. Of the eleven most banned books in the United States, eight of them (73 percent) were novels. See Kasey Meehan and Jonathan Friedman, *Banned in the USA: State Laws Supercharge Book Suppression in Schools* (New York: PEN America, 2023), pen.org/report/banned-in-the-usa-state -laws-supercharge-book-suppression-in-schools.
4. Hixenbaugh, "Mom's Campaign."
5. Elizabeth A. Harris and Alexandra Alter, "Book Ban Efforts Spread across the U.S.," *New York Times*, January 30, 2022, www.nytimes .com/2022/01/30/books/book-ban-us-schools.html.
6. I have left out the moral panic over violent video games in the 1990s–2000s (which still somewhat lingers); clearly, in that case, the cicadas were out of season.
7. The quotes come from Rev. Thomas Fitzgerald, a member of the

National Council of Catholic Men and director of the National Organization for Decent Literature, who played a key role in the 1950s moral panic over paperback books. Kenneth C. Davis, *Two-Bit Culture: The Paperbacking of America* (Boston: Houghton Mifflin, 1984), 220.

8. Amy Werbel, *Lust on Trial* (New York: Columbia University Press, 2018).

9. For more on this history, see contemporary French academic William Marx's terrific book on the subject, William Marx, *The Hatred of Literature*, trans. Nicholas Elliott (Cambridge, MA: Belknap Press of Harvard University Press, 2018).

10. Jonathan Gottschall, *The Story Paradox* (New York: Basic Books, 2021), 14.

11. Elizabeth A. Harris and Alexandra Alter, "A Fast-Growing Network of Conservative Groups Is Fueling a Surge in Book Bans," *New York Times*, December 12, 2022, www.nytimes.com/2022/12/12/books/book-bans-libraries.html.

12. Hannah Allam, "Culture War in the Stacks: Librarians Marshal against Rising Book Bans," *Washington Post*, March 4, 2023, www.washingtonpost.com/national-security/2023/03/02/culture-war-stacks-librarians-marshal-against-rising-book-bans; PEN America, *Booklash: Literary Freedom, Online Outrage, and the Language of Harm* (New York: PEN America, 2023), pen.org/report/booklash.

13. Marx, *Hatred of Literature*, 26–29. The two philosophers in question are Xenophanes of Colophon and Heraclitus.

14. Plato, *Republic*, trans. G. M. A. Grube, revised C. D. C. Reeve (Indianapolis, Ind.: Hackett, 1992) 65.

15. Ibid., 68.

16. "Mimesis" has a several different meanings in literary studies, including the imitation of reality. I'm using it in this book to refer exclusively to the kind of imitative behavior that readers are imagined to bring to the text.

17. Plato, *Republic*, 268.

18. Ibid., 232.

19. Josh Zeitz, "How an Infamous Movie Revived the Confederacy," *Politico*, June 22, 2015, www.politico.com/magazine/story/2015/06/charleston-shooting-confederacy-birth-of-a-nation-119300.

20. See Amy S. Kaufman and Paul B. Sturtevant, *The Devil's Historians:*

How Modern Extremists Abuse the Medieval Past (Toronto, Ontario: University of Toronto Press, 2020) 103–126.

21. Elian Peltier and Nicholas Kulish, "A Racist Book's Malign and Lingering Influence," *New York Times*, November 22, 2019, www.nytimes .com/2019/11/22/books/stephen-miller-camp-saints.html.

22. James Baldwin, "Everybody's Protest Novel," in *Collected Essays* (New York: Library of America, 1998).

23. There's some scholarly debate over whether *What Is to Be Done?* really counts as a work of fiction or intends to portray itself as "real." See Sonia A. Werner, "The Reality Effect and the Real Effects of Chernyshevsky's 'What Is to Be Done?,'" *Novel: A Forum on Fiction* 47, no. 3 (2014): 422–42, www.jstor.org/stable/43830028.

24. Belinda Jack, "Goethe's *Werther* and Its Effects," *Lancet*, April 30, 2014, doi.org/10.1016/S2215-0366(14)70229-9.

25. Matthew S. Schwartz, "Teen Suicide Spiked after Debut of Netflix's '13 Reasons Why,' Study Says," NPR, April 30, 2019, www.npr.org/2019 /04/30/718529255/teen-suicide-spiked-after-debut-of-netflixs-13-reasons -why-report-says.

26. "Because my catastrophic imagination is highly active these days," critic and memoirist Myriam Gurba wrote at the end of her takedown of *American Dirt*, "I can visualize what this film [version of the book] might inspire. I can see Trump sitting in the White House's movie theatre, his little hands reaching for popcorn as he absorbs *Dirt's* screen adaptation. 'This!' he yells. '*This is why we must invade.*'" Myriam Gurba, "Pendeja, You Ain't Steinbeck: My Bronca with Fake-Ass Social Justice Literature," *Tropics of Meta*, December 12, 2019, tropicsofmeta .com/2019/12/12/pendeja-you-aint-steinbeck-my-bronca-with-fake -ass-social-justice-literature.

27. Margaret Anne Doody, *The True Story of the Novel* (New Brunswick, NJ: Rutgers University Press, 1996), 232.

28. Lusane quoted in Collette Coleman, "How Literacy Became a Powerful Weapon in the Fight to End Slavery," History.com, January 29, 2021, www.history.com/news/nat-turner-rebellion-literacy-slavery.

29. M. F. Burnyeat, "Art and Mimesis in Plato's 'Republic,'" *London Review of Books*, May 21, 1998, www.lrb.co.uk/the-paper/v20/n10/m.f.-burn yeat/art-and-mimesis-in-plato-s-republic. It's worth mentioning that Plato's fellow citizens included only free men, not women or slaves, and

the Athens of the time was in many respects not a democracy as we would understand it.

30. "Let's go eat a goddamn snack" was once said by former Jets head coach Rex Ryan to his players at the end of a rousing speech and is proof that in a democracy, great art can truly come from anywhere. "Let's go eat a goddamn snack!," YouTube video, December 28, 2014, www.you tube.com/watch?v=k5yCA9boxzM.

31. Gottschall, *Story Paradox*, 22.

32. Rick Gekoski, "Fast-Food Fiction: Good or Bad for Your Health?," *Guardian*, December 23, 2013, theguardian.com/books/2013/dec/23 /fast-fiction-fifty-shades-grey.

33. See Nadja Spiegelman, "James Joyce's Love Letters to His 'Dirty Little Fuckbird,'" *Paris Review*, February 2, 2018, www.theparisreview.org /blog/2018/02/02/james-joyces-love-letters-dirty-little-fuckbird.

34. Rachel Potter, "Ulysses at 100: Why It Was Banned for Being Obscene," *Conversation*, February 1, 2022, theconversation.com/ulysses -at-100-why-it-was-banned-for-being-obscene-176086.

35. Caroline Davies, "UK Judge Orders Rightwing Extremist to Read Classic Literature or Face Prison," *Guardian*, September 1, 2021, www .theguardian.com/politics/2021/sep/01/judge-orders-rightwing -extremist-to-read-classic-literature-or-face-prison; Lizzie Dearden, "Neo-Nazi Terror Offender Ordered to Read Jane Austen 'Resumed Interest in Far-Right Extremism within Days', Court Told," *Independent*, January 19, 2022, independent.co.uk/news/uk/crime/neo-nazi -ben-john-austen-sentence-b1996148.html.

36. Jennifer Wilson, "The Empathy Industrial Complex," *Bookforum*, March/April/May 2021, www.bookforum.com/print/2801/george -saunders-looks-for-life-lessons-in-russian-literature-24370.

37. Gottschall, *Story Paradox*, 121, 124. The original quote from Roger Ebert comes from *Life Itself*, a documentary about Ebert directed by Steve James. See Linda Holmes, "'A Machine That Generates Empathy': Roger Ebert Gets His Own Documentary," NPR, July 3, 2014, www .npr.org/2014/07/03/328230231/a-machine-that-generates-empathy -roger-ebert-gets-his-own-documentary.

38. Johann Hari, *Stolen Focus* (New York: Crown, 2022), 86.

39. Meehan and Friedman, *Banned in the USA*.

40. Wilson, "Empathy Industrial Complex."

41. Gottschall, *Story Paradox*, 125.

42. Elaine Castillo, *How to Read Now* (New York: Viking, 2022), 15.

43. See D. Kidd and E. Castano, "Reading Literary Fiction and Theory of Mind: Three Preregistered Replications and Extensions of Kidd and Castano (2013)," *Social Psychological and Personality Science* 10, no. 4 (2019): 522–31, doi.org/10.1177/1948550618775410.

44. There's also evidence that the "dark triad" traits of sociopathy tend to cluster in the arts, less, I would suspect, because sociopaths are particularly drawn to the arts and more because sociopaths have the requisite traits for becoming successful creative professionals. See Peter K. Jonason et al., "Occupational Niches and the Dark Triad Traits," *Personality and Individual Differences* 69 (October 2014): 119–23, doi.org/10.1016/j.paid.2014.05.024.

45. Doody, *True Story*, 241.

46. Castillo, *How to Read Now*, 31.

47. Oscar Wilde, *The Picture of Dorian Gray* (1890; repr., New York: Modern Library, 1998), xi.

48. "For in art there is no such thing as a universal truth. A Truth in art is that whose contradictory is also true"; Oscar Wilde, *Intentions* (New York: Brentano's, 1905), 263.

49. The collaboration between U.S. military agencies and Marvel movies is somewhat unclear; they were definitely involved with the production of *Iron Man*, *Captain Marvel*, and others, but not with the first *Avengers* movie and possibly not with the second either. See Rueben Baron, "The MCU's Relationship with the Military, from Iron Man to Captain Marvel," *CBR*, March 16, 2019, www.cbr.com/captain-marvel-mcu-military-relationship.

50. Marvel's and Disney's VFX workers were so frustrated with their poor treatment that they unionized in 2023. See Jazz Tangcay, "Walt Disney Pictures VFX Workers Vote to Unionize with IATSE," *Variety*, October 3, 2023, variety.com/2023/artisans/news/walt-disney-pictures-vfx-workers-unionize-1235730179.

51. Gottschall says that not only does art operate like an infection, but that this claim is backed up by (dubious) science (*Story Paradox*, 77).

52. Stuart Hall, "Notes on Deconstructing 'the Popular,'" in *Cultural Resistance Reader*, ed. Stephen Duncombe (London: Verso, 2002), 186.

53. The number of English majors in the United States has dropped

precipitously over the past decade, as young people who might have wanted to study literature have chosen safer, more obviously cost-effective degrees. See Nathan Heller, "The End of the English Major," *New Yorker*, February 27, 2023, www.newyorker.com/magazine/2023 /03/06/the-end-of-the-english-major.

54. This meme has popped up on Twitter, Tumblr, Reddit, and Quora, but one of its earliest usages online appears to be from David Dunning, "Humans Pay to Live and It's Not Natural," *Thought Catalog*, April 28, 2014, thoughtcatalog.com/david-dunning/2014/04/humans-pay-to-live -and-its-not-natural.

55. Gottschall, *Story Paradox*, 77.

56. See "Kill All the Poor" sketch in *That Mitchell and Webb Look*, series 4, episode 4, 2010, www.comedy.co.uk/tv/that_mitchell_and_webb _look/episodes/4/4.

57. Doody says that in the eighteenth century, a woman reader was considered "forever a minor before the law" and therefore suspect. See Doody, *True Story*, 279.

58. Gottschall says that according to studies, women are "more transportable than men on average" (*Story Paradox*, 61). I was certainly transported by his writing—but not, I think, in the direction he hoped.

59. Davis, *Two-Bit Culture*, xi.

CHAPTER ONE: GET A LOAD OF THESE CRAZY BROADS

1. Tesfaye Negussie and Rahma Ahmed, "Florida Schools Directed to Cover or Remove Classroom Books That Are Not Vetted," ABC News, February 6, 2023, abcnews.go.com/Politics/florida-schools-di rected-cover-remove-classroom-books-vetted/story?id=96884323. A similar event occurred in Escambia County, Florida, in August 2023; see Jennie McKeon, "Some Escambia High School Libraries Are Closed as District Works to Review Titles," WUWF, August 18, 2023, www.wuwf.org/local-news/2023-08-18/some-escambia-high -school-libraries-are-closed-as-district-works-to-review-titles.

2. Hannah Grossman, "Florida School Board Member Demands 'Disciplinary Action' over Pornographic Books in Schools: 'I'm Disgusted,'" Fox News, July 27, 2022, www.foxnews.com/media/florida-school -board-member-demands-disciplinary-action-pornograpic-books

-schools-disgusted; Madison Marques, "Rutgers Alum Wins National Librarian Award for Opposing Book Banning Efforts," *Daily Targum*, December 9, 2022, dailytargum.com/article/2022/12/rutgers-alum -wins-national-librarian-award-for-opposing-book-banning-efforts.

3. Ashley Hope Pérez, "I Wrote 'Out of Darkness' for My High School Students. Now High Schools Are Removing It," *Dallas Morning News*, February 11, 2022, www.dallasnews.com/opinion/commentary/2022 /02/11/i-wrote-out-of-darkness-for-my-high-school-students-now -high-schools-are-removing-it.

4. Kasey Meehan and Jonathan Friedman, *Banned in the USA: State Laws Supercharge Book Suppression in Schools* (New York: PEN America, 2023), pen.org/report/banned-in-the-usa-state-laws-supercharge-book -suppression-in-schools.

5. Kathryn VanArendonk, "The Mortal Queen of Faerie Smut," *Vulture*, February 1, 2024, www.vulture.com/article/sarah-j-maas-acotar -crescent-city-new-book.html.

6. The lawsuit was dismissed by the presiding judge. See Amanda Holpunch, "Virginia Judge Dismisses Case That Sought to Limit Book Sales," *New York Times*, August 31, 2022, www.nytimes.com /2022/08/31/us/virginia-obscenity-book-ban.html.

7. Jennifer Martin, "The 50 Most Banned Books in America," CBS News, November 10, 2022, www.cbsnews.com/pictures/the-50-most-banned -books-in-america; Meehan and Friedman, *Banned in the USA*.

8. "Obscenity," Cornell Law School Legal Information Institute, accessed February 1, 2024, www.law.cornell.edu/wex/obscenity.

9. The politics of curation were major topics of discussion in my graduate program (I have a master's degree in library and information science).

10. Joseph P. Laycock uses the useful phrase "moral entrepreneurs" in *Dangerous Games: What the Moral Panic over Role-Playing Games Says about Play, Religion, and Imagined Worlds* (Oakland: University of California Press, 2015), 277.

11. "Who We Are," Moms for Liberty, accessed January 31, 2024, www .momsforliberty.org/about.

12. See also the use of "woke mind virus," which is feared, unlike literal viruses.

13. Amy Werbel, *Lust on Trial* (New York: Columbia University Press,

2018), 111. The original quote is from the New York Society for the Suppression of Vice's annual meeting in 1876, as covered by the *New York Observer*.

14. See Sarah Fonesca, "The Constitutional Conflationists: On Abigail Shrier's 'Irreversible Damage' and the Dangerous Absurdity of Anti-trans Trolls," *Los Angeles Review of Books*, January 17, 2021, lareviewofbooks.org/article/the-constitutional-conflationists-on -abigail-shriers-irreversible-damage-and-the-dangerous-absurdity -of-anti-trans-trolls.

15. Christopher T. Conner, "Why Are So Many Young People Having Less Sex and Fewer Friendships?," *Salon*, November 6, 2022, www .salon.com/2022/11/06/why-are-so-many-young-people-are-having -less-and-fewer-friendships.

16. Mike Schneider, "Census Shows US Is Diversifying, White Population Shrinking," Associated Press, August 12, 2021, apnews.com/article /census-2020-house-elections-4ee80e72846c151aa41a808b06d975ea.

17. In case you are happily unfamiliar with the phrase, the white supremacist "fourteen words" are "We must secure the existence of our people and a future for white children."

18. Bill Chappell, "A Texas Lawmaker Is Targeting 850 Books That He Says Could Make Students Feel Uneasy," NPR, October 28, 2021, www.npr.org/2021/10/28/1050013664/texas-lawmaker-matt-krause -launches-inquiry-into-850-books.

19. Zeeshan Aleem, "Virginia's Youngkin Spotlights Woman Who Tried to Ban Toni Morrison's 'Beloved,'" MSNBC, October 27, 2021, www .msnbc.com/opinion/virginia-s-youngkin-spotlights-woman-who -tried-ban-toni-morrison-n1282458.

20. Amiah Taylor, "How Florida's Stop WOKE Act Could Impose a Chilling Effect on Diversity Efforts in the Workplace," *Fortune*, May 3, 2022, fortune.com/2022/05/03/florida-governor-desantis-signs-stop -woke-act-for-school-employers-diversity-race-gender; Trip Gabriel, "He Fuels the Right's Cultural Fires (and Spreads Them to Florida)," *New York Times*, April 24, 2022.

21. Zach Beauchamp, "Chris Rufo's Dangerous Fictions," *Vox*, September 10, 2023, www.vox.com/23811277/christopher-rufo-culture-wars-ron -desantis-florida-critical-race-theory-anti-wokeness.

22. Christopher Rufo (@realchrisrufo), "Yes, I envisioned a strategy—turn

the brand 'critical race theory' toxic—and, despite having virtually no resources compared to my opponents, willed it into being through writing and persuasion. Follow my playbook to save America; follow Charlie [Sykes]'s to lose sanctimoniously," Twitter, May 24, 2021, x.com /realchrisrufo/status/1396961964190961665?s=20.

23. Nathalie Baptiste, "Moms For Liberty's School Board Takeover Attempts Fizzled Out on Election Day," *HuffPost*, November 8, 2023, www.huffpost.com/entry/moms-for-liberty-elections_n_654bf7fbe4 b0e63c9dc2172e; Tori Otten, "Moms for Liberty Completely Collapses in Former Strongholds," *New Republic*, February 8, 2024, newrepublic .com/post/178879/moms-liberty-chapters-collapse-strongholds-penn sylvania-florida.

24. Ellen Kolodziej, "Central Bucks School District Swear In New School Board Members, Locals Tailgate to Celebrate," Fox29, December 4, 2023, fox29.com/news/central-bucks-school-district-swear-in-new -school-board-members-locals-tailgate-to-celebrate. The stack of banned books included novels such as Elie Wiesel's *Night* and Toni Morrison's *The Bluest Eye*. See Maddie Hanna, "Central Bucks' New School Board President Was Sworn In on a Stack of Frequently Banned Books. Here's What These Books Mean to Her," *Philadelphia Inquirer*, December 5, 2023, www.inquirer.com/education/cbsd-new-school -board-karen-smith-president-swearing-in-20231205.html.

25. Mitch Perry, "DeSantis and Newsom Clash in TV Debate, Charging Each Other with Lies and Bullying," *Missouri Independent*, December 1, 2023, missouriindependent.com/2023/12/01/desantis-and-newsom -clash-in-tv-debate-charging-each-other-with-lies-and-bullying.

26. A Florida mother who petitioned to remove books said of herself, "I'm not a reader. I'm not a book person. I'm a mom involved in my children's education." She also posted a *Protocols of the Elders of Zion* meme on her Facebook page; in her apology she said she hadn't read the meme in its entirety. Andrew Lapin, "The Florida Mom Who Sought to Ban Amanda Gorman's Poem Says She's Sorry for Promoting the Protocols of the Elders of Zion," *Jewish Telegraphic Agency*, May 24, 2023, jta.org/2023/05/24/united-states/the-florida-mom-who-got-amanda -gormans-poem-restricted-says-shes-sorry-for-promoting-the-proto cols-of-the-elders-of-zion; Isabela Dias, "A 17th Birthday Party, a Stocked Bar, Beer Pong, and a 'Parental Rights' Mom Facing Assault

Charges," *Mother Jones*, December 28, 2023, www.motherjones.com /politics/2023/12/clarice-schillinger-parental-rights-activist-faces -criminal-charges-bucks-county; Lexi Lonas, "Moms for Liberty Faces Growing Challenges amid Florida Sex Scandal," *Hill*, December 23, 2023, thehill.com/homenews/education/4372144-moms-liberty -rocky-year-elections-scandal; Gabriella Ferrigine, "Philadelphia Moms for Liberty Organizer Is a Registered Sex Offender: Report," *Salon*, November 20, 2023, www.salon.com/2023/11/20/philadelphia -moms-for-liberty-organizer-is-a-registered-offender-report.

27. Dorany Pineda, "In Burbank Schools, a Book-Banning Debate over How to Teach Antiracism," *Los Angeles Times*, November 12, 2020, www .latimes.com/entertainment-arts/books/story/2020-11-12/burbank -unified-challenges-books-including-to-kill-a-mockingbird.

28. Jaclyn Diaz, "Changes to New Editions of Roald Dahl Books Have Readers up in Arms," NPR, February 21, 2023, www.npr.org/2023 /02/21/1158347261/roald-dahl-books-changed-offensive-words.

29. PEN America, *Booklash: Literary Freedom, Online Outrage, and the Language of Harm* (New York: PEN America, 2023), pen.org/report /booklash.

30. The PEN America report does include novels that were canceled be- cause their writers behaved badly on social media, but I think that falls slightly outside the scope of this book, although it's related to the matter of professional precarity.

31. Daniel José Older, "The Real Censorship in Children's Books: Smil- ing Slaves Is Just the Half of It," *Guardian*, January 29, 2016, www .theguardian.com/books/2016/jan/29/smiling-slaves-the-real-cen sorship-in-childrens-books.

32. See Daniel Walden, "On the Limits of Books," *Slow Reading* (Sub- stack), September 9, 2023, danielwalden.substack.com/p/on-the-limits -of-books.

33. Ramin Ganeshram, "Why the Banning of 'A Birthday Cake for George Washington' Really Matters," *HuffPost*, February 11, 2016, www.huff post.com/entry/why-banning-a-birthday-cake-george-washington _b_9210992.

34. The *Booklash* report mentions three canceled works of children's fiction by white male writers out of about twenty novels or children's books.

The other authors were white women or women of color, with the exception of one Black male writer; see PEN America, *Booklash*. Outside of children's literature, there's only one real successful cancellation of a work by a cis, heterosexual white man that I can think of: *Confederate*, the intended "what if the South had won the Civil War" show planned by the *Game of Thrones* showrunners. The project was roundly criticized online and then canceled; however, the bungled ending to *Game of Thrones* had somewhat lowered the showrunners' stock at that time, and both have since gone on to score major projects elsewhere. See Violet Kim, "HBO Confirms *Confederate* Is Officially Dead," *Slate*, January 16, 2020, slate.com/culture/2020/01/hbo-cancels-confederate -game-of-thrones-creators.html.

35. Rabess was also subject to harassment including racial slurs. See Alexandra Alter and Elizabeth A. Harris, "How Review-Bombing Can Tank a Book Before It's Published," *New York Times*, June 27, 2023; Helen Lewis, "The Wrath of Goodreads," *Atlantic*, July 26, 2023, www.the atlantic.com/ideas/archive/2023/07/goodreads-review-bombing-ama zon-moderation/674811; and Imogen West-Knights, "The Saga over Elizabeth Gilbert's 'Russian Novel' Has an Uncomfortable Lesson— and It's Not for Her," *Slate*, June 13, 2023, slate.com/culture/2023/06 /elizabeth-gilbert-snow-forest-russia-novel-ukraine-goodreads.html.

36. Older, "Real Censorship."

37. Molière, *Les précieuses ridicules*, in *Tartuffe and Other Plays*, trans. Donald M. Frame (New York: Signet Classics, 2015), 10.

38. Molière, *Les femmes savantes*, trans. Richard Wilbur (New York: Hippocrene Books, 1978), 10.

39. The critic Françoise Jaouën writes that "preciosity may almost be said to have no known material existence . . . No text, no author of the period is a self-described *précieux*; they are described as such by their enemies." Françoise Jaouën, "Civility and the Novel: De Pure's *La prétieuse ou le mystère des ruelles*," *Yale French Studies*, no. 92 (1997): 106, doi.org/10.2307/2930389. One seventeenth-century author (De Pure) claims there were many précieuses and compares them to huge numbers of counterfeit diamonds. According to scholar Domna C. Stanton, "This emphasis on quantification, a characteristic common to the targets of satiric texts, is also achieved by depicting the précieuses

as a mass of bizarre creatures which have 'infected' society"; Domna
C. Stanton, "The Fiction of *Préciosité* and the Fear of Women," *Yale French Studies*, no. 62 (1981): 112, doi.org/10.2307/2929896.

40. Molière took pains in the preface to the printed edition of *Les précieuses* to specify that he wasn't actually talking about Scudéry but only about the writers who imitated her; this caveat is not very convincing. See Stanton, "Fiction of *Préciosité*," 111.

41. When it comes to the disappearance of women writers, the obvious question is which megastar woman novelist of our era will end up forgotten, and the answer is almost certainly J. K. Rowling, who has been campaigning to make herself as forgettable as possible. Regarding Scudéry, some critics think the work would now be considered Orientalist, though it's worth noting that her novels were translated into Arabic in her lifetime and presumably had an audience. See Harriet Stone, "Scudéry's Theater of Disguise: The Orient in 'Ibrahim,'" *L'esprit créateur* 32, no. 3 (1992): 51–61, www.jstor.org/stable/26286450; and Penelope Whitworth, "Madeleine de Scudéry," Project Continua, accessed February 17, 2024, www.projectcontinua.org/madeleine -de-scudery.

42. Boileau waited to publish his *Les héros de roman* until after Scudéry died (and she lived to be ninety-three). He claimed he waited out of respect, but that was a big fat lie; according to Margaret Anne Doody, "He had circulated the *Dialogue*, even given performances of it, and supposedly illicit printings had appeared." See Margaret Anne Doody, *The True Story of the Novel* (New Brunswick, NJ: Rutgers University Press, 1996), 266.

43. Nicolas Boileau Despréaux, *Les héros de roman: Dialogue de Nicolas Boileau-Despréaux* (Boston: Ginn, 1902), 170.

44. The character of Cyrus in *Artamène ou le grand Cyrus* was publicly known to be based on the Prince of Condé. See Joan DeJean, "The Politics of Genre: Madeleine de Scudéry and the Rise of the French Novel," *L'esprit créateur* 29, no. 3 (1989): 43–51, www.jstor.org/stable /26285888.

45. Anne E. Duggan, "Lovers, Salon, and State: La Carte de Tendre and the Mapping of Socio-political Relations," *Dalhousie French Studies* 36 (1996): 15. The original description of the Carte as a "board game of the ways to a woman's heart" is quoted by Duggan from Joan DeJean,

Tender Geographies: Women and the Origins of the Novel in France (New York: Columbia University Press, 1991).

46. It's notable that the exact same anxiety about Tenderland is currently playing out in China, where the government recently cracked down on a surge of depictions of sweet, effeminate men in media. "Danmei" TV shows like *The Untamed* and others (which carefully depict gay relationships in a nonexplicit manner to avoid preexisting censorship) have been very popular with young women in China (as well as crossover hits in the United States and elsewhere). The crackdown on effeminate depictions has also hit Chinese pop idols, who have been forbidden from wearing earrings or excessive makeup like their K-pop counterparts, and there have even been attempts to ban K-pop altogether. This has been an effort to reduce foreign influence but also to promote hypermasculinity at any cost. See Aja Romano, "The Chinese Government's Unlikeliest Standoff Is with . . . Fandom," *Vox*, October 17, 2022, www.vox.com/culture/23404571/china-vs-fandom-danmei-censorship-qinglang-social-media.

47. Doody, *True Story*, 291–93.

48. Samuel Richardson, *Pamela; or, Virtue Rewarded* (1740; repr., London: Penguin Books, 1985), 31.

49. Not every edition of *Pamela* contains this postscript. See the Project Gutenberg edition: Samuel Richardson, *Pamela; or, Virtue Rewarded* (London: Messrs Rivington and Osborn, 1740; Project Gutenberg, 2022), www.gutenberg.org/files/6124/6124-h/6124-h.htm.

50. Ruth Perry, *Women, Letters, and the Novel* (New York: AMS, 1980), xi.

51. Christine Haynes, "The Politics of Publishing during the Second Empire: The Trial of 'Madame Bovary' Revisited," *French Politics, Culture and Society* 23, no. 2 (2005): 3, www.jstor.org/stable/42843394. Per Haynes, the publisher had already made edits against Flaubert's will, fearing a lawsuit, but they weren't enough to stave off prosecution.

52. Ibid., 4.

53. Chantelle Billson, "Ron DeSantis Claims Disney Is 'Transing' Kids in Republican Debate," *Pink News*, January 12, 2024, www.thepinknews.com/2024/01/12/ron-desantis-claims-disney-is-transing-kids-in-republican-debate.

54. Judy Blume put it beautifully: "What are you protecting your children from? . . . No child is going to become transgender or gay or lesbian

because they read a book. It's not going to happen. They may say, 'Oh, this is just like me. This is what I'm feeling and thinking about.'" Quoted in Selome Hailu, "Judy Blume Scoffs at Roald Dahl Books Being Rewritten for Offensive Language: 'I Don't Believe in That,'" *Variety*, March 31, 2023, variety.com/2023/film/news/judy-blume-roald -dahl-censorship-book-bans-queer-books-1235570001.

55. Vivian Gornick, *The End of the Novel of Love* (New York: Picador, 1997), 157.

56. Werbel, *Lust on Trial*, 143.

57. Sarah Weinman, "The Essential Patricia Highsmith," *New York Times*, March 8, 2023, www.nytimes.com/article/best-patricia-highsmith-books .html.

58. Abigail Jones, "The Girls Who Tried to Kill for Slender Man," *Newsweek*, August 13, 2014, www.newsweek.com/2014/08/22/girls-who -tried-kill-slender-man-264218.html.

59. Fred Patten, "Retrospective: An Illustrated Chronology of Furry Fandom, 1966–1996," *Flayrah*, July 15, 2012, updated March 21, 2021, flayrah.com/4117/retrospective-illustrated-chronology-furry-fandom -1966%E2%80%931996.

60. See Sophie Gilbert, "The Dark Morality of Fairy-Tale Animal Brides," *Atlantic*, March 31, 2017, www.theatlantic.com/entertain ment/archive/2017/03/marrying-a-monster-the-romantic-anxieties -of-fairy-tales/521319.

61. P. W. Richardson and J. S. Eccles, "Rewards of Reading: Toward the Development of Possible Selves and Identities," *International Journal of Education Research* 46, no. 6 (2007): 341–56, doi.org/10.1016/j.ijer .2007.06.002.

62. Maldonado quoted in Mary Ellen Flannery, "Why We Need Diverse Books," NEA Today, October 26, 2020, www.nea.org/advocating-for -change/new-from-nea/why-we-need-diverse-books. *The Snowy Day* (1962) is credited as the first American picture book to feature a Black protagonist. Interestingly enough, it was written and illustrated by Ezra Jack Keats—a white Jewish man who changed his name from Katz to Keats due to the antisemitism of the era—and has faced some criticism on the grounds of appropriation and possible stereotyping. See Yvonne Zipp, "'The Snowy Day,' First Picture Book with Black Child as Hero, Marks 50 Years," *Washington Post*, January 1, 2012, www

.washingtonpost.com/entertainment/books/the-snowy-day-first-picture
-book-with-black-child-as-hero-marks-50-years/2011/12/04/gIQA
3a8yUP_story.html.

63. Jay Caspian Kang, "Do I Have to Read My Child Antiracist Books,
Even When They're Bad?," *New York Times*, January 13, 2022, www
.nytimes.com/2022/01/13/opinion/antiracist-childrens-books.html.

64. Quoted in Kara Yorio, "Ellen Oh: Here Be the Real Everyday Heroes
That Our Children Need," *School Library Journal*, November 10, 2022,
www.schoollibraryjournal.com/story/Ellen-Oh-Here-Be-the-Real
-Everyday-Heroes-That-Our-Children-Need-2022-SLJ-Summit.

65. Blair McClendon, "Such Things Have Done Harm," *n+1*, June 23,
2020, www.nplusonemag.com/online-only/online-only/such-things
-have-done-harm.

66. Aja Hoggatt, "An Author Canceled Her Own YA Novel over Accusations of Racism. But Is It Really Anti-Black?," *Slate*, January 31, 2019,
slate.com/culture/2019/01/blood-heir-ya-book-twitter-controversy
.html.

67. Myriam Gurba, "Pendeja, You Ain't Steinbeck: My Bronca with Fake-
Ass Social Justice Literature," *Tropics of Meta*, December 12, 2019,
tropicsofmeta.com/2019/12/12/pendeja-you-aint-steinbeck-my
-bronca-with-fake-ass-social-justice-literature.

68. See PEN America, *Booklash*.

69. See David Auerbach, "Twitter Is Broken," *Slate*, October 7, 2014, slate
.com/technology/2014/10/twitter-is-broken-gamergate-proves-it.html.

70. Jemisin has since issued an apology for her role in the affair; she claims
that she wasn't really attacking the story but that her tweets were badly
worded and misread. See N. K. Jemisin, "Statement on Isabel Fall Comments," nkjemisin.com, July 1, 2021, nkjemisin.com/2021/07/state
ment-on-isabel-fall-comments.

71. Emily St. James, "How Twitter Can Ruin a Life," *Vox*, June 30, 2021,
www.vox.com/the-highlight/22543858/isabel-fall-attack-helicopter.
For lack of further information regarding Fall's current identity, I've
chosen to refer to her with "she/her" pronouns. I apologize if this is
incorrect.

72. Alison Stine, "'I Have No Particular Power': Don't Blame Sensitivity
Readers for the Latest Censored Books," *Salon*, March 12, 2023, www
.salon.com/2023/03/12/sensitivity-readers-book-changes-censor

ship; "About," Inclusive Minds, accessed February 17, 2024, www
.inclusiveminds.com/about.

73. During the comic book panic of the late 1940s–1950s, some children
participated in the public burning of comics. See David Hajdu, *The
Ten-Cent Plague* (New York: Picador, 2008), 148–50.

74. A much-touted 2023 UCLA study purported to show that young people are opposed to sex scenes in movies and was held up as evidence of
widespread "puriteenism." But the study was based on responses from
young people ranging from ten to twenty-four years of age; it's reasonable for ten-year-olds to not be interested in depictions of sex. See
Samantha Bergeson, "UCLA Study: Gen Z Wants Less Sex Onscreen,
Prefers Platonic Relationships Depicted to Romantic Rollercoasters,"
Indiewire, October 25, 2023, www.indiewire.com/news/general-news
/gen-z-wants-less-sex-onscreen-ucla-study-1234919636.

75. See Gretchen Felker-Martin, "I Don't Wanna Grow Up (and Neither Can You)," *Filth* (Patreon), April 9, 2019, www.patreon.com
/posts/25994657. Felker-Martin refers to "certain left-leaning sets of
younger people, particularly teenagers and early twentysomethings"
who engage in "mass harassment and scapegoating . . . [of] independent creators, many of them marginalized themselves." She doesn't
use the word "tenderqueer," but the term didn't come into vogue until
the following year. See Daisy Jones, "Introducing: The Tenderqueer,
the Softboi of the Queer Community," *Vice*, January 24, 2020, www
.vice.com/en/article/939aap/tenderqueer-meaning-define-what-dating
-type-introducing. Interestingly, Jones's early dissection of the term
"tenderqueer" presents them as sexually appealing: "The tenderqueer
has no problem getting laid," but, she also says, they insist on setting
the rules of relationships. "Tenderqueers are especially adept at using
the watery language of therapy as a means to get out of most things.
They'll ghost you for three weeks then, when you call them out on
it, will reply something like, 'Your negative energy is affecting my
ability to heal from past life trauma.'" The tenderqueers even use language in odd and affected ways—clearly, in their past lives, they were
précieuses. (Note also how in this 2020 piece the tenderqueers were
"too sexual" in an uncontrolled sense, while afterward they were more
likely to be viewed as aggressively antisexual. Some odd qualities are
being projected onto a rather amorphous group.)

76. St. James, "How Twitter Can Ruin."
77. "Houston Independent School District," *U.S. News and World Report*, accessed February 16, 2024, www.usnews.com/education/k12/texas /districts/houston-isd-104364.
78. See Margaret Downing, "Bathroom Policies and Libraries Dominate the Public Speaking Portion of Thursday's HISD Board Meeting," *Houston Press*, December 8, 2023, www.houstonpress.com/news /hisd-bathroom-policies-and-library-shutdowns-criticized-once-again -17007144.

CHAPTER TWO: THE VICTORY OF THE NERDS

1. The claim that *Don Quixote* is the first "real" western novel is contested, but it does remain the conventional belief. Harold Bloom's introduction to *Don Quixote* describes it as "stand[ing] forever as the birth of the novel out of the prose romance." Miguel de Cervantes, *Don Quixote*, trans. Edith Grossman, with introduction by Harold Bloom (New York: Ecco/Harper Collins, 2005), xxiii.
2. Ibid., 935.
3. "Fiction Books Sales Statistics," WordsRated, January 30, 2023, wordsrated.com/fiction-books-sales. The movie statistic is true for both domestic and worldwide box office hits as of February 2, 2024; the two lists vary slightly, but in both cases, eight of ten of the most popular movies are science fiction. "Top Lifetime Grosses," Box Office Mojo, accessed February 2, 2024, www.boxofficemojo.com/chart/top_life time_gross.
4. Literary writers disclaiming genre ties was an especially popular move in the mid-to-late 2010s. The most famous example may be Kazuo Ishiguro's 2015 expression of anxiety over the reception of his novel *The Buried Giant*: "Are [readers] going to say this is fantasy?" Ursula K. Le Guin took great umbrage at the remark, and Ishiguro later qualified to *The Guardian* that he simply didn't want readers to avoid his book just because it had a dragon in it. Coming to Ishiguro's defense, fellow genre-eluding writer David Mitchell said, "Bending the laws of what we call reality in a novel doesn't necessarily lead to elves saying 'Make haste! These woods will be swarming with orcs by nightfall.'" This reference to the *Lord of the Rings* movies (not the books) clarifies that the stakes are about literary writers seeking to protect their works from

being lumped in with a perceived miasma of pop culture genre clichés. See Sian Cain, "Writer's Indignation: Kazuo Ishiguro Rejects Claims of Genre Snobbery," *Guardian*, March 8, 2015, www.theguardian.com /books/2015/mar/08/kazuo-ishiguro-rebuffs-genre-snobbery.

5. Olivia Pym, "The Best Escapist Fiction to Distance Yourself from the World," *Esquire*, June 18, 2020; V. M. Burns, "Now, More Than Ever, Is the Time for 'Escapist Fiction,'" *CrimeReads*, February 1, 2021, crimereads.com/escapist-fiction.

6. Jemisin quoted in Noah Berlatsky, "NK Jemisin: The Fantasy Writer Upending the 'Racist and Sexist Status Quo,'" *Guardian*, July 27, 2015, www.theguardian.com/books/2015/jul/27/nk-jemisin-interview -fantasy-science-fiction-writing-racism-sexism.

7. Jemisin identified this group as "a severe minority" of bigots. See N. K. Jemisin, *How Long 'Til Black Future Month?* (New York: Orbit, 2018), xii.

8. Peter Bebergal, "Samuel Delany and the Past and Future of Science Fiction," *New Yorker*, July 29, 2015.

9. Mark Dery has described science fiction as having "sublegitimate status" at the time of Gibson's writing. Mark Dery, "Black to the Future: Interviews with Samuel R. Delany, Greg Tate, and Tricia Rose," in *Flame Wars: The Discourse of Cyberculture*, ed. Mark Dery (Durham, NC: Duke University Press, 1994), 180.

10. A coworker of mine at Marvel once called Sarah Finn, Marvel Studios' longtime casting director, "the real hero of the MCU," a claim that's echoed in a lot of Marvel Studios' media coverage. Marvel's reliance on buzzy stars has had its drawbacks: they pinned the future of the Marvel Cinematic Universe on Jonathan Majors only to be pinned, in turn, by the abuse allegations against him.

11. Umberto Eco, "The Myth of Superman," trans. Natalie Chilton, *Diacritics* 2, no. 1 (1972): 21, doi.org/10.2307/464920.

12. Margaret Anne Doody, *The True Story of the Novel* (New Brunswick, NJ: Rutgers University Press, 1996), 211.

13. Cervantes, *Don Quixote*, 411.

14. "We are all Quixotes in reading novels—inevitably"; Doody, *True Story*, 268.

15. Samuel R. Delany, "The Semiology of Silence" in *Silent Interviews: On Language, Race, Sex, Science Fiction, and Some Comics* (Hanover, NH,

and London: Wesleyan University Press, University Press of New England, 1994), 31.

16. Doody, *True Story*, 18, 260–62.

17. Cervantes's last book was the heroic romance *Los trabajos de Persiles y Sigismunda*.

18. Doody points out that in most European languages, there isn't even a linguistic difference between a romance and a novel: the word used for both is *roman*, meaning a prose story written in the vernacular (Romance) language. Most European languages—even those that don't derive from Latin, such as German and Russian—use the word "roman" to indicate a longer work of fiction. English and Spanish are two of the only European languages to use the word "novel"/"*novela*" (originating from the Italian "*novella*," meaning a shorter story or collection of stories). The use of the new word seems intended to indicate new and particular qualities. Doody, *True Story*, 15, 187.

19. There are all sorts of exceptions and caveats here. Victorian novels were usually written in serial form, and contemporary literary novels sometimes have sequels or exist in sequence, such as Elena Ferrante's Neapolitan Quartet, which has also been adapted into a television show. Not incidentally, many realist Victorian novels remain beloved to this day, and the Neapolitan Quartet is a masterpiece.

20. The easy answer is that dragons aren't real, and divorce is; but other possible distinctions could be drawn. For example, dragons are *cool*, while divorce often is not. But also dragons function symbolically, while divorce, being a thing of the real world, mainly represents itself.

21. Janice A. Radway, *Reading the Romance: Women, Patriarchy, and Popular Literature* (Chapel Hill: University of North Carolina Press, 1984), 198. Radway bases her analysis of romance and myth partly on Umberto Eco's "The Myth of Superman."

22. Sarah Nicholas, "If It Doesn't Have an HEA (or HFN), It's Not Romance," *Book Riot*, April 10, 2017, bookriot.com/if-it-doesnt-have -an-hea-or-hfn-its-not-romance. HFN stands for "happy for now," i.e., temporary romantic fulfillment if not permanent commitment.

23. Amitav Ghosh similarly identifies science fiction and other genres as hybrids and notes the tendency of western modernity to be uncomfortable with hybridity and quash it whenever it arises. See Amitav Ghosh,

The Great Derangement (Chicago: University of Chicago Press, 2016), 71–73.

24. I understand that some people struggle to pay attention while listening to audiobooks, especially when multitasking, and therefore assume that everybody else has the same problem. What they actually have is known colloquially as a "skill issue."

25. The fascist usage of "NPC" to dehumanize other people dates back at least as far as Gamergate in 2014. See Cecilia D'Anastasio, "How Roblox Became a Playground for Virtual Fascists," *Wired*, June 18, 2021, www.wired.com/story/roblox-online-games-irl-fascism-roman -empire.

26. In 2021, Illinois state representative Marcus Evans Jr.—who is Black and represents Chicago's largely Black and impoverished South Side— tried to pass a bill banning the sale of *Grand Theft Auto* and other violent video games to minors, claiming that playing these games had led to a rise in carjackings in the area and elsewhere in the state. But this is a notable exception; it's almost always young white men who are imagined to be the moral victims of video games. Zac Clingenpeel, "Ban Sale of *Grand Theft Auto*, Other Violent Video Games, State Rep Says," *Chicago Sun-Times*, February 22, 2021, chicago.suntimes .com/news/2021/2/22/22295471/grand-theft-auto-illinois-ban-violent-video-games-carjackings-evans-operation-safe-pump.

27. "Sandy Hook Shooter Motivated by Violent Video Games, Norway Massacre (Report)," *Hollywood Reporter*, February 18, 2013, www .hollywoodreporter.com/news/general-news/sandy-hook-shooter -motivated-by-422271; Jane Coaston, "The Top House Republican Is Blaming Video Games for the Weekend's Mass Shootings," *Vox*, August 4, 2019, www.vox.com/2019/8/4/20753725/el-paso-dayton -shootings-video-games-gop-mccarthy.

28. A couple studies: Christopher J. Ferguson, "Does Media Violence Predict Societal Violence? It Depends on What You Look at and When," *Journal of Communication* 65, no. 1 (February 2015): E1–E22, doi.org/10.1111/jcom.12129; P. M. Markey, C. N. Markey, and J. E. French, "Violent Video Games and Real-World Violence: Rhetoric versus Data," *Psychology of Popular Media Culture* 4, no. 4 (2015): 277– 95, doi.org/10.1037/ppm0000030.

29. Alice Robb, "Tipper Gore Was Right, Violent Video Games Are Bad for

You," *New Republic*, August 5, 2014, newrepublic.com/article/118982 /violent-video-games-increase-risky-behaviors-new-study-proves.

30. Idrees Kahloon, "What's the Matter With Men?," *New Yorker*, January 23, 2023, www.newyorker.com/magazine/2023/01/30/whats-the -matter-with-men.

31. Attacks on children's fantasy novels didn't end with the Satanic Panic; *Bridge to Terabithia* was frequently challenged through the 1990s and early 2000s for alleged depictions of witchcraft and Satanism. See "Connecticut Residents Seek to Ban Two Newbery Medal Winners from School," American Booksellers Association, July 29, 2002, www .bookweb.org/news/connecticut-residents-seek-ban-two-newbery -medal-winners-school. The Harry Potter novels continue to be banned; in one 2019 case, the spells in the books were considered by frightened Catholic critics to possess actual power. Holly Meyer, "Harry Potter Books Removed from St. Edward Catholic School Due to 'Curses and Spells,'" *Tennessean*, August 31, 2019, www.tennessean.com/story /news/religion/2019/08/31/harry-potter-books-removed-st-ed-ward-catholic-school/2168489001. And see Aisling McCrea, "Satanic Panics and the Death of Mythos," *Current Affairs*, February 24, 2021, www.currentaffairs.org/2021/02/satanic-panics-and-the-death-of -mythos.

32. Rich Juzwiak, "Half-True Crime: Why the Stranger-Danger Panic of the '80s Took Hold and Refuses to Let Go," *Jezebel*, October 28, 2020, jezebel.com/half-true-crime-why-the-stranger-danger-panic-of -the-8-1845430801.

33. Joseph P. Laycock, *Dangerous Games: What the Moral Panic over Role-Playing Games Says about Play, Religion, and Imagined Worlds* (Oakland: University of California Press, 2015), 76–96. The Canadian cult horror movie *Skullduggery* (1983) was also made in reaction to the Dungeons and Dragons panic, but it's much less coherent and interesting than *Mazes and Monsters*.

34. This line from the film is a slight but possibly meaningful alteration from the line in the book: "The point of the game is to amass a fortune *and* keep from getting killed" (emphasis mine). Rona Jaffe, *Mazes and Monsters* (New York: Delacorte, 1981), 3.

35. These sentences are so significant to the meaning and purpose of *Mazes and Monsters* that they appear, in truncated form, on the jacket copy

of the first edition: "They could have been anybody's kids: attractive young students sent to college to prepare for life, offered the American Dream. Yet they rejected it for their secret fantasy world. Why?"

36. This is the movie version of the line. In the book, Daniel's mother says: "It's a rat race out there." Jaffe, *Mazes and Monsters*, 20.

37. Ibid., 163.

38. Laycock, *Dangerous Games*, 119–20.

39. Ibid., 121.

40. Ibid., 239. Laycock also notes that the belief in the perfection and desirability of the modern world is a departure from traditional Christian theology.

41. As Harold Bloom writes in his introduction, "When [Don Quixote] ceases to assert his autonomy, there is nothing left . . . and no action remaining except to die." Cervantes, *Don Quixote*, xxiii.

42. Douaa El Khaer, "Is Reading Fiction a Waste of Time?," Medium, August 9, 2020, medium.com/change-your-mind/is-reading-fiction-a -waste-of-time-95e85f157e91.

43. Neil Gaiman, "Why Our Future Depends on Libraries, Reading and Daydreaming," *Guardian*, October 15, 2013, www.theguardian.com /books/2013/oct/15/neil-gaiman-future-libraries-reading-day dreaming.

44. J. R. R. Tolkien, "On Fairy-Stories." The essay was originally presented in 1939 and published in 1947 by Oxford University Press; it can now be accessed online through the University of Houston: uh.edu /fdis/_taylor-dev/readings/tolkien.html#:~:text=The%20realm%20 of%20fairy%2Dstory,sorrow%20as%20sharp%20as%20swords.

45. Cervantes, *Don Quixote*, xxv.

46. David Graeber, "Revolutions in Reverse," in *Revolutions in Reverse: Essays on Politics, Violence, Art, and the Imagination* (Brooklyn, NY: Minor Compositions), 56.

47. Jane Austen, *Northanger Abbey* (London: John Murray, 1818; Project Gutenberg, 2023), chap. 25, www.gutenberg.org/cache/epub/121 /pg121-images.html.

48. Samuel R. Delany, introduction to *Starboard Wine: More Notes on the Language of Science Fiction* (Middletown, CT: Wesleyan University Press, 1984), 25. In another essay in the same volume ("Science Fiction and 'Literature'—or, The Conscience of the King") Delany describes

a conversation with a historian of the early nineteenth century who fell in love with science fiction. When the historian picked up *Pride and Prejudice* again—nervous how he would feel about it after reading so much sci-fi—he found that he loved it even more, but not in the same way as before, because he looked at the structure of Austen's world from a different critical distance. Delany says, "As far as I can tell, this man has started to read Austen as if her novels were science fiction. There had been an encounter" (297–80).

49. Ibid., 27.

50. Samuel R. Delany, "Racism and Science Fiction," *New York Review of Science Fiction*, August 1998, www.nyrsf.com/racism-and-science-fiction-.html.

51. Some of these criticisms of Delany were made by the writer Greg Tate; Mark Dery and Delany discuss them in an interview in Dery, "Black to the Future," 189–90.

52. Delany, "Racism and Science Fiction."

53. Berlatsky, "NK Jemisin."

54. This speech—"The Necessity of Tomorrow(s)"—is in Delany, *Starboard Wine*, 113.

55. Dery, "Black to the Future," 180.

56. Julian Lucas, "How Samuel R. Delany Reimagined Sci-Fi, Sex, and the City," *New Yorker*, July 3, 2023, www.newyorker.com/magazine/2023/07/10/samuel-r-delany-profile.

57. At the 2023 Star Trek convention, Levar Burton said that when he watched the original *Star Trek* series as a child and saw Nichelle Nichols's Uhura, it made him believe that "when the future came there would be a place for me."

58. The *DS9* writers toyed with the idea of ending the show with Benny Russell, implying that the entire *Trek* universe is only a dream. But instead, Benny appears in one more episode in the early seventh season, where he's been institutionalized and is scribbling Captain Sisko's adventures on the wall. He's become something of a literal Don Quixote type, or a combination of writer and character, believing that the imaginary world is real, more real than reality. His doctor thinks that writing has driven him mad: "The stories have got to stop," he says. "They're too dangerous." The doctor hands him a paint roller to destroy his stories. "Destroy them," he says, "before they destroy you." Benny thinks

about it for a moment—then punches out the doctor and keeps writing. He's not a Quixote type after all, or rather, *Star Trek* as a whole remains an inverted *Don Quixote*: the dream, which is more real than reality, remains unbroken.

59. Tolkien, "On Fairy-Stories."

60. Luigi Mastrodonato, "Italy's Far-Right Leader Giorgia Meloni Is a 'Lord of the Rings' Stan," *Vice*, October 20, 2022, www.vice.com/en /article/y3p59m/italy-giorgia-meloni-lord-of-the-rings.

61. The usage of "orc" as a dehumanizing insult has an ugly life in the twenty-first century. The term has been used to refer to immigrants and other "dark" outsiders; it's also been used in Ukraine to refer to Russian forces. The latter usage does feel somewhat fair given that Ukraine has been literally and not figuratively invaded. See Mansur Mirovalev, "'Orcs' and 'Rashists': Ukraine's New Language of War," *Al Jazeera*, May 3, 2022, www.aljazeera.com/news/2022/5/3/orcs-and-rashists -ukraines-new-language-of-war.

62. Berlatsky, "NK Jemisin."

63. Mastrodonato, "Italy's Far-Right Leader."

CHAPTER THREE: STOP MAKING FUN OF OUR ÜBERMENSCHEN!!!

1. There are plenty of documented links between American and European versions of fascism and proto-fascism (though these ought to be understood as links rather than identical DNA). According to Robert O. Paxton, it's likely that "the earliest phenomenon that can be functionally related to fascism is American: the Ku Klux Klan"; Robert O. Paxton, *The Anatomy of Fascism* (New York: Vintage Books, 2004), 49. As mentioned in earlier chapters, Sir Walter Scott's historical novels were an influence on the development of the Klan's fashioning of itself as heroic knights battling dark enemies. Paxton also notes that the first person ever described as a "national socialist" was the Marquis de Morès, a French aristocrat and "adventurer" who moved to the United States and become a cattle rancher. When his business failed, he returned to Paris, where he recruited a group of antisemites to attack Jewish businesses, dressing them in "cowboy garb and ten-gallon hats" (48). Later on, Hitler would famously become interested in the United States' Jim Crow laws, and they formed some of the basis for the Nazis' own race-based judicial structure. See Ira Katznelson, "What America

Taught the Nazis," *Atlantic*, November 2017, www.theatlantic.com /magazine/archive/2017/11/what-america-taught-the-nazis/540630.

2. Walter Benjamin, "The Work of Art in the Age of Mechanical Reproduction" (1935), in *Illuminations*, ed. Hannah Arendt, trans. Harry Zohn (New York: Schocken Books, 1969), web.mit.edu/allanmc/www /benjamin.pdf.

3. See Umberto Eco, "Ur-Fascism," *New York Review of Books*, June 22, 1995, www.nybooks.com/articles/1995/06/22/ur-fascism.

4. Jonathan Gottschall, *The Story Paradox* (New York: Basic Books, 2021), 15.

5. Ibid., 147. It should be noted that Gottschall lumps Dahomey warriors in with Nazis and Confederate soldiers, ostensibly for balance, but also so he can add a footnote about African participation in the transatlantic slave trade, itself a telling narrative choice.

6. See Tarisai Ngangura, "'White Supremacy Is Not Just for White People': Trumpism, the Proud Boys, and the Extremist Allure for People of Color," *Vanity Fair*, February 2, 2021, www.vanityfair.com /news/2021/02/trumpism-the-proud-boys-and-the-extremist-allure -for-people-of-color. Enrique Tarrio, the Proud Boys leader who serves as the main subject of Ngangura's article, was sentenced in May 2023 to twenty-two years in prison for his role in the January 6, 2021, Capitol insurrection. See also Sophie Boulter, "When Fascism Is Female," *Public Seminar*, August 31, 2022, publicseminar.org/essays/public seminar-org-2022-08-when-fascism-is-female; and Ben Jacobs, "Marjorie Taylor Greene Was Surprise Speaker at White-Nationalist Event," *Intelligencer*, February 26, 2022, nymag.com/intelligencer/2022/02 /marjorie-taylor-greene-spoke-at-white-nationalist-event.html.

7. See Tori Otten, "Stephen Miller Uses Textbook Definition of Immigration to Call for 'Massive' Deportations," *New Republic*, December 20, 2023, newrepublic.com/post/177685/stephen-miller-immigration -massive-deportations.

8. Jean Guerrero, *Hatemonger: Stephen Miller, Donald Trump, and the White Nationalist Agenda* (New York: William Morrow, 2020), 401.

9. The writer David Simon once tweeted in response to Miller: David Simon (@AoDespair), "Speaking as another Jew: You're a fucking shanda and if there were only nine of us gathered and it was the morning of my father's yahrzeit and you stumbled in and promised

to just sit in the corner and shut up, I'd say, sorry, no, we don't have a minyan," Twitter, September 5, 2023, x.com/AoDespair/status /1699190111189999761?s=20. If you're unfamiliar with Yiddish/ Hebrew, please trust me that this is an extremely sick burn.

10. Elisabeth Young-Bruehl, *Hannah Arendt: For Love of the World* (New Haven, CT: Yale University Press, 2004), 98.

11. Chaya Raichik (@LibsOfTikTok) is another striking example of a modern American Jewish fascist; she has also been involved in right-wing book censorship drives. See Matt Lavietes, "Libs of TikTok Creator Accused of Inspiring School Bomb Threats Named to Oklahoma Library Board," NBCnews.com, January 23, 2024, www.nbcnews .com/nbc-out/out-news/libs-tik-tok-bomb-threats-oklahoma-library -committee-rcna135369.

12. Joseph P. Laycock, *Dangerous Games: What the Moral Panic over Role-Playing Games Says about Play, Religion, and Imagined Worlds* (Oakland: University of California Press, 2015), 114.

13. Guerrero, *Hatemonger*, 8.

14. Ibid., 283–85.

15. Jean Raspail, *The Camp of the Saints*, trans. Norman Shapiro, 4th ed. (Petosky, MI: Social Contract, 1987, ebook), 23, 24, all over the place.

16. "Jean Raspail, French Writer and Hero of the Right Who 'Invaded' the UK—Obituary," *Telegraph*, June 28, 2020, www.telegraph.co.uk /obituaries/2020/06/28/jean-raspail-french-writer-king-patagonia -hero-right-invaded.

17. Elian Peltier and Nicholas Kulish, "A Racist Book's Malign and Lingering Influence," *New York Times*, November 22, 2019, www.nytimes .com/2019/11/22/books/stephen-miller-camp-saints.html.

18. Camille Jackson, "The Turner Diaries, Other Racist Novels, Inspire Extremist Violence," Southern Poverty Law Center, October 14, 2004, www.splcenter.org/fighting-hate/intelligence-report/2004/turner -diaries-other-racist-novels-inspire-extremist-violence.

19. Per the Southern Poverty Law Center's reporting, McVeigh said he was more interested in the pro-gun-rights part of *The Turner Diaries* than the racism. This claim seems improbable. Ibid.

20. Incidentally, the white supremacist "fourteen words" were coined by David Lane, a member of the Order. He drove the getaway car on the night Berg was murdered and was sentenced to life in prison. "David

Lane," Southern Poverty Law Center, accessed February 5, 2024, www
.splcenter.org/fighting-hate/extremist-files/individual/david-lane.

21. Jackson, "Turner Diaries."

22. J. M. Berger, "Alt History," *Atlantic*, September 16, 2016, www.the
atlantic.com/politics/archive/2016/09/how-the-turner-diaries-chan
ged-white-nationalism/500039.

23. Nafisi, quoted in U.S. Holocaust Memorial Museum, "Nazi Book Burning," YouTube video, May 13, 2013, www.youtube.com/watch?v=
yHzMlgXaiVo&t=1s.

24. Jackson, "Turner Diaries."

25. Ibid.

26. Samuel Delany, "Heinlein," in *Starboard Wine: More Notes on the Language of Science Fiction* (Middletown, CT: Wesleyan University Press,
1984, ebook), 132; Mark Dery, "Black to the Future: Interviews with
Samuel R. Delany, Greg Tate, and Tricia Rose," in *Flame Wars: The
Discourse of Cyberculture*, ed. Mark Dery (Durham, NC: Duke University Press, 1994),195.

27. Guerrero, *Hatemonger*, 124.

28. Ibid., 279.

29. Stephanie Pappas, "Is the Alpha Wolf Idea a Myth?," *Scientific American*, February 28, 2023, www.scientificamerican.com/article/is-the
-alpha-wolf-idea-a-myth.

30. A lot of fascist history-remaking imagines Aryans or other groupings
of white people as inhuman descendants of some kind of superior alien
race. Fascists really don't like to see themselves as human—or at least
not the same kind of human as everybody else. See Alexander Zai-
tchik, "Close Encounters of the Racist Kind," Southern Poverty Law
Center, January 2, 2018, www.splcenter.org/hatewatch/2018/01/02
/close-encounters-racist-kind.

31. Hannah Arendt, *Eichmann in Jerusalem* (New York: Penguin Books,
2006).

32. Toni Morrison, *Playing in the Dark* (New York: Vintage Books, 1993),
37.

33. The burgeoning far-right "Anastasia" movement that's currently
spreading over rural areas of Germany and Eastern Europe is based on
a series of fantasy novels written by a Russian businessman; the writer
claims they aren't really fantasy or even fiction at all but descriptions

of real encounters he had with a woman named Anastasia. She's supposedly "a very young woman with long golden hair and a fantastic figure," who taught the businessman traditionalist, exclusionary, back-to-the-land principles and just so happened to have sex with him. See Aaron Labaree, "A 'Right-Wing' Back-to-Land Movement Called Anastasia Is Making Germans Nervous," *Vice*, March 11, 2022, www.vice.com/en/article/epxk7n/germany-anastasia-back-to-the-land-movement.

34. Raspail, *Camp of the Saints*, 2.

35. Norman Spinrad, *The Iron Dream* (New York: Jove, 1978), 373.

36. Klaus Theweleit, *Male Fantasies, Vol. 1, Women, Floods, Bodies, History*, trans. Stephen Conway, with foreword by Barbara Ehrenreich (Minneapolis: University of Minnesota Press, 1987).

37. Raspail, *Camp of the Saints*, 97.

38. Hannah Natanson, "School Librarians Face a New Penalty in the Banned-Book Wars: Prison," *Washington Post*, May 18, 2023, www.washingtonpost.com/education/2023/05/18/school-librarians-jailed-banned-books.

39. Mike Hixenbaugh, "A Mom's Campaign to Ban Library Books Divided a Texas Town—and Her Own Family," *ProPublica*, August 11, 2022, www.propublica.org/article/texas-book-banning-libraries-lgbtq-hood-county.

40. U.S. Holocaust Memorial Museum, "Nazi Book Burning."

41. Patrick Sauer, "The Most Loved and Hated Novel about World War I," *Smithsonian*, June 16, 2015, www.smithsonianmag.com/history/most-loved-and-hated-novel-about-world-war-I-180955540.

42. "The Movie Rating System with Karina Longworth," *You're Wrong About* (podcast), November 16, 2022, podscripts.co/podcasts/youre-wrong-about/the-movie-rating-system-with-karina-longworth.

43. Real critical race theory is an academic-philosophical movement largely created by Black legal thinkers; much like cultural Marxism, it has little to do with the boogeyman version constructed by the Right.

44. "That 'cultural Marxism' is a crude slander, referring to something that does not exist." Samuel Moyn, "The Alt-Right's Favorite Meme Is 100 Years Old," *New York Times*, November 13, 2018, www.nytimes.com/2018/11/13/opinion/cultural-marxism-anti-semitism.html.

45. Theodor W. Adorno, "The Stars Down to Earth," in *The Stars Down to*

Earth and Other Essays on the Irrational in Culture (London: Routledge, 1994).

46. Jean-Paul Sartre, *Anti-Semite and Jew: An Exploration of the Etiology of Hate*, trans. George J. Becker (1948; repr., New York: Schocken Books, 1976), 13–14.

47. Eco, "Ur-Fascism."

48. William Marx comments that literature is "an ideal victim, and an ideal culprit too," and that literature's "powerlessness makes it the ideal scapegoat." William Marx, *The Hatred of Literature*, trans. Nicholas Elliott (Cambridge, MA: Belknap Press of Harvard University Press, 2018), 138, 181.

49. Quoted in Moyn, "Alt-Right's Favorite Meme."

50. Historian and cultural critic John Ganz has described fascism as "simultaneously both silly and sinister." John Ganz, "The Jock/Creep Theory of Fascism," *Unpopular Front* (Substack), March 27, 2023, www.unpopularfront.news/p/the-jockcreep-theory-of-fascism.

51. Peterson has also used the term "postmodern neo-Marxism," which has the advantage of not making even a tiny bit of sense. Tabatha Southey, "Is Jordan Peterson the Stupid Man's Smart Person?," *Maclean's*, November 17, 2017.

52. Gottschall, *Story Paradox*, 12.

53. "Verses did not defeat me," laments a character in *Don Quixote*, "but my own simplemindedness." Miguel de Cervantes, *Don Quixote*, trans. Edith Grossman, with introduction by Harold Bloom (New York: Ecco/Harper Collins, 2005), 709.

54. Katharine Burdekin, *Swastika Night* (Old Westbury, NY: Feminist, 1985), 101.

55. See Matt Lavietes, "Protesters Are Bloodied and Arrested at NYC Drag Story Hour," NBC News, March 20, 2023, www.nbcnews.com/nbc-out/out-news/protesters-bloodied-arrested-nyc-drag-story-hour-rcna75724.

56. Patrick Nathan, *Image Control: Social Media, Fascism, and the Dismantling of Democracy* (Berkeley, CA: Counterpoint, 2021), 69.

57. My nieces and nephews gave up on the reality of monsters and mermaids at a disappointingly young age. If you've ever brought up unicorns around a four-year-old only to hear them scoff, "Unicorns aren't real," you have not experienced true devastation.

58. Ian Lovett and Adam Nagourney, "Video Rant, Then Deadly Rampage in California Town," *New York Times*, May 24, 2014, www.nytimes.com/2014/05/25/us/california-drive-by-shooting.html.

59. Kyle Smith, "Women Are Not Capable of Understanding 'GoodFellas,'" *New York Post*, June 10, 2015.

60. Malcom Harris, "'Breaking Bad': White Supremacist Fable?," *Salon*, September 12, 2012, www.salon.com/2012/09/12/breaking_bad_white_supremacist_fable. There are literally fascist fight clubs in the United States, though they aren't explicitly based on the film or the original novel. See Mack Lamoureux and Sam Eagan, "Neo-Nazi Fight Clubs Are Fat-Shaming Men into White Nationalism," *Vice*, April 11, 2023, www.vice.com/en/article/n7evgw/neo-nazi-fight-clubs-robert-rundo-fat-shaming-white-nationalism.

61. Ursula K. Le Guin's "carrier bag theory of fiction" discusses an original approach to storytelling outside violent and masculinist frames. See Ursula K. Le Guin, "The Carrier Bag Theory of Fiction," in *Dancing at the Edge of the World: Thoughts on Words, Women, Places* (New York: Perennial Library, 1990).

62. To give just one example, War Machine (a Black male character) briefly replaced Iron Man in the 1990s.

63. Elaine Castillo, *How to Read Now* (New York: Viking, 2022), 126.

64. Ibid., 127.

65. Christina Orlando, editor at Tor.com, mentions the "X-Men problem" in an interview with Tasha Robinson. Tasha Robinson, "How the New Diversity Is Transforming Science Fiction's Future," *Polygon*, October 27, 2020, www.polygon.com/2020/10/27/21536783/science-fiction-predictions-book-recommendations.

66. AMC+, "Stan Lee on the Idea for X-Men: Robert Kirkman's Secret History of Comics," YouTube video, November 6, 2017, www.youtube.com/watch?v=xpBxvzrp5Ng.

67. Joshua Isaac, "Professor X and Magneto Were NOT Based On Martin Luther King and Malcolm X," *ScreenRant*, August 21, 2021, screenrant.com/professor-x-xavier-magneto-martin-luther-king-malcolm; Dorian Lynskey, "Exclusive: X-Men's Chris Claremont Talks through Five Key Storylines," *Empire*, June 4, 2016, www.empireonline.com/movies/features/x-men-wolverine-jean-grey-chris-claremont-five-key-storylines.

68. Claremont created Northstar but didn't write the comic where he finally came out as openly gay (1992). It was heavily hinted at until that point.

69. Incidentally the X-Men comics, among others, have also been subject to book bans. See Brandon Schreur, "Missouri Law Bans X-Men, Walking Dead, Watchmen, Batman from Schools," *CBR*, November 17, 2022, www.cbr.com/missouri-law-schools-ban-batman-walking-dead-watchmen-books.

70. Technically Magneto wasn't officially canonized as Jewish until 1981, but this is very deep in the nerdy weeds and doesn't change the fact that the writers were Jewish. See Abraham Josephine Riesman, "How Magneto Became Jewish," *Vulture*, June 5, 2019, www.vulture.com/2019/06/dark-phoenix-how-the-x-men-magneto-became-jewish.html.

71. See—of all people—David J. Bier (of the Cato Institute), "Biden Can't Stop Immigration. Time to Embrace It," *New York Times*, November 3, 2023, www.nytimes.com/2023/11/03/opinion/immigration-border-biden.html.

CHAPTER FOUR: FEAR OF A RED LITERATURE

1. Frances Stonor Saunders, *Who Paid the Piper? The CIA and the Cultural Cold War* (London: Granta Books, 1999), 323, 353, 366, 165, 346.

2. The Pentagon connection isn't a conspiracy theory either: the Department of Defense describes its relationship with Hollywood on its own website. See Katie Lange, "How and Why the DOD Works With Hollywood," U.S. Department of Defense blog, February 28, 2018, www.defense.gov/News/Inside-DOD/blog/article/2062735/how-why-the-dod-works-with-hollywood.

3. There are many examples of this argument, but the best known may be Adam Curtis's documentary *HyperNormalisation* (BBC, 2016).

4. Stonor Saunders, *Who Paid the Piper?*, 83.

5. Ibid., 381–84.

6. Joel Whitney, "Fifty Years of Disquietude," *Baffler*, December 2016, thebaffler.com/salvos/fifty-years-marquez-whitney.

7. "IWW" will be used throughout this chapter to refer to the Iowa Writers' Workshop, not the Industrial Workers of the World. On literary magazines, see Stonor Saunders, *Who Paid the Piper?*, 333.

8. Eric Bennett, *Workshops of Empire* (Iowa City: University of Iowa

Press, 2015), 112–13. The irony of publishing this particular book through the University of Iowa Press is not lost on Bennett.

9. Ibid., 59, 69.

10. Richard Brody of *The New Yorker* suggests the paranoia bred by the HUAC also led to the creation of some subtle and interesting art, as directors translated their fear into fiction that would pass the censors. See Richard Brody, "What Hollywood Lost When the Communists Were Purged," *New Yorker*, August 15, 2014, www.newyorker.com/culture /richard-brody/hollywood-lost-communists-purged.

11. This quote is most commonly associated with Mark Fisher and his book on the subject, but he attributes the original phrase to Slavoj Žižek and Fredric Jameson. See Mark Fisher, *Capitalist Realism: Is There No Alternative?* (Ropley, UK: Zero Books, 2009), 2, files.libcom.org/files /Capitalist%20Realism_%20Is%20There%20No%20Alternat%20 -%20Mark%20Fisher.pdf.

12. The Cold War remains "the contingent foundation on which many American writers have erected structures of ostensibly eternal common sense." Bennett, *Workshops of Empire*, 4.

13. Eric Bennett, "How Iowa Flattened Literature," *Chronicle of Higher Education*, February 10, 2014, www.chronicle.com/article/how-iowa -flattened-literature.

14. Mark McGurl, *The Program Era: Postwar Fiction and the Rise of Creative Writing* (Cambridge, MA: Harvard University Press, 2009), xi.

15. Ibid., 260.

16. Sandra Cisneros, *The House on Mango Street* (1983; repr., New York: Alfred A. Knopf, 2015), xv.

17. McGurl, *Program Era*, 337.

18. Lena Dunham attended Oberlin around the same time that I did; *Girls* is a good example of what the assignment was and that she understood it.

19. Kevin Jackson, "A Glimpse of Zadie Smith," *New Yorker*, October 10, 1999, www.newyorker.com/magazine/1999/10/18/next-generation-l -zadie-smith.

20. Michael Schaub, "Joyce Carol Oates Riles Up Literary Twitter... Again," *Kirkus Reviews*, March 16, 2021, www.kirkusreviews.com /news-and-features/articles/joyce-carol-oates-riles-up-literary-twitter -again.

21. For more on the conglomeration of fiction—and its impact on the

prevalence of autofiction—see Dan Sinykin, *Big Fiction: How Conglomeration Changed the Publishing Industry and American Literature* (New York: Columbia University Press, 2023).

22. McGurl, *Program Era*, 398.

23. Zadie Smith, "Fascinated to Presume: In Defense of Fiction," *New York Review of Books*, October 24, 2019, www.nybooks.com/articles/2019/10/24/zadie-smith-in-defense-of-fiction.

24. Laura Miller, "Real Life," *Slate*, May 22, 2023, slate.com/culture/2023/05/late-americans-brandon-taylor-twitter-novel-review.html.

25. Brandon Taylor, "bobos in ikea," *Sweater Weather* (Substack), August 17, 2021, blgtylr.substack.com/p/bobos-in-ikea.

26. McGurl, *Program Era*, 409. This book came out in 2009, so McGurl gets a little grace on the matter of rising tuition.

27. Bertrand Cooper, "Who Actually Gets to Create Black Pop Culture?," *Current Affairs*, July 25, 2021, www.currentaffairs.org/2021/07/who-actually-gets-to-create-black-pop-culture. I edited this piece.

28. Sophia June, "The Makings of a Literary It-Girl," *Nylon*, October 24, 2023, www.nylon.com/life/the-makings-of-a-literary-it-girl. Elena Ferrante, operating under a pseudonym, is either a lovely exception to this rule or a last gasp—or, arguably, the mystery of her identity is itself a great sales tactic.

29. Brian Merchant of *Vice* compares CIA-influenced workshop writing to an SEO content farm, which is an extreme metaphor but accurate insofar as the mechanics of capitalist reproduction are concerned. See Brian Merchant, "The CIA Helped Build the Content Farm That Churns Out American Literature," *Vice*, February 11, 2014, www.vice.com/en/article/4x3vg3/how-the-cia-turned-american-literature-into-a-content-farm.

30. David Kipen, "85 Years Ago, FDR Saved American Writers. Could It Ever Happen Again?," *Los Angeles Times*, May 6, 2020, www.latimes.com/entertainment-arts/books/story/2020-05-06/post-coronavirus-federal-writers-project.

31. McGurl, *Program Era*, 4.

32. By the late 1940s/early 1950s, many leftist writers had already turned against communism after the double betrayals of Stalin's purges and the Molotov-Ribbentrop Pact; they were ready for a new ideology. See Stonor Saunders, *Who Paid the Piper?*, 160.

33. Bennett, *Workshops of Empire*, 99. Elsewhere, Bennett describes this as "soft containment" of writers (38).

34. Ibid., 36–39.

35. Stonor Saunders, *Who Paid the Piper?*, 144, 162.

36. Bennett, *Workshops of Empire*, 38.

37. Ibid., 41.

38. Ibid., 107. Incidentally, Engle once participated in a homegrown scam called "the Famous Writers School" that tricked aspiring U.S. writers into signing up for a fake correspondence course. See Jessica Mitford, "Let Us Now Appraise Famous Writers," *Atlantic*, July 1970, www .theatlantic.com/magazine/archive/1970/07/let-us-now-appraise-fa mous-writers/305319.

39. It really was all paperback novels; they were regarded as a suspicious medium at this time. See Kenneth C. Davis, *Two-Bit Culture: The Paperbacking of America* (Boston: Houghton Mifflin, 1984).

40. Stonor Saunders, *Who Paid the Piper?*, 284–85. See also Peter Feuerherd, "How Hollywood Thrived through the Red Scare," *Jstor Daily*, December 2, 2017, daily.jstor.org/how-hollywood-thrived-through -the-red-scare.

41. Jackie Mansky, "An Early Run-In with Censors Led Rod Serling to 'The Twilight Zone,'" *Smithsonian*, April 1, 2019, www.smithsonian mag.com/arts-culture/early-run-censors-led-rod-serling-twilight -zone-180971837.

42. Tony Albarella, review of "Noon on Doomsday," by Rod Serling (April 25, 1956), Rod Serling Memorial Foundation, rodserling.com /noon-on-doomsday-1956-reviewed.

43. McGurl, *Program Era*, 178.

44. James Baldwin, "Everybody's Protest Novel," in *Collected Essays* (New York: Library of America, 1998), 18.

45. McGurl, *Program Era*, 346.

46. "Our Withdrawn Review 'Blood Cotton,'" *Economist*, September 5, 2014, www.economist.com/books-and-arts/2014/09/05/our-withdrawn -review-blood-cotton.

47. Toni Morrison, *Beloved* (New York: Vintage International, 2004), 177.

48. McGurl, *Program Era*, 347.

49. Garth Greenwell, "A Moral Education," *Yale Review*, March 20, 2023, yalereview.org/article/garth-greenwell-philip-roth.

50. See Mary Gaitskill's complex and unsettling essay "The Trials of the Young," *Chronicle of Higher Education*, March 8, 2023, www.chronicle .com/article/the-trials-of-the-young.

51. Greenwell, "Moral Education." Greenwell tries to draw a distinction between his perspective and the sort of amoral, art-for-art's-sake criticism that he says was common in the 1990s, but I'm not sure there's that much daylight between them. That version of art for art's sake was generally acting in defense of certain kinds of storytelling, not actually staking out a position outside the theater of judgment, i.e., it was never really *amoral* in any sense.

52. See Becca Rothfeld, "Sanctimony Literature," *Liberties* 1, no. 3 (n.d.), libertiesjournal.com/articles/sanctimony-literature.

53. Thomas Pynchon, *The Crying of Lot 49* (New York: Harper Perennial, 1965), 150.

54. The subhead for an article about Sally Rooney in *Jacobin* reads: "It's not easy to imagine a Marxist love story." Anastasia Baucina, "How Sally Rooney Gave Normal People Radical Politics," *Jacobin*, May 6, 2020, jacobin.com/2020/05/sally-rooney-normal-people-bbc-literature. Jennifer Wilson writes in *The New Republic:* "What would a Marxist novel actually look like? Is it simply about depicting working-class characters? Should it rail against capitalist exploitation? Or should it, as Rooney tends to do in her fiction, work within the confines of the bourgeois novel to expose (and perchance transcend) the transactional nature of relationships under capitalism?" Jennifer Wilson, "How Should a Millennial Marxist Novel Be?," *New Republic*, September 2, 2021, newrepublic.com/article/163505/millennial-marxist-novel-be-sally -rooney-beautiful-world-review.

55. Violet Haeun Kim, "Writing What Bothers: A Conversation with Frances Cha," *Rumpus*, September 3, 2020, therumpus.net/2020/09/03/ the-rumpus-interview-with-frances-cha.

56. David R. Shumway, "What Is Realism?," *Storyworlds* 9, no. 1–2 (Summer–Winter 2017): 192, doi.org/10.5250/storyworlds.9.1-2.0183.

57. Netflix's reported numbers should be understood as fungible and unreliable. Selome Hailu, "'Stranger Things 4' Fails to Break 'Squid Game' Record as Most Popular Netflix TV Season Ever," *Variety*, August 2, 2022, variety.com/2022/tv/news/stranger-things-4-squid-game-net flix-record-ratings-1235331754.

58. Millionaire influencer Chrissy Teigen threw a glamorous *Squid Game*–themed party in 2021. See Chelsea Ritschel, "Chrissy Teigen Accused of Being 'Tone-Deaf' after Hosting Squid Game–Themed Party: 'The Rich Are at It Again,'" *Independent*, November 19, 2021, www.independent.co.uk/life-style/chrissy-teigen-squid-game-party-b1958922.html.

59. Manori Ravindran, "Inside Netflix's 'Squid Game' Reality Show Disaster: 'The Conditions Were Absolutely Inhumane,'" *Variety*, February 3, 2023, variety.com/2023/tv/global/netflix-squid-game-reality-show-frozen-inhumane-welfare-1235511809.

CHAPTER FIVE: THE GENTLEMAN'S CLUB EFFECT

1. See Joanna Russ, *How to Suppress Women's Writing* (Austin: University of Texas Press, 1983); and Alice Walker, "In Search of Zora Neale Hurston," *Ms.*, March 1975.

2. Caleb Crain, "Twilight of the Books," *New Yorker*, December 17, 2007, www.newyorker.com/magazine/2007/12/24/twilight-of-the-books; Caleb Crain, "Why We Don't Read: Revisited," *New Yorker*, June 14, 2018, www.newyorker.com/culture/cultural-comment/why-we-dont-read-revisited. There does appear to be a somewhat separate problem of illiteracy and lack of attention spans in young people, likely due to a combination of poor teaching practices, smartphones, and pandemic-era learning gaps. See Adam Kotsko, "The Loss of Things I Took for Granted," *Slate*, February 11, 2024, slate.com/human-interest/2024/02/literacy-crisis-reading-comprehension-college.html. Additionally, there was a spike in readership in 2020, almost certainly because of the pandemic, but that may have subsided or at least flattened. See Jeffrey M. Jones, "Americans Reading Fewer Books Than in Past," *Gallup*, January 10, 2022, news.gallup.com/poll/388541/americans-reading-fewer-books-past.aspx.

3. Crain, "Twilight of the Books."

4. Phil Christman, *How to Be Normal* (Cleveland, OH: Belt, 2022), 120.

5. The shrinking of season length has also changed TV; for better and for worse, shows now have less room for filler episodes.

6. C. S. Lewis, *An Experiment in Criticism* (Cambridge: Cambridge University Press, 1961), 105.

7. Christman, *How to Be Normal*, 109.

8. See Max Read, "Going Postal: A Psychoanalytic Reading of Social Media and the Death Drive," *Bookforum*, September/October/November 2020, www.bookforum.com/print/2703/a-psychoanalytic-reading-of-social-media-and-the-death-drive-24171.

9. Also, despite popular stereotypes about accessibility and inaccessibility, popularity and elitism, literary fiction frequently outsells YA. See Lincoln Michel, "Who Is Reading What and Why," *Counter Craft* (Substack), January 10, 2024, countercraft.substack.com/p/who-is-reading-what-and-why.

10. See Tatiana Siegel, "Crisis at Marvel: Jonathan Majors Back-Up Plans, 'The Marvels' Reshoots, Reviving Original Avengers and More Issues Revealed," *Variety*, November 1, 2023, variety.com/2023/film/features/marvel-jonathan-majors-problem-the-marvels-reshoots-kang-1235774940.

11. Parul Sehgal, "Is Amazon Changing the Novel?," *New Yorker*, October 25, 2021, www.newyorker.com/magazine/2021/11/01/is-amazon-changing-the-novel-everything-and-less.

12. Cauley's May 2, 2023, tweet is no longer available but appears in a slideshow on W. Kamau Bell's Instagram at www.instagram.com/wkamaubell/p/CrwMAXnPMTT/?img_index=2.

13. On AI, see Ted Chiang, "ChatGPT Is a Blurry JPEG of the Web," *New Yorker*, February 9, 2023, www.newyorker.com/tech/annals-of-technology/chatgpt-is-a-blurry-jpeg-of-the-web.

14. Mark Richardson, "Kelefa Sanneh on Rockism, Disappearing Genres, and His New Book *Major Labels*," *Pitchfork*, October 14, 2021, pitchfork.com/thepitch/kelefa-sanneh-interview-rockism-major-labels-book.

15. Kelafa Sanneh, "The Rap Against Rockism," *New York Times*, October 31, 2004, www.nytimes.com/2004/10/31/arts/music/the-rap-against-rockism.html.

16. Taylor Swift is still a frequent subject of anti-poptimist critiques. The most bizarre, bigoted, and uptight is probably Armond White's 2023 screed in the *National Review*, which compares the "mob madness" of Swift's young female fans to asylum seekers at the border. "It will take a counterrevolution," White insists, "to repair Swift's moral, aesthetic, and political damage." Armond White, "Taylor Swift's Asylum

Seekers," *National Review*, October 18, 2023, www.nationalreview
.com/2023/10/taylor-swifts-asylum-seekers/amp.

17. Sanneh, "Rap Against Rockism."

18. See Rax King's essay on the band Creed. Rax King, "Six Feet from the
Edge," in *Tacky: Love Letters to the Worst Culture We Have to Offer* (New
York: Penguin Random House, 2021).

19. Ruth Franklin, "A Literary Glass Ceiling?," *New Republic*, February
7, 2011, newrepublic.com/article/82930/vida-women-writers-maga
zines-book-reviews.

20. The most recent VIDA count was completed in 2019. See "The 2019
VIDA Count," VIDA, accessed February 8, 2024, web.archive.org
/web/20231003010833/www.vidaweb.org/the-count/2019-vida
-count/.

21. Rebecca Rubin, "Film Criticism Continues to Be Dominated by Men,
Study Shows," *Variety*, May 24, 2022, variety.com/2022/film/news
/film-critics-male-female-study-1235276110.

22. The term "anti-fan" derives from K-pop fandom, and refers to someone
who despises a given artist or musical group so much that they devote
their time, lovingly, to hating them. Jonathan Franzen, "Mr. Difficult:
William Gaddis and the Problem of Hard-to-Read Books," *New Yorker*,
September 30, 2002, www.newyorker.com/magazine/2002/09/30
/mr-difficult.

23. The imaginary *other people* who are perceived to be judging us for our
taste are sometimes fully imaginary and sometimes based on encounters with real people—usually in the late adolescent past. BookToker
Lauren Hower, quoted in a 2023 *Rolling Stone* article about "lit bros,"
describes her foes as "pretentious artsy college boys" and "pea coat–
wearing liberal arts student[s]." These are indeed the kinds of boys you
meet in college—and not often afterward. CT Jones, "Bros Are Coming for BookTok. These TikTokers aren't Having It," *Rolling Stone*,
October 19, 2023, www.rollingstone.com/culture/culture-features
/tiktok-bro-lit-booktok-infinite-jest-lolita-1234857879.

24. Franzen, "Mr. Difficult."

25. Sanneh, "Rap Against Rockism."

26. Incidentally, Franzen sniffs in his "Mr. Difficult" essay that a dislike
of twentieth-century music belongs to the consumerist "Contract"
model of art appreciation. "If the local symphony plays too much

twentieth-century music," he says, "you cancel your subscription. You're the consumer; you rule." But even most serious classical music aficionados (including me) are largely indifferent to serial music; not that many people want to listen to music that's irritating by design. Serial music was simply never gonna happen.

27. See Ursula K. Le Guin's unpublished interview with Sam Thielman: "Perhaps the real problem," she said, "is that people to whom the arts are extremely important—who listen to popular music, watch movies on screen or TV, or take their kids to the public library—often don't think of them as arts. American culture encourages 'art' to present itself as necessarily irreverent, revolutionary, distressing, formidable, esoteric, etc. People whose art is country music or *Zits* see NEA as elitist money going to elitist projects—nothing to do with them." Sam Thielman, "Unpublished Correspondence with Ursula K. Le Guin," samthielman.com, July 20, 2020, samthielman.com/2020/07/20/un published-correspondence-with-ursula-k-le-guin.

28. Jess Crispin, "Portals of Discovery," *Baffler*, March 2022, thebaffler .com/outbursts/portals-of-discovery-crispin.

29. Adrian Rennix, "The Politics and 'Pretentiousness' of Reading James Joyce," *Current Affairs*, April 28, 2020, www.currentaffairs .org/2020/04/the-politics-and-pretentiousness-of-reading-james -joyce.

30. Sanneh, "Rap Against Rockism."

31. Caitlin O'Kane, "The Federal Reserve Says Taylor Swift's Eras Tour Boosted the Economy. One Market Research Firm Estimates She Could Add $5 Billion," CBS News, July 18, 2023, www.cbsnews.com/news /taylor-swift-eras-tour-boosted-economy-tourism-federal-reserve -how-much-money-made; Brendan Morrow, "Why Taylor Swift Keeps Releasing All Those Re-recorded Albums," *Week*, May 10, 2023, the week.com/taylor-swift/1013413/why-taylor-swift-keeps-releasing -all-those-re-recorded-albums.

32. Martin Scorsese, "I Said Marvel Movies aren't Cinema. Let Me Explain," *New York Times*, November 4, 2019, www.nytimes.com/2019/11/04 /opinion/martin-scorsese-marvel.html.

33. See David Hajdu, *The Ten-Cent Plague* (New York: Picador, 2008).

34. Michael Schulman, "How the Marvel Cinematic Universe Swallowed Hollywood," *New Yorker*, June 5, 2023, www.newyorker.com

/magazine/2023/06/12/how-the-marvel-cinematic-universe-swal
lowed-hollywood.

35. Scorsese, "I Said Marvel Movies."

36. See Amanda Hanna-McLeer, "Melt the Crown," *Current Affairs*, July 18, 2021, www.currentaffairs.org/2021/07/melt-the-crown. I edited this piece.

37. Leslye Headland (as told to Michael O'Connell), "'Russian Doll' Co-Creator: Why the Auteur Myth Is Misogynistic," *Hollywood Reporter*, May 24, 2019.

38. Rebecca Theodore-Vachon, "The Next Generation of Auteur Film-makers Isn't Waiting Its Turn," *Shondaland*, November 11, 2021, www .shondaland.com/inspire/a38214317/next-generation-of-auteur-film makers.

39. Per UCLA's 2022 *Hollywood Diversity Report*, people of color make up one to two of every ten directors of theatrical films, and women make up one to two out of ten. For theatrical film writers, one to two out of ten are people of color, and two to three out of ten are women. Only one woman of color took a writing/directorial role on a "top theatrical film" in 2022. See Ana-Christina Ramón, Michael Tran, and Darnell Hunt, *Hollywood Diversity Report 2023* (Los Angeles: UCLA Entertainment and Media Research Initiative, 2023).

40. Sam Adler-Bell, "Marvel World," *Dissent*, Winter 2024, www.dissent magazine.org/article/marvel-world.

41. Charles Bramesco, "Ishtar at 30: Is It Really the Worst Movie Ever Made?," *Guardian*, May 15, 2017, www.theguardian.com/film/2017 /may/15/ishtar-30th-anniversary-worst-movie-ever-elaine-may.

42. Richard Brody, "To Wish Upon Ishtar," *New Yorker*, August 9, 2010, www.newyorker.com/culture/richard-brody/to-wish-upon-ishtar.

43. Zack Sharf, "Quentin Tarantino Says Marvel Actors aren't Movie Stars: 'Captain America Is the Star,' Not Chris Evans," *Variety*, November 22, 2022, variety.com/2022/film/news/quentin-tarantino-marvel -killed-movie-star-1235439798.

44. Pauline Kael, "Whipped," review of *Raiders of the Lost Ark*, *New Yorker*, June 15, 1981, scrapsfromtheloft.com/movies/raiders-of-the-lost-ark -pauline-kael.

45. A.O. Scott, "Steven Spielberg Gets Personal," *New York Times*, November

9, 2022, www.nytimes.com/2022/11/09/movies/steven-spielberg-the
-fabelmans.html.

46. Scorsese, "I Said Marvel Movies."

47. *Spider-Man: No Way Home* is technically an MCU film co-released with
Sony.

48. Claudia Eller, "Is the Soaring 'Spider-Man: No Way Home' Box Office
Success a Harbinger or an Outlier?," *Variety*, January 6, 2022, variety
.com/2022/film/columns/spider-man-no-way-home-box-office-west
-side-story-matrix-covid-1235147465.

49. Todd Spangler, "Amid 'Spider-Man: No Way Home' Box-Office Boom,
Most Americans Remain Wary of Going to Movie Theaters," *Variety*,
January 6, 2022, variety.com/2022/film/news/americans-wary-movie
-theaters-covid-1235147969.

50. David Hajdu points out that comic books became popular at a time
when movies lacked the technical ability to really show heroic spectacle, so if you wanted to see that kind of thing, you had to find it in
illustrated form. The transition from comics to film is in many ways
a natural development predicated on improved special effects. Hajdu,
Ten-Cent Plague, 30.

51. Charles Pulliam-Moore, "Stellan Skarsgård Hit the Nail on the Head
When It Comes to the State of the Film Industry," *Gizmodo*, September
28, 2021, gizmodo.com/stellan-skarsgard-hit-the-nail-on-the-head-when
-it-come-1847760941.

52. Mark McGurl, *Everything and Less: The Novel in the Age of Amazon*
(London: Verso, 2021).

53. Ibid., 44.

54. Ibid., 22.

CHAPTER SIX: THE ENEMY OF MY ENEMY IS—

1. Media Matters Staff, "Daily Wire Host Says It Is Unscientific to Cast a
Black Person as a Mermaid," *Media Matters*, September 14, 2022, www
.mediamatters.org/daily-wire/daily-wire-host-says-it-unscientific-cast
-black-person-mermaid; Benny Johnson (@bennyjohnson), "We are
a Nation in Decline," Twitter, July 14, 2023, x.com/bennyjohnson
/status/1679858804127854597.

2. Brad Lang, "How Rings of Power's Cast Dealt with Death Threats,

Banking Hacks and Racism," *CBR*, May 25, 2023, www.cbr.com
/rings-of-power-death-threats-banking-hacks-racism.

3. It's difficult to collect data on this particular usage of the culture war
    for far-right radicalization, as the reaction to pop culture events tends
    to be lumped in with other conservative complaints about "wokeness"
    that fall outside the scope of this project. Anecdotally, however, we
    know that some violent far-right criminals—such as the man who at-
    tacked Paul Pelosi—have been radicalized by reactionary events such
    as Gamergate. See Tim Arango et al., "How the Pelosi Attack Suspect
    Plunged into Online Hatred," *New York Times*, November 20, 2022,
    www.nytimes.com/2022/11/20/us/pelosi-attack-suspect-david
    -depape.html.

4. Ryan Beitler, "Walt the Quasi-Nazi: The Fascist History of Disney Is
    Still Influencing American Life," *Paste*, June 16, 2017, www.pastemag
    azine.com/politics/walt-disney/walt-the-quasi-nazi-the-fascist-history
    -of-disney. Per a 2022 investigation, many of Disney's employees, es-
    pecially those working in blue-collar jobs at its theme parks, don't make
    a livable wage. See Michael Sainato, "'Grossly Underpaid': Disney
    Workers Demand Higher Wages as Living Costs Soar," *Guardian*, De-
    cember 8, 2022, www.theguardian.com/us-news/2022/dec/08/flor
    ida-disney-employees-higher-wages-cost-of-living-soars. According
    to Disney's own numbers, its lower-level positions are disproportion-
    ately filled by women and people of color, while the management level
    is disproportionately white and male. See "The Walt Disney Company
    Workforce Diversity Dashboard," Fiscal year 2021, Disney Social Re-
    sponsibility (website), impact.disney.com/app/uploads/2022/01/FY
    21-Workforce-Dashboard.pdf.

5. Actress Daisy Ridley was also harassed. See "Star Wars Actress Kelly
    Marie Tran Deletes Instagram Posts after Abuse," BBC, June 6, 2018,
    www.bbc.com/news/world-asia-44379473.

6. It's very difficult to define what constitutes a "woke" film in the first
    place. If the term refers to diverse casting in a pop culture prop-
    erty, then several of the biggest box office hits were "woke" mov-
    ies (*Avengers: Endgame*, *Avengers: Infinity War*, *Star Wars Episode
    VII: The Force Awakens*), as were many flops. Poor ticket sales in
    China have often been blamed on anti-Black racism; see Shannon
    Power, "Disney's China Problem," *Newsweek*, June 16, 2023, www

.newsweek.com/disney-china-problem-little-mermaid-racism-diversity-bob-iger-1805992. Even this article, framed in a way that would suggest Disney's efforts at Black representation are doomed overseas, admits that most U.S. and European movies have done poorly in China since the start of the pandemic regardless of their casting choices. China also has its own robust film and TV industry.

7. On ordinary nerd bigotry, see Samuel Delany in his 1994 interview with Mark Dery: "The rightist streak in SF fandom has always been there—and has always been vigorously discussed. But, in a field inhabited largely by liberal eccentrics, the rightists have been seen as our most misguided eccentrics." Mark Dery, "Black to the Future: Interviews with Samuel R. Delany, Greg Tate, and Tricia Rose," in *Flame Wars: The Discourse of Cyberculture*, ed. Mark Dery (Durham, NC: Duke University Press, 1994), 202. Before Gamergate, there were also some smaller incidents prefiguring this sort of harassment. See Rachelle Hampton, "The Black Feminists Who Saw the Alt-Right Threat Coming," *Slate*, April 23, 2019, slate.com/technology/2019/04/black-feminists-alt-right-twitter-gamergate.html.

8. Rich McCormick, "Intel Buckles to Anti-feminist Campaign by Pulling Ads from Gaming Site," *Verge*, October 2, 2014, www.theverge.com/2014/10/2/6886747/intel-buckles-to-anti-feminist-campaign-by-pulling-ads-from-gaming.

9. The chili incident really happened: a woman was harassed on Twitter after she posted that she had made a big bowl of chili and was offering it to her neighbors. See Emily Heil, "A Woman Made Chili for Neighbors, and Outrage Ensued. Was She Wrong?," *Washington Post*, November 18, 2022, www.washingtonpost.com/food/2022/11/18/chili-neighbors-twitter-etiquette. As for Taylor and BTS, I would obviously never criticize them; please tell the Swifties and ARMY that I will do anything they say.

10. Kyle Wagner, "The Future of the Culture Wars Is Here, and It's Gamergate," *Deadspin*, October 14, 2014, deadspin.com/the-future-of-the-culture-wars-is-here-and-its-gamerga-1646145844.

11. See Aja Romano, "What We Still Haven't Learned from Gamergate," *Vox*, January 7, 2021, www.vox.com/culture/2020/1/20/20808875/gamergate-lessons-cultural-impact-changes-harassment-laws.

12. Wagner, "Future of the Culture Wars."

13. Pop culture writer Katharine Trendacosta refers to these as "transformative" and "curatorial" fandoms, respectively, terms which are in use in contemporary media studies. See Katharine Trendacosta, "The Decade Fandom Went Corporate," *Gizmodo*, December 19, 2019, gizmodo.com/the-decade-fandom-went-corporate-1840531064.

14. Roger Ebert, "The Fandom Menace: People, Get a Life!," *RogerEbert*, February 4, 2009, www.rogerebert.com/reviews/fanboys-2009.

15. See critic Simon McNeil: "A consumptive fan has staked his own self-recognition on a series of identities he can try on . . . He seeks himself in these product identities and ultimately finds nothing." Simon McNeil, "Fanishness, Consumption and Desire," SimonMcNeil.com, April 10, 2021, simonmcneil.com/2021/04/10/fanishness-consumption-and-desire.

16. Rod Lampard, "William Shatner: 'Gene Roddenberry Would Hate Woke Star Trek,'" *Spectator*, July 30, 2022, www.spectator.com.au/2022/07/william-shatner-gene-roddenberry-would-hate-woke-star-trek.

17. Adam Serwer, "Fear of a Black Hobbit," *Atlantic*, September 14, 2022, www.theatlantic.com/ideas/archive/2022/09/lord-of-the-rings-rings-of-power-fantasy-sci-fi-racist-criticism/671421.

18. For example, see Elon Musk's apparent belief that the hero of *Blade Runner* is a person named "Bladerunner." The world's most famous nerd, who has formed the stuff of his identity out of science fiction probably more so than anybody else, seems to know very little about it. See Max Read, "Let's Clear Up a Few Things about 'Blade Runner' and the Cyber Truck," *Read Max* (Substack), November 1, 2023, maxread.substack.com/p/lets-clear-up-a-few-things-about.

19. John Blake, "When 'Wokeness' Comes to Middle-Earth: Why Some Say Diverse Casting Ruins the New 'Lord of the Rings' Series," CNN, September 5, 2022, www.cnn.com/2022/09/03/entertainment/lord-of-the-rings-amazon-controversy-blake-cec/index.html.

20. The *Rings of Power* will reportedly cost $1 billion to produce. See Eliana Dockterman, "The Secretive, Extravagant, Bighearted World of *The Rings of Power*, the Most Expensive Show Ever Made," *Time*, August 15, 2022, time.com/6205837/the-rings-of-power-amazon-most-expensive.

21. C. S. Lewis noticed this same phenomenon when it came to paintings. "It is inaccurate to say that the majority [of people] 'enjoy bad pictures.'

They enjoy the ideas suggested to them by bad pictures. They do not really see the pictures as they are. If they did, they could not live with them." C. S. Lewis, *An Experiment in Criticism* (Cambridge: Cambridge University Press, 1961), 20–21. When it comes to the *really* bad IP shows and movies, the majority of people don't even like the bad pictures—they are too bad and can't be lived with.

22. Nicolas Vega, "Why Amazon Put Its $715 million 'Lord of the Rings' Series in the Hands of Two First-Time Showrunners," CNBC, September 9, 2022, www.cnbc.com/2022/09/09/amazon-the-rings-of-power-firsttime-showrunners.html.

23. As Meredith Blake wrote for the *Los Angeles Times*: "Jeff Bezos coughed up nearly a billion dollars on a 'Lord of the Rings' series that debuted last year and generated as much buzz as the latest season of 'Love Is Blind.'" Meredith Blake, "How Consumers and Creators Soured on Streaming," *Los Angeles Times*, June 13, 2023, www.latimes.com/entertainment-arts/story/2023-06-13/netflix-hbo-max-disney-hulu-lost-promise-of-streaming.

24. Ryan Cooper, "Unions Are Trying to Save Hollywood from Its Own Foolish Executives," *American Prospect*, July 20, 2023, prospect.org/labor/2023-07-20-unions-save-hollywood-foolish-executives.

25. Amazon claimed that the "completion rate" for overseas viewers was up to 45 percent; a completion rate of 50 percent or higher is usually considered respectable. See Kim Masters, "Inside Amazon Studios: Big Swings Hampered by Confusion and Frustration," *Hollywood Reporter*, April 3, 2023, www.hollywoodreporter.com/business/business-news/inside-amazon-studios-jen-salke-vision-shows-1235364913; Dylan Roth, "Star Trek Has Truly Reinvented Itself," *Polygon*, September 27, 2022, www.polygon.com/23345284/star-trek-tv-show-best-start.

26. Data per a 2022 screenshot I took of the Rotten Tomatoes rating.

27. One typically vague review of *The Rings of Power* called it "too big to fail" and gave little detail regarding what the show is actually about and what happens in it, as if reviewing a trailer. See Kathryn VanArendonk, "The Rings of Power Is Too Big to Fail," *Vulture*, August 31, 2022, www.vulture.com/article/lord-of-the-rings-the-rings-of-power-prime-video-series-review.html.

28. Wagner, "Future of the Culture Wars."

29. As Oscar Wilde wrote in 1905: "The poor reviewers are apparently

reduced to be the reporters of the police-court of literature, the chroniclers of the doings of the habitual criminals of art. It is sometimes said of them that they do not read all through the works they are called upon to criticise. They do not. Or at least they should not." Oscar Wilde, *Intentions* (New York: Brentano's, 1905), 126.

30. Laura Pitcher, "Woke-Washing: What Is It and How Does It Affect the Fashion Industry?," *Teen Vogue*, November 3, 2021, www.teenvogue.com/story/what-is-woke-washing.

31. Katherine Anne Long, "Amazon's Workforce Split Sharply along the Lines of Race and Gender, New Data Indicates," *Seattle Times*, September 23, 2021, www.seattletimes.com/business/amazon/amazons-workforce-split-sharply-along-the-lines-of-race-gender-and-pay-new-data-indicates.

32. Annie Palmer, "Amazon Faces Senate Probe over Warehouse Safety," CNBC, June 20, 2023, www.cnbc.com/2023/06/20/amazon-faces-senate-probe-over-warehouse-safety.html.

33. Jason Del Rey, "Bias, Disrespect, and Demotions: Black Employees say Amazon Has a Race Problem," *Vox*, February 26, 2021, www.vox.com/recode/2021/2/26/22297554/amazon-race-black-diversity-inclusion.

34. Daniel Wiessner, "Fired Amazon Organizer Loses Bid to Revive Race Bias Lawsuit," Reuters, December 8, 2022, www.reuters.com/world/us/fired-amazon-organizer-loses-bid-revive-race-bias-lawsuit-2022-12-08.

35. Catherine Thorbecke, "Amazon Fires Alabama Warehouse Worker Who Led Union Push," CNN, June 2, 2023, www.cnn.com/2023/06/02/tech/amazon-jennifer-bates-fired/index.html.

36. Jason Del Rey, "Leaked Amazon Memo Warns the Company Is Running Out of People to Hire," *Vox*, June 17, 2022, www.vox.com/recode/23170900/leaked-amazon-memo-warehouses-hiring-shortage.

37. Lucas Shaw, "Amazon CEO Asks His Hollywood Studio to Explain Its Big Spending," Bloomberg, July 5, 2023, www.bloomberg.com/news/newsletters/2023-07-05/amazon-ceo-asks-his-hollywood-studio-to-explain-its-big-spending.

38. On Bezos, see ibid.

39. See Cory Doctorow, "How Monopoly Enshittified Amazon," Medium,

November 28, 2022, doctorow.medium.com/how-monopoly-enshit tified-amazon-83f42a585c3c.

40. Anthony Pascale, "The Future of Star Trek TV Remains Unclear as Paramount Announces Streaming Spending Cuts," *TrekMovie.com*, March 1, 2023, trekmovie.com/2023/03/01/the-future-of-star-trek-tv -remains-unclear-as-paramount-announces-streaming-spending-cuts.

41. At the 2023 Star Trek convention in Las Vegas, I noticed that there were far fewer toys and accessories available for the new shows. There was some amount of cosplay—much of it for the animated *Lower Decks*, which I think is easily the best of the lot—and almost none for *Picard*.

42. Pascale, "Future of Star Trek TV"; Katie Bowlby, "Everything You Need to Know about the 'Yellowstone' Spinoffs," *Country Living*, July 9, 2023, www.countryliving.com/life/entertainment/g44482422/yel lowstone-spinoffs.

43. For legal reasons I am not recommending that you watch *Picard* and drink every time a character names an emotion or other mental state. I am not recommending that you do this, and I cannot be held account-able for any damages that may ensue.

44. Vega, "Why Amazon."

45. The stolen *Battlestar Galactica* plot point came in the otherwise ade-quate *Picard* season three; the stolen *Mass Effect* plot (including an out-right filched obvious visual reference) came in season one. This sort of thing isn't illegal, just lazy.

46. Josef Adalian and Lane Brown, "The Binge Purge," *Vulture*, June 6, 2023, www.vulture.com/2023/06/streaming-industry-netflix-max-disney -hulu-apple-tv-prime-video-peacock-paramount.html.

47. Elaine Castillo, *How to Read Now* (New York: Viking, 2022), 271.

48. Michael Schulman, "Why Are TV Writers So Miserable?," *New Yorker*, April 29, 2023, www.newyorker.com/culture/notes-on-hollywood /why-are-tv-writers-so-miserable.

49. Adam Kotsko, "Moralism Is Ruining Cultural Criticism," *Atlantic*, July 26, 2023, www.theatlantic.com/ideas/archive/2023/07/oppen heimer-movie-moralizing-reviews-social-media/674823.

50. Jamelle Bouie, "'Andor' Is the Best Star Wars Anything in Quite a While," *New York Times*, December 3, 2022, www.nytimes.com /2022/12/03/opinion/andor-star-wars-disney.html.

51. Leah Bannon, "The US Military Compares Itself to the Rebel Alliance. In Reality, It's the Evil Empire," *Jacobin*, January 2023, jacobin.com/2023/01/us-military-industrial-complex-star-wars-rebel-alliance-evil-empire-fantasy-heroism.

52. Adam Fleming Petty, "'Andor' Shows Us Star Wars Without Heroes," *Bulwark*, December 8, 2022, www.thebulwark.com/andor-shows-us-star-wars-without-heroes.

53. Jacob Oller, "The IP Era's Venture Capital Philosophy Has Poisoned Movies," *Paste*, May 10, 2023, www.pastemagazine.com/movies/intellectual-property/ip-era-franchises-venture-capital-filmmaking.

54. Ben Shapiro, who set Barbies on fire during his hour-long video critique of *Barbie*, is clearly much more interested in playing with dolls than I ever was. See Amanda Marcotte, "'They Need Us. We Don't Need Them': The Fall of Twitter Is Making the Trolls and Grifters Desperate," *Salon*, August 1, 2023, www.salon.com/2023/08/01/they-need-us-we-dont-need-them-the-fall-of-twitter-is-making-the-and-grifters-desperate.

55. CT Jones, "Inside TV Writers' Fight to Keep Their Shows from Disappearing," *Rolling Stone*, March 24, 2023, www.rollingstone.com/tv-movies/tv-movie-features/streaming-cancellations-hbo-max-breaking-point-1234680746; Alex Cranz, "The Golden Age of the Streaming Wars Has Ended," *Verge*, December 14, 2022, www.theverge.com/2022/12/14/23507793/streaming-wars-hbo-max-netflix-ads-residuals-warrior-nun.

56. Emma Nolan, "Warner Bros. 'Cut Its Losses' by Axing $90 Million 'Batgirl' Movie: Lawyer," *Newsweek*, August 11, 2022, www.newsweek.com/warner-bros-hbo-max-batgirl-movie-cancelled-tax-1732963.

57. Anthony D'Alessandro, "'Coyote Vs. Acme': Warner Bros Shelves Finished Live-Action/Animated Pic Completely as Studio Takes $30M Tax Write-Off," *Deadline*, November 9, 2023, deadline.com/2023/11/coyote-vs-acme-shelved-warner-bros-discovery-writeoff-david-zaslav-1235598676.

58. Michael Sun, "Why Are Movies and TV Shows Disappearing from Streaming Services?," *Guardian*, June 28, 2023, www.theguardian.com/tv-and-radio/2023/jun/28/why-are-movies-and-tv-shows-disappearing-from-streaming-services.

59. Alison Foreman and Wilson Chapman, "87 Titles Unceremoniously

Removed from HBO Max," *Indiewire*, May 17, 2023, www.indiewire
.com/gallery/removed-hbo-max-movies-shows-warner-bros-discov
ery-merger-list.

60. Jamie Lang, "Without Warning, HBO Max to Slash Dozens of Animated Series from Its Service," *Cartoon Brew*, August 18, 2022,
www.cartoonbrew.com/streaming/hbo-max-removes-animated
-series-warner-220212.html.

61. GLAAD Media Institute, *Where We Are on TV: 2022–2023* (Los Angeles: GLAAD, 2023), assets.glaad.org/m/114d72edf8a779a6/original
/GLAAD-2022-23-Where-We-Are-on-TV.pdf.

62. Asyia Iftikhar, "New A League of Their Own Series Declared One of
the Greatest Queer Shows of All Time," *Pink News*, August 16, 2022,
www.thepinknews.com/2022/08/16/a-league-of-their-own-gets
-queer-fan-reaction.

63. See Masters, "Inside Amazon Studios"; and BJ Colangelo, "Let's Not
Mince Words: Canceling A League of Their Own Due to Focus Group
Feedback Is Homophobic," *Slashfilm*, April 4, 2023, www.slashfilm
.com/1247769/canceling-a-league-of-their-own-homophobic.

64. Leen Dweik (@vivafalastin), "classics can be retold in whatever way
like idc but i think this era of colorblind casting is actually harming bipoc storytellers. why are we taking traditionally white stories
and throwing in poc instead of just... making new media based on
bipoc stories?," Twitter, April 4, 2023, x.com/vivafalastin/status
/1643306482375483412?s=20.

CHAPTER SEVEN: THE DRAMATIC CONDITION

1. Alyssa Rosenberg, "How Police Censorship Shaped Hollywood,"
Washington Post, October 24, 2016, www.washingtonpost.com/sf
/opinions/2016/10/24/how-police-censorship-shaped-hollywood.

2. Sophia Kovatch, Pamela Colloff, and Brett Murphy, "Is It Forensics
or Is It Junk Science?," *ProPublica*, January 31, 2023, www.propublica
.org/article/understanding-junk-science-forensics-criminal-justice.

3. Spencer S. Hsu, "FBI Admits Flaws in Hair Analysis over Decades,"
Washington Post, April 18, 2015, www.washingtonpost.com/local
/crime/fbi-overstated-forensic-hair-matches-in-nearly-all-criminal
-trials-for-decades/2015/04/18/39c8d8c6-e515-11e4-b510-962fcfabc
310_story.html; Ed Pilkington, "Thirty Years in Jail for a Single Hair:

The FBI's 'Mass Disaster' of False Conviction," *Guardian*, April 21, 2015, www.theguardian.com/us-news/2015/apr/21/fbi-jail-hair-mass -disaster-false-conviction.

4.   Hsu, "FBI Admits Flaws."

5.   *NCIS* has frequently been rated as the most popular show on U.S. television and sometimes the most popular show in the entire world. See Tim Kenneally, "'NCIS' Is the Most-Watched Drama in the World," *Wrap*, June 11, 2014, www.thewrap.com/ncis-is-the-most-watched -drama-in-the-world. According to Nielsen ratings for the 2022–23 broadcast season, *NCIS* was the most popular TV drama in the United States; only live football had more viewers. See Rick Porter, "TV Ratings 2022-23: Final Seven-Day Averages for Every Network Series," *Hollywood Reporter*, June 7, 2023, www.hollywoodreporter.com /tv/tv-news/tv-ratings-2022-23-every-primetime-network-show -ranked-1235508593.

6.   Jason M. Chin and Larysa Workewych, "The CSI Effect," *Oxford Handbook Topics in Law* (online edition, Oxford Academic, May 2, 2016), accessed September 19, 2023, doi.org/10.1093/oxfordhb /9780199935352.013.28.

7.   C. S. Lewis, *An Experiment in Criticism* (Cambridge: Cambridge University Press, 1961), 68.

8.   Mario Vittone, "Drowning Doesn't Look Like Drowning," Slate, June 1, 2013, slate.com/technology/2013/06/rescuing drowning children -how-to-know-when-someone-is-in-trouble-in-the-water.html. Originally published as Mario Vittone, "Drowning Doesn't Look Like Drowning, Mario Vittone, May 3, 2010, mariovittone.com /2010/05/154/.

9.   David Graeber points out that even the philosophical concept of "reality" carries an automatic association with state violence and state power—the English word "real" derives from Latin *res* and Spanish *real*, meaning "royal," i.e., the king's property. In fiction, state violence and state power usually have an automatic pass as something "real" and neutral, while alternatives tend to be instantly regarded as "political." David Graeber, "Revolutions in Reverse," in *Revolutions in Reverse: Essays on Politics, Violence, Art, and the Imagination* (Brooklyn, NY: Minor Compositions), 45.

10.   *Dragnet* the radio show debuted in 1949. See Rosenberg, "How

Police Censorship." See also Constance Grady, "How 70 Years of Cop Shows Taught Us to Valorize the Police," *Vox*, April 12, 2021, www.vox.com/culture/22375412/police-show-procedurals-hollywood-history-dragnet-keystone-cops-brooklyn-nine-nine-wire-blue-bloods.

11. See Matt Webb Mitovich, "What Were the TV Season's Top-Rated and Most-Watched Shows? And Which Cancelled Drama Did the 'Best'?," *TVLine*, May 31, 2023, tvline.com/lists/most-popular-tv-show-rankings-2022-2023-ratings/top-rated-new-comedy-18-to-49-demo. Of the top ten overall most popular shows in the United States for 2022–23—including sports, reality shows, and news programming—three were about the police.

12. Lois Beckett, "One in 20 US Homicides Are Committed by Police—and the Numbers aren't Falling," *Guardian*, February 15, 2023, www.theguardian.com/us-news/2023/feb/15/us-homicides-committed-by-police-gun-violence; Curtis Bunn, "Report: Black People Are Still Killed by Police at a Higher Rate Than Other Groups," NBC News, March 3, 2022, www.nbcnews.com/news/nbcblk/report-black-people-are-still-killed-police-higher-rate-groups-rcna17169.

13. Abené Clayton, "'Far from Justice': Why Are Nearly Half of US Murders Going Unsolved?," *Guardian*, February 27, 2023, www.theguardian.com/us-news/2023/feb/26/us-murders-unsolved-homicide-police-san-francisco-brandon-cheese.

14. Tamar Sarai, "Scripted Cop Dramas Paint a Dangerously False Picture," *Prism*, July 7, 2020, prismreports.org/2020/07/07/scripted-cop-dramas-paint-a-dangerously-false-picture; Shima Baradaran Baughman, "Crime and the Mythology of Police," *Washington University Law Review* 99, no. 65 (2021), 1-67, fingfx.thomsonreuters.com/gfx/legaldocs/gkplwmqlbvb/CRIME%20AND%20THE%20MYTHOLOGY%20OF%20POLICE.pdf. Lisa Avalos, "The Under-enforcement of Crimes against Black Women," *Case Western Law Review*, forthcoming, digitalcommons.law.lsu.edu/cgi/viewcontent.cgi?article=1461&context=faculty_scholarship.

15. K. M. Donovan and C. F. Klahm, "The Role of Entertainment Media in Perceptions of Police Use of Force," *Criminal Justice and Behavior* 42, no. 12 (2015): 1261–81, doi.org/10.1177/0093854815604180.

16. Julia Métraux, "How Police Work the Media When Civilians Die in

Custody," *Mother Jones*, August 10, 2023, www.motherjones.com/crime
-justice/2023/08/baltimore-police-violence-media-freddie-gray.

17. There have been promising recent efforts by journalists to set better
professional standards and change the general relationship between
news media and the police. See Tamar Sarai, "A New Kind of Crime
Reporting," *Prism*, January 25, 2023, prismreports.org/2023/01/25
/crime-reporting-journalism-initiatives.

18. Leslie Nemo, "How Do Police Dramas Shape What We Think of Real-Life Officers?," *Discover*, June 11, 2020, www.discovermagazine.
com/mind/how-do-police-dramas-shape-what-we-think-of-real-life
-officers; "Why Do People Become Cops?," *Dolan Consulting Group*,
July 9, 2019, www.dolanconsultinggroup.com/news/why-do-people
-become-cops.

19. Nick Martin, "Tear Gas Doesn't Deploy Itself," *New Republic*, June 1,
2020, newrepublic.com/article/157942/tear-gas-doesnt-deploy; Em-
erson Malone, "We Need to Abolish the 'Exonerative Tense' of Headlines," *BuzzFeed News*, May 4, 2023, www.buzzfeednews.com/article
/emersonmalone/police-traffic-safety-headline-language-exoneration.
For a broader look at attempts to shift the language used in journalistic
coverage of crime in general, see Tamar Sarai, "Journalistic Integrity
Requires a Reckoning with How News Media Covers the Criminal Legal System," *Prism*, January 24, 2023, prismreports.org/2023/01/24
/newsrooms-crime-reporting-media.

20. The first two ads were broadcast during football season in late 2022 and
the other one in 2023. I only watch ads during football games.

21. Kate Summerscale, *The Suspicions of Mr. Whicher* (New York: Walker,
2008), 223, 269.

22. I made up the names Hetlock and Shayfield. If you're a cigar person (or
a Sherlock Holmes person), I bet you clocked that immediately; but if
you aren't, I bet you didn't.

23. Stewart King, Alistair Rolls, and Jesper Gulddal, "How Crime Fiction Went Global, Embracing Themes from Decolonisation to Climate
Change," *Conversation*, August 30, 2022, theconversation.com/how
-crime-fiction-went-global-embracing-themes-from-decolonisation
-to-climate-change-185584.

24. Iceland had four murders in 2022, a shocking 200 percent increase from
2021 (two murders). But criminologist Margrét Valdimarsdóttir told

Iceland Review that, if judged in per capita terms against Iceland's increasing population, the homicide rate is actually going down. See Ragnar Tómas, "Homicide Rate in Iceland Not Increasing, Criminologist Explains," *Iceland Review*, June 20, 2023, www.icelandreview.com/news /homicide-rate-in-iceland-not-increasing-criminologist-explains. About one out of every ten Icelanders is a writer; see Rosie Goldsmith, "Iceland: Where One in 10 People Will Publish a Book," BBC, October 14, 2013, www.bbc.com/news/magazine-24399599.

25. Summerscale, *Suspicions of Mr. Whicher*, 303–304.

26. Lesley Goldberg and Daniel Fienberg, "'TV's Top 5': A Conversation about Police and Hollywood with the 'Law & Order: SVU' Showrunner," *Hollywood Reporter*, June 5, 2020, hollywoodreporter.com/tv/tv -news/tvs-top-5-a-conversation-police-hollywood-law-order-svu-show runner-1297222.

27. See Chimamanda Ngozi Adichie, "The Danger of a Single Story," TEDGlobal 2009, July 2009, www.ted.com/talks/chimamanda_ ngozi_adichie_the_danger_of_a_single_story

28. See Paul Achter, "Have You Seen 'The Wire?,'" *HuffPost*, July 21, 2015, www.huffpost.com/entry/have-you-seen-the-wire_b_7840604.

29. Taya Graham, interview with the author over the *Real News* Slack channel, August 10, 2023.

30. David Simon has done some charitable work for Baltimore and its residents, but given the fame and fortune he made from the show, Graham still feels it isn't sufficient.

31. Alyssa Rosenberg, "Shut Down All Police Movies and TV Shows. Now," *Washington Post*, June 4, 2020.

32. Rick Porter, "'Cops' Quietly Resumes Production," *Hollywood Reporter*, October 1, 2020, www.hollywoodreporter.com/tv/tv-news/cops -quietly-resumes-production-4069865.

33. Steven Thrasher (@thrasherxy), "But Brooklyn Nine-Nine is an even more effective form of social control than Dragnet. Jack Webb was a stoic white man—stern & unfunny & alone. But I seen so many of y'all on here—many of you Black Lives Matter suppoerts [*sic*] & social critics!—unreflectively singing Brooklyn's renewal," Twitter, May 12, 2018, x.com/thrasherxy/status/995283366059630592?s=20.

34. Graham interview.

35. Dexter Thomas, "Michael Brown Was Not a Boy, He Was a 'Demon,'"

Al Jazeera, November 26, 2014, www.aljazeera.com/opinions/2014
/11/26/michael-brown-was-not-a-boy-he-was-a-demon.

36. Liat Marks, "Whose Side Are We On? The Truth behind True Crime,"
Berkeley Journal of Criminal Law blog, April 13, 2021, www.bjcl.org
/blog/whose-side-are-we-on-the-truth-behind-true-crime.

37. Emma Berquist, "True Crime Is Rotting Our Brains," *Gawker*, October
12, 2021, web.archive.org/web/20231006162530/gawker.com/cul-
ture/true-crime-is-rotting-our-brains; Amelia Tait, "The Rise of 'Citizen Sleuths': The True Crime Buffs Trying to Solve Cases," *Guardian*,
October 2, 2021, www.theguardian.com/tv-and-radio/2021/oct/02
/the-rise-of-citizen-sleuths-the-true-buffs-trying-to-solve-cases.

38. Scott A. Bonn, "Why the True Crime Audience Is Predominantly
Female," *Psychology Today*, June 5, 2020, www.psychologytoday
.com/us/blog/wicked-deeds/202306/why-the-true-crime-audience
-is-predominantly-female.

39. Summerscale, *Suspicions of Mr. Whicher*, 220; Noor Al-Sibai, "True
Crime Ghouls Are Using AI to Resurrect Murdered Children," *Byte*,
May 31, 2023, futurism.com/the-byte/true-crime-children-ai.

40. Tait, "Rise of 'Citizen Sleuths.'"

41. McKay Coppins, "The Gross Spectacle of Murder Fandom," *Atlantic*,
June 14, 2023, www.theatlantic.com/ideas/archive/2023/06/idaho
-university-murders-true-crime-frenzy/674384.

42. *I'll Be Gone in the Dark*, six-part series directed by Liz Garbus (New
York: HBO Documentary Films Story Syndicate, 2020), www.hbo
.com/ill-be-gone-in-the-dark.

43. Men in the United States (and elsewhere) are more likely to be victims
of violent crime in general, including assault and murder, while women
are more likely to be victims of sex crimes specifically. See Rachel E.
Morgan and Alexandra Thompson, "Criminal Victimization, 2020 –
Supplemental Statistical Tables," U.S. Department of Justice, February 2022, bjs.ojp.gov/content/pub/pdf/cv20sst.pdf; and "Scope of
the Problem: Statistics," RAINN, accessed February 13, 2022, www
.rainn.org/statistics/scope-problem.

44. The most commonly cited study on the matter comes from Fin-
land: M. Näsi et al., "Crime News Consumption and Fear of Violence: The Role of Traditional Media, Social Media, and Alternative

Information Sources," *Crime and Delinquency* 67, no. 4 (2021): 574–600, doi.org/10.1177/0011128720922539.

45. On the fandom phenomenon, note that one of the most popular true crime podcasts is named *My Favorite Murder*, and there are a number of true crime conventions for fans, including CrimeCon. On turning crime into content, see Annie Nichol, "The True Harm of True Crime," *New York Times*, June 8, 2024, www.nytimes.com/2024/01/08/opin ion/movies-books-true-crime.html.

46. Critic Charlie Tyson has convincingly compared internet drama to stage drama: "There is, first, the performativity involved in calling out wrongdoers in front of an audience. Second, these shame events involve acts of collective fiction-making. When we shame people, we create a narrative that justifies our treatment of them." See Charlie Tyson, "Theater of Shame," *Yale Review*, September 1, 2022, yalereview.org /article/online-shaming-twitter-culture-tyson.

47. Summerscale, *Suspicions of Mr. Whicher*, 242.

48. There are a shocking number of examples of people faking cancer for money and attention, but the best known may be Amanda C. Riley, featured in the true crime podcast *Scamanda*. The Fyre Festival has been covered in multiple documentaries.

49. Juli Weiner, "West Wing Babies," *Vanity Fair*, March 6, 2012, www .vanityfair.com/news/2012/04/aaron-sorkin-west-wing.

50. Ibid.

51. Sarah Lyall, "They Can't Get Enough of 'The West Wing' Right Now," *New York Times*, December 29, 2019, www.nytimes.com/2019/12/29 /us/politics/west-wing-politics.html.

52. Luke Savage, "How Liberals Fell in Love with the West Wing," *Current Affairs*, June 7, 2017, www.currentaffairs.org/2017/04/how-liberals -fell-in-love-with-the-west-wing.

53. According to a February 2022 poll, one in four Republicans believes in some version of the QAnon conspiracy. See Susan Milligan, "A Quarter of Republicans Believe Central Views of QAnon Conspiracy Movement," *U.S. News*, February 24, 2022, www.usnews.com/news /politics/articles/2022-02-24/a-quarter-of-republicans-believe-central -views-of-qanon-conspiracy-movement.

54. Colin Dickey, "From Sound of Freedom to Ron DeSantis: How QAnon's

Crazy Conspiracy Theories Went Mainstream," *Guardian*, August 16, 2023, www.theguardian.com/us-news/2023/aug/16/qanon-conspiracy -theory-sound-of-freedom-trump-desantis.

55. Steven Monacelli, "The Fringe QAnon 'Cult' Is Still Waiting for a JFK Jr. Miracle in Dallas," *Rolling Stone*, December 1, 2021, www.rolling stone.com/culture/culture-features/qanon-dallas-conspiracy-theo rist-jfk-still-there-1264953.

56. For a representative example, see Awesomely Luvvie, "This Season of 'America' Has Jumped the Shark," October 16, 2020, awesomelyluvvie .com/2020/10/america-season-finale.html.

57. Mike Rothschild (@rothschildmd), "2024 could be the series finale for America as we've known it. It's all too easy to imagine a scenario where state legislatures are given the green light by SCOTUS to throw out results they don't like, nobody having any idea who won the election, and civil war kicking off," Twitter, June 30, 2022, x.com/rothschildmd /status/1542546686626525185?s=20.

58. There are of course novels and movies *about* conspiracies, some of which even sometimes contribute to the creation of new conspiracy frameworks (e.g., *The Manchurian Candidate*). What I mean is that ded- icated conspiracists themselves appear to be somewhat less likely to *cre- ate* fiction about conspiracies, since they already believe in them as true.

59. The QAnon marketing tie-in was reportedly against the wishes of the director. See Sammy Gecsoyler, "Sound of Freedom Director Denies Film Linked to QAnon Theory," *Guardian*, August 29, 2023, www .theguardian.com/film/2023/aug/29/sound-of-freedom-director-denies -film-linked-to-qanon-theory.

60. See Anna Merlan, "A Famed Anti-Sex Trafficking Group Has a Prob- lem with the Truth," *Vice*, December 10, 2020, www.vice.com/en /article/k7a3qw/a-famed-anti-sex-trafficking-group-has-a-problem -with-the-truth. Ballard has also been accused of sexual coercion by at least five women; see Anna Merlan, "Five of Tim Ballard's Alleged Victims Have Filed a Lawsuit against Him," *Vice*, October 10, 2023, www.vice.com/en/article/4a378p/five-of-tim-ballards-alleged-vic tims-have-filed-a-lawsuit-against-him.

61. Miles Klee, "'Sound of Freedom' Is a Superhero Movie for Dads with Brainworms," *Rolling Stone*, July 7, 2023, www.rollingstone.com/tv

-movies/tv-movie-reviews/sound-of-freedom-jim-caviezel-child
-trafficking-qanon-movie-1234783837.

62. Miles Klee, "They Made 'Sound of Freedom' a Hit—but Were They Deceiving Their Audience?," *Rolling Stone*, December 14, 2023, www .rollingstone.com/culture/culture-features/sound-of-freedom-angel -studios-audience-business-practices-1234928374.

CHAPTER EIGHT: HOW TO BLOW UP REALITY

1. Clayton Davis, "'Don't Look Up' or: How Netflix Learned to Stop Worrying and Love the Discourse," *Variety*, December 30, 2021, vari ety.com/2021/awards/awards/dont-look-up-critics-leonardo-dicaprio -netflix-oscars-1235144756.

2. On climate change's connection to other political issues, see United Nations Human Rights Office of the High Commissioner, "The Global Climate Crisis Is a Racial Justice Crisis: UN Expert," press re- lease, October 31, 2022, www.ohchr.org/en/press-releases/2022/11 /global-climate-crisis-racial-justice-crisis-un-expert; Julie Watson, "Climate Change Is Already Fueling Global Migration. The World Isn't Ready to Meet People's Changing Needs, Experts Say," *PBS NewsHour*, July 28, 2022, www.pbs.org/newshour/world/climate -change-is-already-fueling-global-migration-the-world-isnt-ready -to-meet-peoples-needs-experts-say; and "Climate Change and Con- flict," International Committee of the Red Cross, accessed February 14, 2024, www.icrc.org/en/what-we-do/climate-change-conflict.

3. The episode is actually titled "Gnomes" and is the seventeenth episode of *South Park's* second season.

4. Rotten Tomatoes ratings as of February 14, 2024; Catie Keck, "Don't Look Up Narrowly Misses Becoming Netflix's All-Time-Best Film Debut," *Verge*, January 25, 2022, www.theverge.com/2022 /1/25/22878712/netflix-dont-look-up-red-notice-bird-box-top-10.

5. Katherine Richardson et al., "Earth beyond Six of Nine Planetary Boundaries," *Science Advances* 9, no. 37 (2023), www.science.org/doi /10.1126/sciadv.adh2458.

6. "NASA Announces Summer 2023 Hottest on Record," NASA, Sep- tember 14, 2023, www.nasa.gov/news-release/nasa-announces-sum mer-2023-hottest-on-record.

7. The official death toll for the Derna disaster is over four thousand, though early reports estimated the death toll might top twenty thousand. See Ismaeel Naar, "Libya Floods Investigation Puts Derna Death Toll at 4,540," *National News*, January 6, 2024, www.thenationalnews.com/mena/2024/01/06/libya-floods-investigation-puts-derna-death-toll-at-4540; Hendia Alashepy, "Months after Deadly Floods in Libya, Migrants' Families Still Await News of the Missing," *Guardian*, November 21, 2023, www.theguardian.com/global-development/2023/nov/21/months-after-deadly-floods-in-libya-migrants-families-still-await-news-of-the-missing.

8. The literary critic Becca Rothfeld has pointed out that this view of fiction puts those who love it in "a losing position, for it is simply not plausible that literature will ever tank capitalism or keep the ice caps from melting." Becca Rothfeld, "Sanctimony Literature," *Liberties* 1, no. 3 (Autumn 2022), libertiesjournal.com/articles/sanctimony-literature.

9. Kendra Pierre-Louis, "Hollywood Has a Climate Problem," *Mother Jones*, July/August 2023, www.motherjones.com/environment/2023/06/hollywood-scripts-climate-change-plot-screenwriting.

10. A near-future episode of the Marvel TV show *Loki* centers around an apocalyptic "Category 8" hurricane and was praised by critics for tackling climate change. See Gregory Lawrence, "How Did 'Loki' Episode 2 Sneak In Terrifying, Prescient Satire about Climate Change?," *Collider*, June 19, 2021, collider.com/loki-episode-2-climate-change. The CBS show *Fire Country*—about incarcerated firefighters battling wildfires—is also sort of a climate show.

11. Melena Ryzik, "Can Hollywood Movies about Climate Change Make a Difference?," *New York Times*, October 2, 2017, www.nytimes.com/2017/10/02/movies/mother-darren-aronofsky-climate-change.html; "Research Findings: Climate Silence in TV and Film," Good Energy, accessed February 14, 2024, www.goodenergystories.com/playbook/research-findings-climate-silence-in-tv-and-film.

12. Amitav Ghosh, *The Great Derangement* (Chicago: University of Chicago Press, 2016), 72.

13. Ibid., 16.

14. Ibid., 6.

15. Lincoln Michel, "Everything Everywhere All in One Novel," *Esquire*,

July 13, 2022, www.esquire.com/entertainment/books/a40434090/genre
-bending-books/.

16. Derrick O'Keefe, "Kim Stanley Robinson Imagines a Future Where
We Don't All Die," *Jacobin*, December 10, 2020, jacobin.com/2020/12
/kim-stanley-robinson-ministry-for-the-future; Ezra Klein, "The Most
Important Book I've Read This Year," *Vox*, November 30, 2020, www
.vox.com/2020/11/30/21726563/kim-stanley-robinson-the-ezra-klein
-show-climate-change.

17. The original quote comes from a review on the website *That Shelf* and
was used in TV marketing campaigns in September 2023. Pat Mullen,
"TIFF 2023: Dumb Money Review," *That Shelf*, September 8, 2023,
thatshelf.com/tiff-2023-dumb-money-review.

18. Aubrey Plaza's line comes from episode 1, season 2, of *White Lotus*.

19. See Jia Tolentino, "What to Do with Climate Emotions," *New Yorker*,
July 10, 2023, www.newyorker.com/news/annals-of-a-warming-planet
/what-to-do-with-climate-emotions.

20. Ghosh, *Great Derangement*, 11.

21. Mary Annaïse Heglar, "To Build a Beautiful World, You First Have
to Imagine It," *Nation*, October 24, 2021, www.thenation.com/article
/environment/climate-world-building.

22. For legal reasons, I am not—legally—suggesting that you should go
blow up a pipeline.

23. See Gina Vivinetto, "Quinta Brunson Explains Why There Won't Be a
Shooting Episode of 'Abbott Elementary,'" NBC News, May 27, 2022,
www.nbcnews.com/news/nbcblk/quinta-brunson-explains-wont
-shooting-episode-abbott-elementary-rcna30827.

24. Ibid.

25. Carlos De Loera, "Nancy Pelosi Just Cited This Poet in Her Reaction
to Roe vs. Wade Reversal," *Los Angeles Times*, June 24, 2022, www
.latimes.com/entertainment-arts/story/2022-06-24/roe-vs-wade-nancy
-pelosi-poem-reaction-ehud-manor.

26. Bryan Metzger, "House Democrats Cheerfully Sang 'God Bless America' on the Steps of the Capitol as Crowds Protested the Overturning of
Roe v. Wade at the Supreme Court across the Street," *Business Insider*,
June 24, 2022, businessinsider.com/video-god-bless-america-demo
crats-supreme-court-roe-v-wade-2022-6.

27. Phil Klay, "False Witnesses," *Point*, April 26, 2022, thepointmag.com /criticism/false-witnesses.

28. Racquel Gates, "The Problem with 'Anti-racist' Movie Lists," *New York Times*, July 17, 2020, www.nytimes.com/2020/07/17/opinion /sunday/black-film-movies-racism.html.

29. Ursula K. Le Guin, speech in acceptance of the National Book Foundation Medal for Distinguished Contribution to American Letters, November 19, 2014, transcript, www.ursulakleguin.com/nbf -medal.

30. Le Guin doesn't reference Amazon directly, but she refers to "a profiteer" that recently "tr[ied] to punish a publisher for disobedience" (ibid.). This is a clear reference to the infamous 2014 dispute between Amazon and Hachette over ebook sales. Hachette had refused to accede to Amazon's price-fixing standards, and Amazon responded with "aggressive" tactics including disallowing preorders of Hachette books on the platform. See Hannah Ellis-Petersen, "Amazon and Publisher Hachette End Dispute over Online Book Sales," *Guardian*, November 13, 2014, www.theguardian.com/books/2014/nov/13 /amazon-hachette-end-dispute-ebooks.

31. Emily Wilson, the acclaimed feminist translator, says that after the publication of her 2023 *Iliad* she was contacted by a deodorant company interested in making a promotional tie-in product, so we've really come full circle on the whole deodorant issue. Emily Wilson (@EmilyRCWilson), "Sometimes I wonder bleakly whether my work has any real 'impact' beyond the academy. But I got an email from a company planning to manufacture A DEODORANT INSPIRED BY MY HOMERIC TRANSLATIONS. My life has not lacked purpose," Twitter, September 21, 2023, x.com/EmilyRCWilson/status /1704943088605573456?s=20.

32. The terms of the WGA agreement specify that writers can still use AI at their own discretion and companies have to disclose if "any materials" (presumably treatments, summaries, etc.) given to writers have been AI generated. See "Summary of the 2023 WGA MBA," WGA Contract 2023 (website), accessed February 15, 2023, www.wga contract2023.org/the-campaign/summary-of-the-2023-wga-mba.

33. Sarah Jones, "The Strikes Are Working," *Intelligencer*, September 26, 2023, nymag.com/intelligencer/2023/09/the-strikes-are-working.html.

34. On the Sun Valley Conference, see Sissi Cao, "What We Know about the Ultra-private Sun Valley Conference Host," *Observer*, June 27, 2023, observer.com/2023/06/allen-co-sun-valley. Iger quoted in Tim Mullaney, "How Netflix Can End the Hollywood Strike in a Way Disney, Paramount Can't Afford," CNBC, July 20, 2023, www.cnbc .com/2023/07/20/how-netflix-can-end-the-hollywood-strike-in-a -way-disney-cant-afford.html.

35. Kylie Kirschner, "Disney CEO Bob Iger Called Hollywood Strikers 'Not Realistic.' His Critics Are Calling His $27 Million Pay Package Unrealistic," *Business Insider*, July 22, 2023, www.businessinsider.com /disney-ceo-bob-iger-writers-strike-comments-criticism-salary-pay -2023-7.

36. The Authors Guild press release on the AI lawsuit mentioned that the median writer makes just twenty thousand dollars a year. See Authors Guild, "The Authors Guild, John Grisham, Jodi Picoult, David Baldacci, George R. R. Martin, and 13 Other Authors File Class-Action Suit against OpenAI," press release, September 20, 2023, authorsguild.org/ news/ag-and-authors-file-class-action-suit-against-openai. Per MIT's 2023 living wage calculator, a living wage for a single worker without children is around $38,000 a year, or nearly twice that of the median writer's salary (dependent on location). See Amy K. Glasmeier, "NEW DATA POSTED: 2023 Living Wage Calculator," Living Wage (website), February 1, 2023, livingwage.mit.edu/articles/103-new-data -posted-2023-living-wage-calculator.

37. Authors Guild, "Authors Guild."

38. Andrew Deck, "Why Silicon Valley's Biggest AI Developers Are Hiring Poets," *Rest of World*, September 20, 2023, restofworld.org/2023 /ai-developers-fiction-poetry-scale-ai-appen.

39. Michael J. Coren, "Luddites Have Been Getting a Bad Rap for 200 Years. But, Turns Out, They Were Right," *Quartz*, April 30, 2017, qz.com/968692/luddites-have-been-getting-a-bad-rap-for-200-years -but-turns-out-they-were-right.

40. Vauhini Vara, "Confessions of a Viral AI Writer," *Wired*, September 21, 2023, www.wired.com/story/confessions-viral-ai-writer-chatgpt.

41. At least one award-winning science fiction novel has already relied on the use of generative AI. See Benedict Smith, "Author Admits She Used ChatGPT to Write Parts of Prize-Winning Novel," *Telegraph*,

January 18, 2024, www.telegraph.co.uk/world-news/2024/01/18/author
-used-chatgpt-ai-to-write-prize-winning-novel-japan.

42. An early version of this argument appeared in my newsletter. See Lyta
Gold, "The Cult of Mediocrity," *Lyta's List* (Substack), May 5, 2023,
lytagold.substack.com/p/the-cult-of-mediocrity.

43. The advice to write a novel every three months is often presented in
scammy terms by a person who claims to write this quickly (and may
have been relying on generative AI prior to its wider mainstream adop-
tion). For a representative example, see T. R. Harris, "I've Made Over
$1.2 Million Writing Self-Published Novels," *Ascent Publication* (Me-
dium), May 20, 2020, medium.com/the-ascent/how-ive-made-over-1
-2-million-dollars-from-my-writing-92a307b5bce2.

44. Dawson's tweets, dated April 21, 2023, have since been deleted but have
been archived at en.rattibha.com/thread/1649492170062155779.

45. "Rather than the outcome of human creativity and craft, book-writing
by machines shall transform it into a commodity—commodification of
culture." P. J. James, "On Understanding Generative AI as a Corporate-
Fascist Weapon," *Counter Currents*, October 6, 2023, countercurrents
.org/2023/06/on-understanding-generative-ai-as-a-corporate-fascist
-weapon.

46. See Elizabeth A. Harris, "The Most Powerful Person in Publishing
Doesn't Like to Talk about Himself," *New York Times*, January 30,
2024, www.nytimes.com/2024/01/30/books/penguin-random-house
-nihar-malaviya.html.

47. The energy cost of AI also contributes to the climate crisis. See Sha-
ron Adarlo, "Critics Furious Microsoft Is Training AI by Sucking Up
Water During Drought," *Futurism*, September 26, 2023, futurism.com
/critics-microsoft-water-train-ai-drought.

48. See Brewster Kahle, "The US Library System, Once the Best in the
World, Faces Death by a Thousand Cuts," *Guardian*, October 9, 2023,
www.theguardian.com/commentisfree/2023/oct/09/us-library-sys
tem-attack-digital-licensing; and Zane McNeill, "NYC Budget Cuts
Forces Public Libraries to Close on Sundays, Reduce Services," *Truth-
out*, November 20, 2023, truthout.org/articles/nyc-budget-cuts-forces
-public-libraries-to-close-on-sundays-reduce-services.

49. Michelle Tea, *Black Wave* (New York: Feminist Press, 2016), 291.

50. Sally Rooney, *Beautiful World, Where Are You* (New York: Farrar, Straus and Giroux, 2021), 244.

51. Talia Lavin, "The Confession," *The Sword and the Sandwich* (Substack), September 26, 2023, theswordandthesandwich.substack.com/p/the -confession.

52. B. D. McClay, "Pleasure Needs No Politics," *Gawker*, November 11, 2021, web.archive.org/web/20230609035353/www.gawker.com/culture /pleasure-needs-no-politics.

53. Alexander Chee, "On Becoming an American Writer," *Paris Review*, April 19, 2018, www.theparisreview.org/blog/2018/04/19/on-becoming -an-american-writer.

© Nikita Artinian

LYTA GOLD is a critic, essayist, and fiction writer living in Massachusetts. Her work has appeared in *The Baffler*, *Protean*, *New York Review of Architecture*, and *Current Affairs*.